URN TO THE RECIPE
DIRECTORIES ON
PAGES 305–27 TO FIND A
SIDE DISH TO SUIT WHATEVER,
WHENEVER AND HOWEVER
YOU ARE COOKING.

This book is for anyone who already realises that the best bits of a Sunday roast are the trimmings.

And for everyone else too – because you'll see the light soon.

B L O O M S B U R Y
LONDON · OXFORD · NEW YORK · NEW DELHI · SYDNEY

ON THE SIDE

A SOURCEBOOK OF INSPIRING SIDE DISHES

ED SMITH

PHOTOGRAPHY BY JOE WOODHOUSE

Contents

On side dishes

This book will change how you think about your meals. A bold statement, I know, but bear with me.

I've been writing a food blog, RocketandSquash.com, for six years. For nearly three of those I was also beavering away as a corporate lawyer; I then trained as a chef and started working in the food industry. My blog covers the usual things – recipes, restaurant write-ups, the odd doodle – but a few years ago I added a new element to it: every Monday I publish a digest of the recipes in that weekend's newspaper supplements. It's been an illuminating and only occasionally laborious process. I've witnessed the way seasons and annual events inspire food writers; I've watched trends arrive, and some of them crash and burn; I've seen a million and one ways with chicken, hundreds of crumbles and nearly as many chocolate fondants. And yet, in all this time, barely a handful of side dishes. Which is madness. A key part of every meal time is being ignored.

To my mind, roast chicken or pork belly is naked without a few good sides. Slow-cooked lamb flounders without something to punctuate the rich meat and juices, and even the perfect seasonal vegetable tart is lost without a perky partner on the plate. I'm deflated whenever I read a cursory 'eat with potatoes and greens' or 'goes well with rice', as if the trimmings don't really matter. In restaurants and at friends' houses, I'm quietly despondent if the mains are let down by overcooked or poorly matched vegetables or stodgy, bland, unsuitable carbs.

What we call side dishes actually make up the bulk of a meal. They have the potential to be as inspirational as the main event itself. In fact, they're often the best bit, whether it's roast potatoes and Yorkshire pudding alongside a rib of beef; cheesy polenta with luscious cavolo nero underneath a meaty Italian ragù; or refreshing, crunchy salads and pickles to go with a Japanese or Korean dinner.

Yes, I'd like to push the oft-neglected supporting acts to centre stage. It's the 'two veg' rather than the meat that I focus on here, because whether they're plain or fancy, side dishes should never be an afterthought. On the contrary; they can be the starting point.

Good sides lift a meal from being just fine to being truly delicious or memorable. They might be comforting and moreish, complex and impressive, or simply a handful of vegetables harvested at their peak and cooked to perfection. Some sides have the power to inspire a whole menu, while others happen to be exactly the right thing for the centrepiece you've already set your heart on. It's so satisfying, isn't it, when each ingredient on your plate is independently delectable as well as complementing and enhancing the rest? That moment you realise that you need seconds of *everything*... oooof.

Just to calm things down a bit, although many of the recipes in this book could very well be the star of your lunch or dinner, I don't mean this to be a mains-versus-sides, us-versus-them thing. A meal is the sum of its parts, and the recipes and words below are really aimed at ensuring everything comes together in harmony. My point is simply that by thinking about the elements that are sometimes disregarded, your overall eating experience will be more gratifying.

For me, it's all about balance: of tastes, textures, flavours, colours and, just as importantly, effort versus results. With that in mind, it seems worth setting down a few principles of eating well on the side. Which, of course, also means eating well in the round.

On matching sides to the centrepiece

Match your sides to the meat. Or fish. Or vegetables. Or cheese. Or tofu. Or egg. Or, indeed, a gaggle of other sides. This seems obvious, but perhaps it's so obvious it gets overlooked.

Some things just work well together, and few of those combinations are a secret or as yet undiscovered. Think leeks and pumpkin with lamb; onions and cauliflower cheese with beef; or sweet things like corn, carrots or fruit with pork. There's no harm in following tradition, even clichés. In fact, you can make that classic match your starting point and work the other accompaniments around it.

But how do we know what goes well together? In part, it's trial and error, which is what some people call 'experience'. I'm afraid this largely comes with time and effort. But there's no shame in piggy-backing on other people's work too, by paying attention to flavour combinations in restaurants and scanning the recipe titles in cookery books and the weekend supplements. It's rare that any chef or food writer is truly laying down new discoveries for the rest of us to eat, read and generally marvel over; most reaffirm or reinterpret age-old traditions and flavour matches. So we can learn from them and do the same!

I'm a voracious collector and reader of recipes. Though I rarely follow them to the letter, I'm constantly inspired by flavour combinations within them. Some of my most thumbed and dog-eared cookbooks include Niki Segnit's *The Flavour Thesaurus*, which examines ingredients that go well with each other, and considers why; *Bar Tartine* by Cortney Burns and Nicolaus Balla, because the techniques it introduces and the taste and textural combinations in its recipes are instructive and inspirational; and Nigel Slater's *Tender*, volumes 1 and 2, because it's a tremendous resource for ideas, across a variety of cuisines, about which vegetables, fruits and meats work together. You'll probably have your own favourites too; it's really worth dipping into books and the papers from time to time to keep the creative juices flowing.

On which note, do use the directories at the back of the book and the 'Alongside' notes with each recipe. These are just suggestions, but I hope the ideas persuade you to try something new as well as reinforcing your well-rehearsed preferences.

On the number of sides

How many sides to prepare? There is no single right answer, thank goodness. In Britain we've been schooled with the phrase 'meat and two veg'. As it happens, I think that's a pretty strong rule of thumb to go by, largely because there's a law of diminishing returns when it comes to home cooking. Is it really worth doubling your work to make four instead of two sides? Is the meal better for it? Will anyone else appreciate the effort? Sadly for us cooks, the answer is usually no.

More often than not, it's best to keep things simple. Three, two or sometimes just one side dish tends to be the right way to go, even (especially) for a Sunday roast. That way you can concentrate on making sure that everything you're cooking is perfect. You might simply serve a bunch of purple sprouting broccoli dressed with olive oil and tarragon and nothing else (page 42); or a serene, calming bowl of spring greens in shiitake dashi broth (page 14) with perfectly cooked but otherwise plain rice. Choose your sides and build your meal according to the centrepiece, the season, your mood, the other trimmings and the practical realities of your kitchen and ability.

Naturally, rules of thumb are there to be broken. Perhaps the best way to do that is to ignore the meat part completely. I think as eaters we're creeping away from the idea that there must always be a standout piece of meat or fish in a meal; at least I hope we are. You could quite easily make a well-balanced feast from three, four or five of the recipes in this book, and I encourage you to do just that. Look to the 'Alongside' section in each recipe for inspiration, though feel free to diverge from them too.

On texture

Ideally, your meal will feature a mixture of complementary textures. Fried and roasted things are awesome, aren't they? From Southern fried or katsu breaded chicken, to steaks pan-fried to a rich brown crust, roast potatoes, okra chips and deep-fried sprouts (pages 170, 70 and 32)... or anything else with a crisp and caramelised edge. But you need variety – you can have too much of a good thing.

Conversely, while Yeasted cauliflower purée (page 130), Anchoïade mashed potatoes (page 180) and Roast butternut squash purée (page 188) might each individually go well with, say, lamb, together they're basically baby food. Try to ensure that there's always something with crunch or bite (whether fried, roasted, raw, or topped with nuts, seeds, toasted breadcrumbs, and so on); something that's soft (a mash, a purée, something braised or well boiled); and something in between (such as al dente vegetables) on your plate.

Save for bread and romesco sauces (pages 236 and 106), this book doesn't really cover condiments, sauces, broths or gravy unless they're used within a specific dish. But it's still a good idea to think about them when making a meal. Does your centrepiece have a natural sauce, or is it quite lean and dry? If it's the former, you won't want more than one other heavily dressed, wet or creamed side dish. If it's the latter, then definitely make sure that somewhere in the side dishes there's a liquid, purée or dressing to punctuate the savoury flavours and to lift and bind your meal. There are plenty of recipes to suit here, from pulses, beans and grains served with a broth to creamy gratins and luscious bakes.

On flavour

At the risk of sounding like a broken record, the key to a truly pleasing meal is balance. If your centrepiece is sweet through saucing or spices, or you're planning on roasting root vegetables, onions and leeks, or serving the likes of sweetcorn and peas, then you'll need something plain and earthy alongside. For instance, blanched brassica leaves (cabbages and kales), potatoes, pasta, rice or grains like couscous, pearl barley, freekeh and so on.

You might find sour, bitter or peppery flavours offer a good contrast, too; look for recipes containing citrus, radishes, radicchio or chicory, among others. On the other hand, if your centrepiece or sides are plain, earthy, sour, bitter or peppery, then seek out something sweet!

On colour

We really do eat with our eyes, so it's worth ensuring that your plate is a pretty one. If you take away the odd sprinkle of fresh herbs or pomegranate seeds, you'll see that the vast majority of meat, fish and vegetable main courses are brown. It's up to the side dishes to bring a flash of colour. A pile of chopped kale (page 26), spoonfuls of caponata (page 140) or ratatouille (page 114) or simple but gorgeous salad leaves (pages 78, 82, 86) will transform even the boggiest-looking plate.

There's more to this point than looks alone. You'll notice that the colours of your vegetables and other trimmings reflect how they taste. Grains, rice and pasta are pale browns and yellows; they're neutral colours and relatively neutral in flavour. By contrast, carrots, sweet potato, pumpkin aren't all just orange, they're all sweet too. It follows that if your meal is mono-coloured, it's also likely to taste a bit one-note and won't satisfy. See if you can make things vibrant and varied; I honestly think it tastes better that way.

On the practicalities of cooking

Your oven is not a Tardis – I'm afraid it won't fit more than three things at once. Even then, the tray at the top is going to take the best part of the heat, so forget about a nice brown crust or crisp edges on the items underneath.

Similarly, you probably can't boil more than three pans of vegetables at once, if that; at least one of your hot spots is basically useless; and do you really want to think about cooking each of those things to perfection at the same time?

Though initially disappointing, the limitations of our kitchens are not disastrous; instead they provide a helpful hint. We don't want everything to be roasted anyway (too greasy), nor everything boiled or steamed (too clean). So, for the benefits of taste and logistics, I suggest mixing things up. If you fancy something that requires significant and dedicated time in a hot oven, like Chorizo roast potatoes (page 170), perhaps your other sides should be verdant, fresh and quick, like French-ish peas (page 58) cooked on a hob, or shaved fennel (page 118), which needs no cooking at all.

Have a think about where you're going to cook things, how long that will take and whether anything could or should be done in advance. The 'Preparation' and 'Time Needed' notes on the recipe pages are there to help your planning, as are the directories on the same topics (see pages 324 and 326). I always find it's worth taking a moment to consider whether my grand plans will come together before I launch into them.

On being realistic

There's no point trying to do something interesting with *everything* on the plate. Select one, maybe two things to make an effort with, whether that's adding an interesting dressing or garnish, cooking something unusual or assembling the world's best-ever root vegetable gratin. If more sides need to be added, just cook them plainly (but perfectly) and allow the ingredients to speak for themselves.

So, although you'll see five examples of sides that might go well 'Alongside' each recipe, you need only pick one or two, or just cook the main ingredients in the suggested recipes simply.

On the seasons

Finally, when thinking about side dishes there is the important question of seasonality.

The most satisfying and successful sides are often a bunch or basket of seasonal vegetables, and if you start with one seasonal item the other parts of your meal tend to fall into place around it. There's much to be said for the phrase 'what grows together goes together'. In autumn and winter, for example, you'll see brassica leaves like kale, cavolo nero and cabbages growing next to root vegetables and winter squash. It's nature's not-so-subtle hint.

Moreover, all the recipes will taste better when the vegetables that feature in them are in season locally. There's nothing more disappointing than a tomato salad or asparagus side in December, and no point looking (or paying) for sprout tops or parsnips in July.

Think seasonally too about the nature of the sides (and centrepieces). Cheesy and creamy gratins might seem the perfect match in the cold months for things like beef, chicken and lamb. But in late spring and summer? A baby gem lettuce or tomato salad; herby, citrusy grains and pulses; or crunchy dressed vegetables would be more appropriate, and appreciated.

Using this book

As it's not possible to hang around in your kitchen to answer any questions that might arise whilst you are cooking, below are a few pointers that apply to all the recipes, and which should help you to interpret my instructions.

Serving size

As a guideline, most of the recipes in this book are labelled as serving four to six people, as a side dish (obviously). The quantity is roughly suitable for four if there's only one (or no) other side dish, or people are hungry; and for six if several other things are to be served and/or appetites are low. All the recipes are easily scaled up or down. If you make too much, most ingredients are relatively inexpensive and/or could be reheated or eaten cold as leftovers.

Measurements

Perhaps more than any other part of a meal, side dishes suit pragmatic cooking. A little bit of intuition goes a long way, not least with quantities. Vegetable and fruits, for example, vary in size. I might have suggested that you need, say, 800g cauliflower or pumpkin, but if the one you've bought weighs 950g, of course use it all – you might just want to adjust the cooking time and seasoning a little.

That said, the details of my recipes have been carefully considered. Use digital scales where possible, and I heartily recommend getting your hands on a set of measuring spoons; tablespoons and teaspoons are real measurements (15ml and 5ml respectively), not just a rough guide.

Timings and details

I have opted to provide detail rather than assume knowledge in the recipe methods. That might mean that, at first glance, some relatively simple tasks appear onerous. However, none of these sides should prove disproportionately time consuming. Certainly, once you've cooked them once, you'll be able to whizz through according to the timings suggested, find your own shortcuts and fit the preparation of that dish seamlessly around the rest of your meal.

Ingredients

Salt Unless stated otherwise, all references to salt mean natural, granular or flaked sea salt. I use Halen Môn, Maldon or Cornish sea salt or French *sel gris.*

Butter and dairy The recipes call for full-fat dairy products. These taste better, are better value and have now been proven to be better for us than low-fat or 'skimmed' versions. For the same reasons, I also suggest using organic dairy products where possible.

Herbs You'll see that herb quantities are mostly specified as leaves from a number of sprigs or stems. 'Sprig' means the several stems and branches of a woody herb, like thyme or rosemary, that attach to the same base point; 'stem' is used for a significant shoot of greener, leafy herbs like parsley, tarragon, mint and basil, which may have a few smaller ones coming off it. I hope this is a more useful description than 'a tablespoon of chopped', 'a handful' or 'a bunch' (of unspecified size), which I've always found wildly unhelpful. Ultimately, though, it's just intended to be an indication. As a general rule, it's best to be generous.

Spices and condiments Your ground cinnamon might be more aromatic than the pot I have; the ratio of spices in my za'atar is probably different from yours; and your thirst for fish sauce or pomegranate molasses could well be greater than mine. No recipe in this book will live or die by seasoning or spice quantities, so use your judgement and season and spice to taste.

'Exotic' ingredients There are a few ingredients in this book that probably weren't on many supermarket shelves ten years ago, and may not be on yours now (such as the likes of sumac, 'nduja, mirin, freekeh and smoked water). If not, they are easy to find online. See page 334 for a full list of useful suppliers and websites.

Kitchen tools

Two or three good knives, a few wooden spoons and silicone spatulas, decent saucepans and frying pans, a couple of roasting tins and baking trays, a colander and/or a sieve: these are the bare essentials for a functioning kitchen, and I suspect you've got them all. However, your cooking life will be made easier, and the recipes in this book will be completely accessible, if you also have the following: ovenproof earthenware and a pyrex or enamel dish (or two); a cast-iron griddle pan; a mandolin; a pestle and mortar; a basic vegetable 'speed' peeler; a julienne peeler; a microplane grater; tongs; an electric stand mixer; a jug blender, stick blender or food processor; measuring spoons; and a digital weighing scale.

Serving side dishes alongside each other

Each recipe page includes multiple suggestions as to which sides might go 'Alongside' that dish. This is not a recommendation that you cook six side dishes from this book at the same time; for practical reasons, it's normally best to only do one or two sides that require extra effort. You could, however, use the Alongside suggestions to prompt plainer sides using similar ingredients. Or, alternatively, build a whole meal from three or four of them, without the need for a main.

Choosing your side dish

There are a few different routes into the recipes that follow. The most intuitive way is through browsing the chapters: Greens, leaves & herbs; Vegetables, fruits, flowers & bulbs; Roots, squash & potatoes; and Grains, pulses, pasta & rice. But crucial life decisions such as *what shall we have for dinner?* don't always fit neatly into a single stream of themes. So on occasion you might prefer to use the recipe directories at the back of the book, which address the following questions:

1. What's your main dish? (pages 308–23)
2. Where is the side dish prepared? (pages 324–5)
3. How long does it take to make? (pages 326–7)

I hope *On the Side* will be a source of inspiration, both for sides to go with the things you're already cooking, and as the starting point for a memorable meal.

GREENS, LEAVES & HERBS

Eat your greens. No, seriously, do – they give so much to a meal. It's a rare occasion when I don't have at least one type on my plate (and that's probably because a purple or yellow variety of leaf, bean or brassica has jumped on instead). Greens, leaves and herbs bring vibrancy and texture whether raw or cooked, unadorned or dressed. They provide a crucial contrast to other foods through the cool crunch of a bitter leaf, the squeaky bite of a green bean, the comforting chew of tender broccoli or the frilly tickle of wilted kale or flower sprouts.

Regardless of their unique flavours, eating leaves, greens and herbs always seems to leave you with a sense of vitality. Unless over-boiled, sulphurous and lifeless, greens make you feel good for having eaten them, and are often the essential balancing act alongside heavy or rich mains.

On which note: there are numerous ways to cook greens and leaves, and just about the only method that doesn't suit them is boiling them for too long, which dulls colour, taste, texture and, frankly, purpose. That is not to say don't boil greens at all; many of the recipes in this chapter involve blanching (in other words, cooking briefly in boiling water, and sometimes chilling quickly to reheat later) and some are better, I think, when floppy and wet from a pot (purple sprouting broccoli, for example). For similarly satisfying results, consider wilting leaves or sautéing beans and brassicas in a heavy-bottomed pan with a little oil or butter. Add a spoonful or two of water after a few minutes to generate steam and speed up the process.

Steaming greens is another good option, although you must take care not to overdo it, as this is as heinous a crime as over-boiling. You'll also find that greens and leaves enjoy a hit of high direct heat, whether that's the char of the grill or the fierce temperature of a wok or deep-fryer.

Avoiding overcooking is key, but ensuring your greens are smartly finished is important too. Even if the greens are very much the simple element of your meal (and there's nothing wrong with a bag of frozen peas), always season them, and perhaps dress them as well. A good pinch or two of salt is necessary every time, and black pepper often helps. You'll find a squeeze of fresh lemon provides a huge lift, particularly if the greens have been fried or charred. Lashings of peppery, grassy extra-virgin olive oil or nutty cold-pressed rapeseed oil are excellent additions to steamed or boiled greens. Ditto butter. Chopped fresh herbs – particularly mint, tarragon, chervil, parsley and chives – are an easy but extremely effective flourish.

It's worth noting that salad leaves make great sides. Avoid the bagged salads that wilt and rot, and seek instead sweet and crisp baby gem, cos or Romaine lettuce; bitter chicory, endive or radicchio; peppery wild rocket and watercress; and bunches of parsley, mint and sorrel. These are all good at mopping up hot juices, providing a crisp, refreshing contrast against soft, rich, tender meat and fish, or simply pairing with centrepiece dishes that need something cool.

As a final note, if you'd like to go beyond a simple side of greens and delve into the recipes that follow, bear in mind that many of the dressings and sprinklings are interchangeable. For example, the flavours in Cavolo nero with garlic, chilli and orange (page 24) would work just as well with purple sprouting broccoli instead of tarragon oil (page 42) and vice versa; the yolks in Asparagus with cured egg yolk (page 60) could be grated over a multitude of al dente greens; and the umami crumbs on the grilled tenderstem broccoli (page 40) go with pretty much everything. Please do experiment.

Chard with chilli, shallot and cider vinaigrette

PREPARATION: *on a hob*
TIME NEEDED: *less than 15 minutes*

Chard is an odd one. The difference in texture between the hard stalks and the leaves that disappear at the merest hint of heat makes it a bit of a pain to cook, and I'm sure some people question how rewarding an eat it is.

But it really is! The obvious thing to do is simply to wilt the stalks and leaves separately, season with salt and pepper and maybe add a glug of olive oil or a knob of butter. Which is fine, but this dressing enlivens things further. The sweet-sour of the vinegar and chilli and the hint of raw shallot work so well against the earthy and ever-so-slightly bitter stem and warm-but-barely-wilted leaf; I love it. *Fatty pork chops or shoulder steaks*, *lamb* and *beef* are big fans of the combination too.

It takes barely three minutes to cook this dish, so make sure you have all the other components of your meal ready before throwing the leaves into the pan. Large-leaf spinach works well as a substitute for the chard.

Serves 4–6

800g Swiss or rainbow chard
2 tablespoons sunflower or vegetable oil
1 garlic clove, crushed
Freshly ground black pepper

Vinaigrette
1 teaspoon caster sugar
2 tablespoons light olive oil
2 tablespoons cider vinegar
1 small shallot (40g), very finely diced
1 mild red chilli, very finely diced
Sea salt

First, prepare the vinaigrette. Put the sugar, olive oil, cider vinegar, a pinch of salt and 2 teaspoons tepid water in a bowl or jar and stir or shake well to emulsify. Add the shallot and chilli. Put a third of the dressing in a large serving bowl.

Trim the chard stems and leaves to remove any unsightly bits. Remove the thick stems from the leaves. Chop the stems into 3cm lengths and set aside, then cut the leaves into large pieces about 8–12cm wide.

Set a large heavy-bottomed frying pan, saucepan or wok over a high heat. Add the oil and allow it to heat up. Add the chard stems and cook for 90 seconds, pushing them around a few times so they don't catch and burn. Add the leaves and garlic. Cook for 90 seconds longer, moving the chard around the pan so all the pieces get a little heat, seasoning with salt and pepper as you go. Remove from the pan once two thirds of the leaves have wilted; the rest will cook in the residual heat.

Tip the chard into the serving bowl containing one third of the vinaigrette and toss well. Transfer to a serving platter and spoon the rest of the vinaigrette liberally over the top.

ALONGSIDE: *Boulangère potatoes* (page 168); *Chorizo roast potatoes* (page 170); *Roast butternut squash purée* (page 188); *'Young Turk' celeriac* (page 196); *Haricot beans with tomato and persillade* (page 278)

Creamed chard

PREPARATION: *on a hob*
TIME NEEDED: *less than 15 minutes*

Oh my. While I feel sure this recipe is about right for 4–6 people as a side, I know from experience that it's entirely possible that the cook will eat it all in one go and then have to rustle up a quick salad for everyone else.

If you're more disciplined than me and do end up sharing the spoils, you might also consider varying the recipe by topping the creamed chard with breadcrumbs and turning it into a gratin. To do that, preheat the oven to 190°C/ Fan 170°C/ Gas 5, spoon the mixture into a gratin dish or shallow casserole, sprinkle 30g umami crumbs (page 40) over the top and an extra 10g grated Parmesan. Pour a little olive oil from the anchovy tin over the crumbs, then bake in the upper section of your oven for 20–25 minutes until the breadcrumbs are golden brown and the cream is bubbling through.

Whether you plump for crunchy-topped bake or the simple creamed version, this is very good with *rich meats*, *chicken*, *root vegetables* and *mushrooms*.

Serves 4–6

800g Swiss or rainbow chard, or large-leaf spinach
20g butter
½ onion, finely diced
1 garlic clove, very thinly sliced
4 salted anchovies, roughly chopped
400ml double cream
80g Parmesan, grated
Freshly ground nutmeg
Juice and finely grated zest of ½ lemon
Sea salt and freshly ground black pepper

Put a large pan of salted water on to boil. Prepare the chard by cutting the stems off the leaves. Trim any gnarly bits off stem ends and discard, then cut the stems into 5cm lengths. Blanch the stems in the boiling water for 1 minute. In the meantime, if the chard leaves are bigger than your hand, cut them in half. Add them to the boiling water and blanch for a further 30 seconds. Drain, rinse until cool, then squeeze the water from the leaves with your hands. Unravel each leaf like a hanky and spread them out on a clean tea towel to dry.

Return the pan to a medium heat. Add the butter, onion and a pinch of salt and cook for 3–4 minutes to soften before adding the garlic and anchovies. Cook for about 90 seconds until the anchovies start to melt, then add the cream and Parmesan. Stir until the cheese has melted. Turn off the heat and season with plenty of black pepper and a couple of gratings of fresh nutmeg.

Stir the chard stems and leaves into the cream. Season with the lemon zest, juice and some black pepper; you'll find it's fairly salty already thanks to the anchovies and Parmesan. Serve immediately (although it's still pretty good if reheated).

ALONGSIDE: *French-ish peas* (page 58); *Hasselback potatoes with bay and caraway* (page 172); *Sweet potato and rosemary hash-rösti* (page 192); *Wine-poached salsify with gremolata* (page 200); *Cannellini beans with sweetcorn and pickled mushrooms* (page 276)

Grilled hispi cabbage with anchovy and crème fraîche

PREPARATION: *on a hob*
TIME NEEDED: *15 to 30 minutes*

Hispi is also known as 'sweetheart' cabbage, which points to the fact that it's sweeter and more tender than most, and can even be eaten raw. Perhaps unsurprisingly, then, it's also excellent when quickly grilled to leave the edges charred, soft and muted, while the inner bits remain uncooked and crunchy.

Add a salty-sharp anchovy and crème fraîche dressing and you've a cracking accompaniment to cut through *rich, fatty lamb dishes*, *calves' liver* or, frankly, *any roast meat*. You could use the anchovy and crème fraîche dressing on things like broccoli, kale and other types of cabbage too, regardless of how they've been cooked.

In this instance, the hispi cabbage is first cut into wedges. After it has been charred, I suggest you cut the hard centre out and separate the leaves, then dress them with the anchovy sauce, as this makes it much easier to serve and eat than when left in wedges.

Serves 4–6

1 tablespoon sunflower oil
2–3 medium (about 800g) hispi cabbages, cut into 6 segments through the root

Anchovy and crème fraîche dressing
50g tinned anchovies in olive oil, roughly chopped
3 garlic cloves, crushed
30g cold butter, cubed
100g crème fraîche
1 teaspoon red wine vinegar

Heat the anchovies, their oil and the garlic in a small saucepan over a low heat. Once the anchovies have started to dissolve into a mush and the garlic is softening, add the butter, 2 small cubes at a time, stirring with a wooden spoon so that the sauce emulsifies. Add the crème fraîche, stir, then add the vinegar and take off the heat. You could make this in advance, but warm it just a little before using, whisking in more cold butter if it has split.

Put a griddle or heavy-based frying pan on the hottest part of your hob and use a wad of kitchen paper to grease it with the oil. When the pan is smoking hot, place the cabbage segments on it, cut-side down. Cook until blackened, about 3–4 minutes. Turn over and blacken the other cut side for another 3 minutes. You may need to do this in two batches.

Once well charred, use tongs to hold the cabbage segments steady on a chopping board while you quickly cut the cores away, so the leaves become loose. (Don't discard the cores.)

Spoon about a third of the dressing onto a serving plate or bowl. Put the cabbage leaves and cores on top and dress liberally with the remaining dressing. Serve immediately.

ALONGSIDE: *Boulangère potatoes* (page 168); *Roast butternut squash purée* (page 188); *'Young Turk' celeriac* (page 196); *Nutmeg neeps* (page 202); *Wheat berries with capers and tomatoes* (page 250)

Charred fermented cabbage

PREPARATION: *on a hob*
TIME NEEDED: *more than an hour*

This side requires forethought and patience (for 2 weeks or so while the cabbage ferments), but in return you get fizz and tang, as well as the depth of flavour a bit of aggressive griddling can bring. To my mind, it's a project worth embarking on; it cuts brilliantly through *rich meats like mutton, venison and beef*, *sweetly sauced barbecue cuts* and *stews* too.

You will need a jar or fermentation crock at least 3 litres in size (a Kilner jar or similar is fine). If the vessel you use is much bigger than that, you could consider doubling the recipe so you have enough cabbage to keep you going for more than just one meal. The fermented cabbage can also be eaten raw, without the charring, just like a pickle – it's excellent with cold meats or spicy stir-fries.

The brine is 3.5 per cent salt. If you need to top up the jars with more liquid than the recipe suggests, just dissolve more salt in water using the same ratio.

Serves 6

105g natural salt, with no anti-caking agents
2 medium green cabbages
8 garlic cloves, peeled
6 or 7 stems dill
6 bay leaves
10 black peppercorns
2 teaspoons caraway seeds

Make a brine by slightly heating 3 litres water in a large pan, then adding the salt and stirring until it has fully dissolved. Leave to cool. Ensure your fermentation crock or jars are clean and sterilised.

Wash the cabbages. Cut them in half through the core, then each of the halves into 4 wedges, angling your knife through the core so the wedges remain intact. Place the wedges in the jars, adding the aromatics as you go. Pour the brine over the cabbage, and keep the cabbage pieces submerged by placing on top a weight or sealed freezer bag filled with a little water. Leave a 2–3cm gap between the brine and top of the jar and seal it. Store it out of direct sunlight but in a warm room (21–24°C) for about 2 weeks. Unless you have an air-lock lid, open the lids to 'burp' the jars by releasing any build-up of gases a couple of times a day during the first week, resealing them each time. The cabbage should be pleasingly fizzy after 2 weeks, at which point decant it, with the brine, into smaller sterilised jars and store in a cool place, where it will keep for at least 2 months more.

To char the cabbage, remove the required number of wedges from the brine and allow to dry for at least an hour before cooking. Put a griddle pan on the hottest spot on your hob. Brush with oil and heat until smoking. Add the wedges and char for 4–5 minutes per side, turning just once. Eat immediately.

ALONGSIDE: *Sprout tops with Jerusalem artichokes and apple* (page 36); *Smoky ratatouille* (page 114); *Creamed sweetcorn with feta* (page 122); *Scorched sweet potatoes with sobrasada butter* (page 190); *Spelt grains with wild mushrooms* (page 256)

Spring greens in shiitake dashi

PREPARATION: *on a hob*
TIME NEEDED: *more than an hour*

Dashi is a Japanese broth made from water, kombu (dried kelp) and bonito flakes. It forms the base of miso soup and numerous other dishes, but in itself is a soothing blend of saline and umami flavours. This recipe adds dried shiitake, fresh ginger and a splash of light soy for seasoning.

The idea of serving greens in a stock derives from a Japanese dish called *ohitashi*, which involves blanched, squeezed and rolled spinach. You could use spinach or chard with this dashi, or kale and turnip tops too, but I like the body and bite of spring greens.

This is one of those dishes that I find myself wanting before I've thought about what it will go with. It works really well, though, in tandem with *soba noodles and pickled vegetables*, or alongside things like slices of *bavette steak*, *venison* or *duck breast* that have been seared brown on the outside and left blushing pink within. It's also good with *hake* and *salmon fillets*, or the *baked portobello mushrooms* on page 152.

The dashi can be made well in advance and refrigerated for up to 3 days, then reheated when required – but cook the greens at the very last minute.

Serves 4–6

1 piece kombu, about 8cm square
10g bonito flakes
1 dried shiitake mushroom
10g fresh ginger, sliced into 3mm discs
1 tablespoon light soy sauce
500–600g spring greens

For the dashi, put 1.2 litres cold water and the kombu in a pan and leave to soak for 15 minutes. Place it over a medium heat and bring to a light simmer (don't allow it to boil), before reducing the heat so that it's barely bubbling. Cook for 45 minutes–1 hour until you have a saline, slightly gelatinous liquid. Turn the heat off. Add the bonito and leave it to infuse for 4 minutes without stirring, then strain the dashi through a sieve into another container. Return the dashi to the heat, add the mushroom, ginger and soy sauce and simmer for 15 minutes.

———

To prepare the spring greens, trim the stems from each leaf at their base, and cut each leaf into 2 or 3 palm-sized pieces. Bring a large pan of salted water to the boil. When the water is at a rapid boil, add the leaves and blanch for 90 seconds, until they are tender and a vivid green. Drain.

———

Serve in individual bowls with a ladle or two of dashi over the top. The meat, fish, noodles or pickles could go in the same bowl, or just be nearby for picking at.

———

ALONGSIDE: *Courgette and edamame salad* (page 110); *Quick cucumber and daikon kimchi* (page 160); *Quick-pickled daikon* (page 210); *Buckwheat with celery and walnuts* (page 252); *Sesame soba noodles* (page 254)

Chinese cabbage with black vinegar

PREPARATION: *on a hob*
TIME NEEDED: *less than 15 minutes*

Chinkiang (black rice) vinegar has a malty, woody flavour that you may recognise from dim sum dipping sauces, where it's often combined with soy or just served on its own. Adding it in the last moments of wok-frying lends a slightly sour but also a mellow quality to the pale, crisp but relatively bland Chinese cabbage; I find myself eating masses of it when cooked like this.

That flavour, along with the crunch and water content of the cabbage, makes it a killer side for fatty, rich or sweet dishes. I'm thinking *soy and chilli-braised beef shin*; *teriyaki chicken, beef or salmon*; or *miso-braised aubergine*.

Serves 4–6

1 Chinese cabbage
2 tablespoons light soy sauce
2 tablespoons Chinkiang vinegar
2 teaspoons golden caster sugar
4 tablespoons sunflower oil
4cm fresh ginger, peeled and cut into fine matchsticks
2 teaspoons dried chilli flakes
1 teaspoon lightly crushed Sichuan peppercorns (optional)

Prepare all the ingredients first, as the cooking process is quick. Cut the cabbage in half lengthways, then each of those halves in two again. Cut out the core from the base of each quarter, then roughly chop the lengths into 5 or 6 pieces widthways. Mix the soy sauce, vinegar and caster sugar together in a bowl and set to one side.

Place a large wok over a very high heat, add the oil and allow it to heat almost until it smokes. Drop the ginger into the hot oil and let this soften for 30 seconds before adding the chilli flakes and Sichuan peppercorns (if using), then pretty much immediately start to add the pieces of cabbage cut from the harder (root) end. Stir-fry for 30 seconds, before adding the softer top part of the cabbage. Cook for 45 seconds more, stirring occasionally, before pushing the cabbage to one side and pouring the soy sauce mixture in. Quickly move the cabbage around for 20–30 seconds, then remove from the heat so that the cabbage takes on the flavours of vinegar and soy but retains its bite. Serve immediately.

ALONGSIDE: *Grilled tenderstem broccoli with umami crumbs* (page 40); *Smacked cucumbers* (page 158); *Quick cucumber and daikon kimchi* (page 160); *Sesame soba noodles* (page 254); *Coconut jasmine rice* (page 296)

Bacon and buttermilk cabbage

PREPARATION: *on a hob*
TIME NEEDED: *less than 15 minutes*

Bacon and sautéed cabbage is a well-rehearsed and flawless match. The two are often combined with double cream or crème fraîche, but I find it then becomes a heavier, richer side than I personally want. The idea behind this recipe was to add buttermilk for a lighter touch. It's certainly worth trying, particularly if you're planning a meal involving things like *pan-fried scallops*, or *white fish such as cod or pollock*.

Don't be tempted to pour the buttermilk into the pan while the cabbage is cooking, as it'll curdle and turn lumpy. Also, avoid cooking Savoy – or indeed any cabbage (you could use spring greens here too) – for too long. Once the vivid green colour dulls, so does the flavour.

Serves 4–6

700–800g Savoy or green cabbage
150–200g smoked dry-cured lardons
1 tablespoon vegetable or sunflower oil
Leaves from 6 sprigs thyme
200g cultured buttermilk
Finely grated zest of ½ lemon
Freshly ground black pepper

Quarter the cabbage, cutting from root to tip. Cut out and discard the hard core, then cut each of the wedges in half widthways. (I prefer leaving cabbage leaves relatively large, rather than shredding them.)

Put the lardons in a large heavy-bottomed pan over a medium-high heat. You could use a wok if none of your frying pans look big enough to hold the cabbage just a few layers deep. The fat will render from the lardons as the pan warms, but add a drizzle of oil to help things get started. Fry the lardons for 4–6 minutes, or until golden and crisp. Don't panic if they stick a little and the base of the pan colours; we'll release much of that flavour in a second.

Add the cabbage to the pan once the lardons are crisp. Push around for 20 seconds, then make a space and pour in 150ml water. Again, move the cabbage around. The steam from the water will help it wilt. Add the thyme, stir and leave the cabbage to soften for 2–3 minutes. Stop cooking while most of the leaves are still bright green and retain a little bite. Let it sit for 3 minutes to cool slightly.

Spoon the buttermilk into a large mixing bowl or serving dish. Give it 15–20 grinds of the pepper mill, then transfer the cabbage and bacon to the buttermilk, taking care not to add any excess liquid, and toss well. Sprinkle over the lemon zest and serve immediately.

ALONGSIDE: *Asparagus with cured egg yolk* (page 60); *Anchoïade mashed potatoes* (page 180); *Scorched sweet potatoes with sobrasada butter* (page 190); *Sweet potato and rosemary hash-rösti* (page 192); *White wine and dill carrots* (page 222)

Cabbage with juniper butter

PREPARATION: *on a hob*
TIME NEEDED: *less than 15 minutes*

Cabbages are massively underrated. The problem, I imagine, is that many of us associate the word 'cabbage' with soggy, dull, overcooked, near-sulphurous shredded leaves. In fact, there's a huge variety of cabbages and, when cooked to just tender, they're a versatile, tasty, cheap and filling side that shouldn't be left in the shadow of the more fashionable kales and broccolis.

I almost always cook Savoy, green, white and January King cabbages and spring greens as described below, though only occasionally adding the juniper berries. By part boiling, part steaming the cabbage in a shallow depth of water, the risk of overcooking the leaves and leaching out all their goodness is reduced. The butter and milk glaze doesn't just add gloss; it also seems to accentuate and round off the best bits of the cabbage's flavour profile. Try it with other leaves too.

This is best when cooked at the last minute as cabbage loses vibrancy if you cook it in advance and try to keep it warm. It's autumn and winter material – think *casseroles*, *pies* and mouthwatering *roast meats*. The juniper lends itself to *beef*, *venison* and *game birds*.

Serves 4–6

700–800g cabbage, such as Savoy, green, January King or spring greens
15 juniper berries
50g butter
1 tablespoon milk
Sea salt and freshly ground black pepper

I like cabbage in large, almost hand-sized pieces; it's more attractive and more enjoyable to eat like this than if it were shredded. To do this, cut the cabbage in half from root to tip, then separate the leaves from each other, leaf by leaf, starting from the outside. Cut out and discard the rib from the middle of each leaf, and cut the leaves in half along the rib line at the same time.

Crush the juniper berries with a pestle and mortar until they're nearly a dust. Fill a large pan with 6–7cm water, add a generous pinch of salt and bring to a rapid boil. Blanch the cabbage for 1–2 minutes, until just tender. Drain and return the pan to a medium heat.

Put the butter and milk in the pan with the ground juniper, 7 or 8 grinds of black pepper and a pinch of salt. When the butter has melted, add the cabbage and stir for 30 seconds, until the leaves are well glossed. Transfer to a serving bowl, pouring any residual milk, butter and juniper dressing over the leaves.

ALONGSIDE: *Chorizo roast potatoes* (page 170); *Honey and Marmite-glazed parsnips* (page 182); *Celeriac baked in a salt and thyme crust* (page 198); *Nutmeg neeps* (page 202); *Carrot-juice carrots* (page 218)

Braised red cabbage and beetroot

PREPARATION: *on a hob*
TIME NEEDED: *more than an hour*

It's amazing how far red cabbages seem to stretch (the answer to your panicked question in the shop is: yes, it is big enough). They're best cooked gently and slowly for a long time, or not cooked at all (such as in a slaw); this recipe plumps for the former option, because no book on side dishes should be without braised red cabbage – so good from autumn through to spring.

My version of the classic dish includes beetroot, which brings its own sweetness and earthiness to the party. The redcurrant jelly at the end is the secret weapon, though. Imagine this alongside a *venison suet pudding or pie*, a *beef casserole* or a *roast game bird*.

Serves 4–6

½ red cabbage (450–600g)
2 tablespoons vegetable or sunflower oil
1 onion, finely diced
250g cooked (not pickled) beetroot, cut into 2cm dice
50g demerara sugar
100g cider vinegar
5 juniper berries, crushed
⅕ nutmeg, freshly grated
1 heaped tablespoon redcurrant jelly
20g butter
Sea salt and freshly ground black pepper

Cut the cabbage in half, then in half again from root to tip. Shred each piece widthways with a large sharp knife.

Heat the oil in a large pan or flameproof casserole over a medium heat. When it is hot, add the onion and a pinch of salt, stir and cook to soften without colouring for 3–4 minutes.

Add the cabbage and cook for 10 minutes more, stirring occasionally, then add the beetroot, sugar, cider vinegar, crushed juniper berries and nutmeg. Cover and reduce the heat to medium-low. Cook slowly for 60 minutes, disturbing it only 2 or 3 times to stir it. (You could also cook it in the oven at 160°C/Fan 140°C/Gas 3.)

Stir in the redcurrant jelly and cook for 10 minutes more, or until the cabbage is tender and flavourful. Add the butter and stir it through, then season with plenty of salt and at least 10 good turns of the black-pepper mill. You can make this in advance and reheat it. In fact, it's usually better after a day or two in the fridge.

ALONGSIDE: *Runner beans with bacon and walnuts* (page 66); *Colcannon* (page 178); *Butter-glazed turnips with horseradish* (page 204); *Baked Jerusalem artichokes with yoghurt and sunflower seeds* (page 206); *Carrot-juice carrots* (page 218)

Cavolo nero with garlic, chilli and orange

PREPARATION: *on a hob*
TIME NEEDED: *less than 15 minutes*

You can sauté cavolo nero (also sometimes known as Tuscan kale or black cabbage) in a pan, perhaps with a splash of water to speed things up. More often than not, though, I take the quick-blanch approach described here, in part because you can do much of the work in advance before reheating when needed. But I also like the fact that boiling seems to make the leaves plump and juicy.

Garlic, chilli and orange is an excellent combination with cavolo nero, though you could also use it to enliven flower sprouts, purple sprouting broccoli or agretti (and, in return, use the dressings on pages 30, 42 and 62 with cavolo nero). *Chicken* and *pork* are massive fans, especially when polenta, pulses or rice are involved.

Serves 4

300–350g cavolo nero leaves
1 orange
4 tablespoons extra-virgin olive oil
½ mild red chilli, finely diced
1 garlic clove, thinly sliced
Sea salt and freshly ground black pepper

Cut out the central rib from the cavolo nero leaves and discard it, leaving you with long, thin, dimpled ribbons. Fill a wide saucepan (large enough to comfortably hold the cavolo nero) with water to a depth of 10cm, add a good pinch of salt and bring to a rapid boil. Add the cavolo nero and blanch it for 90 seconds. Drain, then plunge it into iced water or rinse it under a running cold tap. You could do this bit in advance.

Use a vegetable peeler to remove the zest of the orange. Scrape off any white pith from the underside, then cut the fragrant zest into very thin strips. Squeeze the juice and reserve it for later.

When you're almost ready to eat, set a large frying pan or wok over a medium-high heat. Add 2 tablespoons oil, the chilli, garlic and orange zest. Once the oil starts to bubble around the ingredients, allow them to soften and flavour the oil for 30 seconds more.

Before the garlic starts to colour and turn bitter, add the cavolo nero to the pan. The leaves may have become tangled as they drained, so you might need to separate them as you go. Move them around with tongs or a spatula and cook for a couple of minutes, during which time they will soften further and pick up the flavours in the pan. Add the orange juice, remove from the heat and transfer to a serving dish. Pour the remaining oil over the top and season with salt and lots of freshly ground pepper. Mix well so there's an even distribution of aromatics. Serve immediately.

ALONGSIDE: *Chorizo roast potatoes* (page 170); *Sweet potato, celeriac and porcini bake* (page 194); *Spiced roast carrots* (page 216); *Cheesy polenta* (page 238); *Cannellini beans with sweetcorn and pickled mushrooms* (page 276)

Chopped kale with edamame, miso and sweet chilli

PREPARATION: *on the counter*
TIME NEEDED: *15 to 30 minutes*

Raw kale started out as a 'clean eating' thing, thanks to kale's status as the most 'super' of foods. I just think it tastes great and produces a variety of enjoyable, fresh and flexible sides.

When kale is shredded finely and salt and acid are massaged into it, the relatively tough and fibrous leaves are broken down and become good to eat, while still technically raw. It can handle a variety of flavours, though here they're vaguely Japanese. The miso paste in the dressing adds sweetness and umami – I suggest using yellow shinshu miso if possible, as it's relatively mild compared to dark red aka miso, but bolder than white shiro miso.

This is perfect with *red meats*, *offal*, *tofu* and *white fish*.

Serves 4–6

300–350g kale
2g sea salt
150g podded edamame beans, defrosted if frozen
2 teaspoons sesame seeds

Sweet pickled chilli
3 tablespoons rice vinegar
1 teaspoon golden caster sugar
1 red chilli, finely diced

Miso dressing
2 tablespoons white or yellow miso paste
3 tablespoons sesame oil
1 tablespoon maple syrup
4 tablespoons mirin
2 tablespoons rice vinegar

First, pickle the chilli. Heat the rice vinegar and sugar in a small saucepan and stir until the sugar has dissolved. Add the chilli and remove from the heat to cool while preparing the rest of the dish.

———

Wash and dry the kale. Tear the leaves from the central rib of each leaf and discard the ribs. You should end up with around 200–250g leaves. Working in batches, make a stack of leaves, roll them into a cigarette shape and use a large knife to shred that into very fine strips. Chop across the strips a few times before transferring to a large bowl. Once all the kale is chopped, add the salt and massage with your hands for 2–3 minutes – the kale will soften and become wet.

———

Whisk all the dressing ingredients together until they have emulsified. Stir in the pickled chilli and its liquid, stir again, then pour over the kale. Add the edamame beans and sesame seeds and mix well. Leave for about 5 minutes so that the dressing mingles with the kale. It's good if there's still a bit of bite to this salad, so it's best eaten within an hour, as the kale will continue to soften. That said, it's also perfectly fine after a few hours in the fridge.

———

ALONGSIDE: *Buttermilk, dill and soy-seed wedge salad* (page 88); *Spiced roast carrots* (page 216); *Buckwheat with celery and walnuts* (page 252); *Sesame soba noodles* (page 254); *Coconut jasmine rice* (page 296)

Kale, Romanesco, Parmesan and pine nut salad

PREPARATION: *on the counter*
TIME NEEDED: *15 to 30 minutes*

If you need something that's fresh, verdant, lively and zesty but also works well with warm meats and fish, consider this kale salad. It's raw and cool but sturdy enough to counter something hot like *grilled or roast chicken*, *fatty pork belly* or *whole baked sea bream and bass*.

The pine nuts, Parmesan and lemon remind me of pesto (obviously without the basil, though feel free to add some), and little nuggets and crumbs of Romanesco add colour and crunch. This is great as part of a banquet, not least because you can prepare it in advance and it requires no last-minute cooking.

Serves 4–6

300–350g kale
1g sea salt
4 tablespoons cold-pressed rapeseed oil
1 teaspoon golden caster sugar
Juice and finely grated zest of 1 large lemon
400g (about ½ head) Romanesco
30g pine nuts, toasted
35g Parmesan, grated
Freshly ground black pepper

Wash and dry the kale. Tear the leaves from the central rib of each leaf, discard the ribs and roughly chop any leaves if they're bigger than 4–5cm. You should end up with around 200–250g leaves. Add the salt and massage it into the kale with your hands for 2–3 minutes. The leaves will soften and become wet.

Make the dressing by mixing the oil, sugar, lemon juice and black pepper until they have emulsified. Stir in the lemon zest, then pour the dressing into the kale and mix well.

To prepare the Romanesco, trim the florets off the stalk, then cut the little buds off each floret to end up with lots of fingernail-sized pieces, reserving the stalks for another occasion. Add the buds, any Romanesco crumbs, the pine nuts and most of the Parmesan to the kale. Mix well, then sprinkle the remaining cheese over the top.

It's good if there's still a bit of bite to this salad, so it's best eaten within an hour, as the kale will continue to soften. It's still fine if left in the fridge for a few hours.

ALONGSIDE: *Tomato tonnato* (page 96); *Green tomato, salted celery and chervil salad* (page 100); *Steamed marinated fennel* (page 116); *New potatoes with pickled samphire and sorrel* (page 174); *Mixed quinoa with radish and pea shoots* (page 246)

Flower sprouts with lemon and anchovy butter

PREPARATION: *on a hob*
TIME NEEDED: *less than 15 minutes*

My default approach to cooking brassicas (aka the cabbage family) is simply to blanch and then dress them with anchovies and melted butter. Flower sprouts (a hybrid of kale and Brussels sprouts, also known as kalettes) are no exception. In this instance, though, I also add lemon zest to lighten things a little.

Boiling vegetables seems unfashionable at the moment, but I find cooking flower sprouts (or, for that matter, kale, sprout tops or purple sprouting broccoli) that way results in a certain luscious, juicy quality that you miss out on when sautéing or stir-frying. It takes barely 90 seconds, after which the wet, frilly leaves seem particularly happy to put on a heavy jacket of flavoured butter.

The anchovy, lemon and brassica scream out for *lamb – whether chop, roast joint or stew* – but I love it with *eggs* or *smoked haddock* too. Come to think of it, a pile of these on the side of a *fish pie* would be awesome.

Serves 4–6

400–500g flower sprouts
20g butter
50g tinned anchovies in olive oil
Juice and finely grated zest of 1 lemon
1 large garlic clove, very thinly sliced
Sea salt and freshly ground black pepper

Trim any woody-looking ends off the flower sprouts, then wash them thoroughly. The best way to do this is to fill a large bowl with cold water, put the flower sprouts in it, shake them around, then remove them, discard the dirty water and repeat until the water is clear.

———

Bring a large pan of salted water to the boil. Meanwhile, melt the butter in another saucepan. Roughly chop the anchovies and add them to the butter along with a tablespoon or two of their oil, most of the lemon zest and all the garlic. Cook over a low-medium heat for 1–2 minutes until the anchovies start to melt, the garlic softens and the lemon zest mellows, but nothing takes on any colour. Remove from the heat and add the lemon juice.

———

When the water is at a rapid rolling boil, add the flower sprouts and cook them for 60–90 seconds, no more. Drain them thoroughly, then tip them back into the pan. Pour the flavoured butter and oil over the flower sprouts, followed by 5 or 6 turns of the pepper mill. Toss them until all the leaves are well glossed and sprinkle the last of the lemon zest over the top.

———

ALONGSIDE: *Butter-braised chicory* (page 72); *Chicken stock and orange-braised fennel* (page 120); *Cauliflower cheese* (page 132); *Sweet potato, celeriac and porcini bake* (page 194); *Beetroot gratin* (page 224); *Butter beans with sage* (page 272)

Deep-fried Brussels sprouts

PREPARATION: *on a hob*
TIME NEEDED: *15 to 30 minutes*

Deep-frying sprouts provides crunch, caramel and browning flavours on the outside, but because the process is quick, the centre is sweet, not sulphurous, and retains a pleasing bite. It's an ace way to cook and serve these tightly packed little brassicas, and fun to make and serve too.

I suggest seasoning them with celery salt and white pepper, though standard sea salt and many twists of the black-pepper mill would be good too. You could even try a sprinkling of sweet spices, such as cinnamon, cardamom or nutmeg.

Turkey, in any form, is an obvious match for deep-fried sprouts. I'd love them next to *goose*, a *rib of beef* or a *veal chop*, too. Serve alongside something soft, like a mash or a purée, to provide textural contrast and a balance of fried and 'clean'.

Serves 4–6

600g Brussels sprouts
1 litre sunflower or vegetable oil
1 heaped teaspoon celery salt
⅓ teaspoon ground white pepper

Bring a large pan of salted water to the boil. Preheat the oven to 60°C/Fan 50°C/the lowest gas setting and line a baking tray with kitchen paper.

Trim any woody bits off the base of the sprouts and cut the largest ones in half, so they are all roughly the same size. When the water is boiling, add the sprouts and cook for 2 minutes. Drain, then rinse under cold water until cool (or plunge them into a bowl of iced water). Tip them onto a clean tea towel to dry completely.

Put the oil in a deep fryer or high-sided pan and heat it to 180°C (use a kitchen thermometer to check). Cook the sprouts in 3 or 4 batches until they start to turn gold – about 2 minutes per batch. Tip them onto the prepared tray and keep warm in the oven until all the sprouts are cooked. Remove the kitchen paper, then season the sprouts with celery salt and white pepper. Mix well and serve immediately.

ALONGSIDE: *Creamed chard* (page 8); *Creamed sweetcorn with feta* (page 122); *Yeasted cauliflower purée* (page 130); *Anchoïade mashed potatoes* (page 180); *Roast butternut squash purée* (page 188); *Sweet potato, celeriac and porcini bake* (page 194)

Rosemary and chestnut sprouts

PREPARATION: *on a hob*
TIME NEEDED: *less than 15 minutes*

There are myriad ways to spruce up the much-maligned Brussels sprout, but cooked chestnuts are by far the best addition, their sweetness lifting the sprouts' natural bitterness (and sulphurous odour if overcooked). I also like adding finely chopped rosemary, which means they go as well with *lamb*, *pork* and *game birds* as they do with the *traditional turkey*.

Other tricks in this recipe that ensure sprout-eating pleasure include parboiling the sprouts, then plunging them into iced water to keep them vivid and perky; adding sprout tops to the mix; sautéing in plenty of butter and seasoning with lots and lots and lots of black pepper.

Serves 4–6

400g Brussels sprouts
150–200g sprout tops (1–2 heads)
40g butter
Leaves from 4 sprigs rosemary, finely chopped
200g cooked, peeled whole chestnuts, roughly chopped
Sea salt and freshly ground black pepper

Bring a large pan of salted water to the boil. Trim any woody bits off the base of the sprouts. If you have lots of different sizes, cut the largest ones in half so they're a similar size to the smallest. Separate the sprout-top leaves from their stalk, rinse and drain. Cut the 6–8 largest outer leaves in half. You will reach a bud at the top that's about the size of a golf ball. Cut this in half (it's the best bit), and ensure you keep any mini sprouts hidden among the leaves.

Cook the sprouts (but not the tops) in the boiling water for 2 minutes. Drain and plunge them into a bowl of iced water or rinse under cold running water to stop the cooking and prevent them from turning dull and sulphurous, then drain them well.

Place a large pan or wok over a medium-high heat and add the butter. When it starts to froth, add the cold part-cooked sprouts and rosemary. Sauté for 1 minute before adding the sprout tops and 3 tablespoons water. Cook for 3–4 minutes, until the leaves are tender, then stir in the chestnuts and leave the pan on the heat for 30 seconds more. Season with a good pinch of salt and many grinds of the pepper mill. Serve immediately.

ALONGSIDE: *Honey and Marmite-glazed parsnips* (page 182); *Scorched sweet potatoes with sobrasada butter* (page 190); *Carrot-juice carrots* (page 218); *White wine and dill carrots* (page 222); *Bread sauce and parsnip crisps* (page 236)

Sprout tops with Jerusalem artichokes and apple

PREPARATION: *on a hob*
TIME NEEDED: *15 to 30 minutes*

The three core ingredients in this dish work incredibly well together: the sprout tops are earthy but fresh, the knobbly artichokes bring a nutty sweetness, and the apple is sharp, which both accentuates and binds the other two. They combine to make a lively, warm autumnal salad, which could be your only side dish or form part of a larger selection.

The sweet-and-savoury nature of it works really well next to *pork* and *chicken* in pretty much any style, as well as *rich beef dishes* and *things with cheesy or sweet sauces*.

Serves 4–6

1 lemon, halved
250g Jerusalem artichokes
2 tablespoons sunflower or vegetable oil
40g butter
350g sprout tops (2–3 heads)
1 sharp apple, such as Cox, Granny Smith or Braeburn
½ onion, diced
Sea salt and freshly ground black pepper

Squeeze one of the lemon halves into a bowl and add 2 tablespoons water. Peel the artichokes one by one and immediately drop them into the acidulated water. Cut the artichokes in half lengthways, then in half again widthways.

———

Set a large heavy-bottomed frying pan or wide saucepan over a medium-high heat. Add the oil and 10g butter and let them heat up for a minute. Drain the artichokes, add them to the pan and sauté for 5–6 minutes, or until browned a little at the edges but tender within.

———

Separate the sprout-top leaves from their stalk, then rinse and drain. Cut the 6–8 largest outer leaves in half. You will reach a bud at the top that's about the size of a golf ball. Cut this in half (it's the best bit), and ensure you keep any mini sprouts hidden among the leaves.

———

Core the apple, cut it into 1–2cm dice, then add the juice of the remaining lemon half to prevent the apple discolouring and to add a little zing.

———

When the Jerusalem artichokes are just tender, add the remaining butter and, once that's melted, the onion and a pinch of salt. After 2–3 minutes the onions should be soft and the butter frothing. Add the sprout tops, bud and mini sprouts. Stir, then add 3 tablespoons water, which will steam and help warm, wilt and soften the leaves. Stir occasionally to ensure even cooking (it will take about 3–4 minutes). Remove from the heat and add the diced apple, a pinch of salt and lots of freshly ground black pepper. Decant into a serving dish, making sure you pour any pan juices over the top.

———

ALONGSIDE: *Cauliflower cheese* (page 132); *Boulangère potatoes* (page 168); *Maple and pecan roast squash* (page 186); *Beetroot gratin* (page 224); *Mac 'n' cheese* (page 286)

Sweet cauliflower greens

PREPARATION: *on a hob*
TIME NEEDED: *less than 15 minutes*

Cauliflower greens are arguably the best freebie in the vegetable world. At first glance they're a natural packaging of little interest. But they are, in fact, crunchy, vibrant, nutritious and not without a hint of cauliflower flavour. They're a brilliant match with *fatty meats* and *rich sauces*, or as something light and crunchy to go alongside *white fish*. So only discard the most withered and brown outer leaves (if any). If you want to use them later, they'll store well enough in the fridge for 2–3 days in a paper or ziplock bag, or wrapped in clingfilm.

The key is to cook each leaf appropriately. I find that, once trimmed from the base of a cauliflower, they can be sorted into three types: the small, thin bright green-yellow leaves close to the vegetable, which need no cooking; the medium bright green leaves, which need only 10 seconds of direct heat; and the tougher outer leaves with thick stems, which require a quick blanch.

Serves 4–6

350–500g cauliflower leaves (from 2 cauliflower heads)
2 tablespoons cold-pressed rapeseed oil
1 tablespoon cider vinegar
1 teaspoon golden caster sugar
Sea salt and freshly ground black pepper

Bring a large pan of salted water to the boil. Meanwhile, wash and drain the cauliflower leaves. Sort the leaves into three types: set the small bright green-yellow and the medium green leaves aside in separate piles; cut the largest and thickest stems in half down the middle of the stem so they cook quickly.

———

In a large bowl, make the dressing by whisking the oil, vinegar, sugar and a pinch each of salt and black pepper.

———

Once the water is boiling, and when the rest of your meal is very nearly ready, blanch the largest greens for 45–60 seconds. Put the medium leaves in a colander, then drain the large greens through the colander so that the hot water wilts the medium leaves. There will still be a little crunch in the thickest stems, which is a good thing. Tip the leaves into the bowl with the dressing. Toss, then add the smallest, still-raw leaves. Serve immediately.

———

ALONGSIDE: *Grilled tenderstem broccoli with umami crumbs* (page 40); *Yeasted cauliflower purée* (page 130); *Vermouth-braised red onions* (page 146); *Sweet potato, celeriac and porcini bake* (page 194); *Red wine, anise and orange lentils* (page 264)

Grilled tenderstem broccoli with umami crumbs

PREPARATION: *on a hob and in the oven*
TIME NEEDED: *15 to 30 minutes*

It would be perfectly reasonable to say that broccoli doesn't need to be messed around, whether in its normal, tenderstem or sprouting form – just steam or blanch and enjoy it as the super food that it is. But that ignores the fact that when charred and blistered and crisp at the edges, there's a whole other level of broccoli to be enjoyed. You can achieve this effect by roasting or grilling (though the broccoli should be blanched first, so that the vegetable is tender and juicy as well as crisp). I love charred broccoli – with the crumbs – alongside *salmon*, *tofu* or *slow-braised pork belly*. But it's a pretty adaptable side.

The umami crumbs are a garnish to accentuate the gnarly browned bits. Panko breadcrumbs (available in supermarkets and online) make for a better crunch when cooked than plain breadcrumbs. And although you can buy mushroom powder now, you'll get more bang for your buck if you buy dried porcini and whizz them in a spice grinder. This recipe provides far more crumbs than you need, but they keep well and can be used to garnish many vegetable side dishes, or top the odd gratin or cheesy sauce. The crumbs will store well in an airtight container for at least a month.

I've suggested tenderstem broccoli because those long stems seem to particularly enjoy a little grill time. But the florets from a standard broccoli work well too; keep them large and cut them in half, exposing the cut sides to the heat.

Serves 4–6

600g tenderstem broccoli
1 tablespoon cold-pressed rapeseed oil

Umami crumbs
4 tablespoons cold-pressed rapeseed oil
100g panko breadcrumbs
30g dried porcini mushrooms
Sea salt

To make the umami crumbs, preheat the oven to 220°C/Fan 200°C/Gas 7. Spread around 2 tablespoons oil over a shallow baking tray. Sprinkle the panko breadcrumbs on top, and the remaining oil over that, then stir well so all the crumbs have a chance to soak up the oil. Shake the tray to level the contents, then bake on the top shelf for around 10 minutes, or until golden brown. If your tray is small and the crumbs deep, you may need to move the crumbs around with a spoon so they are evenly cooked, and they will take longer to brown.

———

Tip the crumbs into a container and allow to cool. Meanwhile, use an electric spice grinder or small food processor to process the porcini to a powder. Sprinkle this over the cooled breadcrumbs along with 2 good pinches of salt and mix well. Store in an airtight container.

———

When you're ready to eat, preheat the grill to its highest setting Bring a large pan of salted water to a rolling boil. Blanch the broccoli for 4 minutes, then drain well.

———

Spread the broccoli over a baking tray, drizzle with the oil and toss to ensure all the stems are coated. Place the tray 5–8cm from the heat and grill for 3 minutes. Turn the vegetables over and grill for 2–3 minutes more, or until the broccoli is browned and blistering. Decant the broccoli into a serving bowl and scatter with generous handfuls of umami crumbs (you'll need around half the batch; see pages 8, 72 and 286 for other uses).

ALONGSIDE: *Butter-braised chicory* (page 72); *Wilted bitter leaves with blue cheese dressing* (page 76); *Chicken stock and orange-braised fennel* (page 120); *Aubergine purée* (page 138); *Caponata* (page 140)

Purple sprouting broccoli with tarragon

PREPARATION: *on a hob*
TIME NEEDED: *less than 15 minutes*

This, quite probably, is the side I cook most often, and the first one I think of to go with *lamb* or *white fish*. Once you tune into it, the match of iron-y purple sprouting broccoli and anise-heavy tarragon is hard to turn from. In fact, I'm not sure I even liked tarragon before I ate it with broccoli, and now I can't stop using it; if you have the same response, try adding it to spring greens, tenderstem broccoli, green beans or asparagus.

In this instance I prefer to steam the broccoli a little beyond al dente, so that it's juicy and floppy but not yet dulled in colour; and to be liberal with the herb, the oil and the black pepper. It's perfectly fine to boil it instead (see page 44) but steaming seems to keep things particularly green.

Serves 4–6

600g purple sprouting broccoli
Leaves from 12 stems tarragon, roughly chopped
Juice and finely grated zest of ½ lemon
4–5 tablespoons extra-virgin olive oil
Sea salt and freshly ground black pepper

Trim any woody ends off the purple sprouting stems. Cut the leaves from the stalks and any little florets branching from the main stalk (these cook more quickly and go in the steamer later).

Prepare a steamer or pan of boiling water with a steamer basket on top. Once the water is boiling, add the main broccoli stems and cover with a lid. After 4 minutes, add the little florets and leaves, then steam for 3–4 minutes more, deliberately going just beyond al dente. (Cooking it directly in boiling water will take less time.)

Remove the broccoli and put it in a serving bowl, then add the tarragon, lemon zest, plenty of salt and black pepper. Pour the lemon juice and oil over the top and toss thoroughly but gently, so all pieces are well dressed. Serve immediately.

ALONGSIDE: *Creamed sweetcorn with feta* (page 122); *Caponata* (page 140); *Roman rosemary polenta* (page 240); *Wheat berries with capers and tomatoes* (page 250); *Haricot beans with tomato and persillade* (page 278)

Purple sprouting broccoli with ricotta and orzo

PREPARATION: *on a hob*
TIME NEEDED: *15 to 30 minutes*

There is deliberately more broccoli than pasta here (hence its presence in the greens chapter); the orzo is there to add a little texture and a certain silkiness. In just one mouthful you get warming broccoli and tarragon, cold, creamy and refreshing ricotta and lemon, and then the buzz of a little red chilli. Things like *chicken* and *chargrilled fatty lamb chops and cutlets* are particular fans.

I like to cook purple sprouting broccoli until it's just a little floppy; it takes on aromatics better and is particularly satisfying to eat like this. You could easily use classic or tenderstem broccoli if you can't get hold of the purple stuff.

Serves 4–6

400g purple sprouting broccoli
80g orzo pasta
1 garlic clove, thinly sliced
2 tablespoons extra-virgin olive oil
Leaves from 8–10 stems tarragon, roughly chopped
Juice and finely grated zest of 1 lemon
1 small, mild red chilli, finely chopped
60–80g ricotta
Sea salt and freshly ground black pepper

Trim any woody ends off the broccoli stems. Cut the leaves from the stalks and any little florets branching from the main stalk (these cook more quickly and will be added to the pan later).

———

Bring a large pan of heavily salted water to the boil. Add the orzo and cook at a gentle simmer for the time stated on the packet. (The broccoli will be cooked in the same water, so you need far more than normal for this quantity of pasta.)

———

With 6 minutes remaining on the orzo cooking time, add the main broccoli stems to the pasta water. Throw in the small florets 3 minutes later, and 1 minute later add the sliced garlic and any leaves.

———

Drain the broccoli and orzo thoroughly, then return them to the pan. Add the oil, tarragon, lemon zest and juice, chilli, lots of black pepper and a good pinch of salt. Gently toss so that the pasta and sprouting is well coated, check for seasoning, then decant to a serving dish. Dot teaspoons of ricotta in and around the broccoli and allow it to melt just a little before serving.

———

ALONGSIDE: *Roast Romano peppers* (page 104); *Quick romesco* (page 106); *Smoky ratatouille* (page 114); *Portobello mushrooms baked with oregano* (page 152); *Maple and pecan roast squash* (page 186)

Charred Romanesco

PREPARATION: *on a hob*
TIME NEEDED: *less than 15 minutes*

To my mind there are only two ways to eat Romanesco: charred or raw. If you boil or steam this remarkable-looking brassica it becomes pretty bland and dull: a real waste. This recipe is all about the blackened option (for raw Romanesco see page 28). It's best to use a frying pan or ridged grill pan to achieve a char. You could roast it in a hot oven for 30 minutes or so to similar effect, but you lose vibrancy, crunch and moisture.

If eating Western cuisine, go with the squeeze of lemon and glug of peppery, grassy extra-virgin olive oil. If Eastern or 'fusion' food is on the menu, try the soy, sesame, chilli and lime. The char and crunch complements *flaky white fish*, *slow-cooked pork*, *beef cheeks* or *stews*. You could also give broccoli the same treatment. Now go forth and burn things.

Serves 4–6

1 large head Romanesco (about 1kg, including green leaves)
3–4 tablespoons sunflower or vegetable oil

Olive oil and lemon dressing
3 tablespoons good extra-virgin olive oil
Juice and finely grated zest of ½ lemon
½ teaspoon sea salt

Soy, chilli and lime dressing
2 tablespoons light soy sauce
2 tablespoons sesame oil
Juice and finely grated zest of 1 lime
2 teaspoons sesame seeds
1 medium red chilli, very thinly sliced

Starting from the bottom of the Romanesco head, remove the outer leaves, then cut the florets off at their base. Cut the florets in half lengthways and put them in a large bowl with the sunflower oil. Cut the core into slices 2cm thick and each of these into shapes broadly the same size as the florets. Add to the florets and mix well to coat in the oil.

———

Bring a large pan of salted water to the boil and blanch any leaves for 30 seconds, then immediately plunge into iced water or rinse under cold water until cool. Drain.

———

Put your largest ridged grill pan, frying pan or wok over a high heat and arrange the Romanesco pieces flat-side down. Cook for around 4 minutes until well browned, then flip them over (don't even think of turning them if they're not charred). Cook for another 3–4 minutes to get a little colour on the bumpy side of the florets, then turn the heat off and stir the blanched leaves through to warm in the residual heat of the pan.

———

Make either of the dressings by combining all the ingredients in a large bowl, then toss the warm Romanesco in that. It's best served immediately, though still mighty enjoyable when cooled to room temperature.

———

ALONGSIDE: *Yeasted cauliflower purée* (page 130); *Anchoïade mashed potatoes* (page 180); *Mum's bulgar wheat salad* (page 244); *Sesame soba noodles* (page 254); *Chicken stock orzo* (page 282)

Baby pak choi with sticky garlic and ginger

PREPARATION: *on a hob*
TIME NEEDED: *less than 15 minutes*

Pak choi seems to have become the most ubiquitous and readily available of the Chinese greens. I like the fresh, crisp contrast it provides to a *spicy or sticky Asian-spiced meal such as braised pork, deep-fried tofu or sweetly sauced salmon*. But because it's not exactly flavoursome, I like to give the edges a little bit of colour and add some extra aromatics in the form of garlic and ginger.

Serves 4–6

600g baby pak choi
1 large banana shallot or small red onion
2 tablespoons sunflower or vegetable oil
6cm fresh ginger, peeled and cut into fine matchsticks
2 garlic cloves, sliced thinly
3 tablespoons light soy sauce
Juice of ½ lime

Prepare all the ingredients first, as the cooking process is quick. Cut the pak choi into halves or quarters lengthways, depending on their size. Cut the shallot in half from root to tip, remove the skin, then slice each half very finely, again from root to tip.

Pour the oil into a wok or large frying pan and place over a high heat. When the oil is nearly smoking, add the shallot and ginger. Cook for 30 seconds, stirring once or twice, then add the garlic and cook for 20 seconds or so until you have a fragrant mixture. Put the pak choi quarters in the pan, cut-side down if you can. Cook without stirring for 30 seconds, so they take on a bit of colour but remain crisp. You'll probably need to do this in 2 or 3 batches if your wok isn't huge, in which case remove the part-cooked pak choi after each batch, returning them all to the wok to finish.

Once all the pak choi is coloured and back in the wok, add the soy sauce and cover with a lid. Let the greens steam for 30–60 seconds, or until they just wilt a little. Remove the wok from the heat, stir in the lime juice and serve immediately.

ALONGSIDE: *Courgettes with soy, sesame, mint and chilli* (page 112); *Smacked cucumbers* (page 158); *Buckwheat with celery and walnuts* (page 252); *Sesame soba noodles* (page 254); *Three pepper rice* (page 294)

Asian greens with shrimp paste

PREPARATION: *on a hob*
TIME NEEDED: *less than 15 minutes*

This is based on a revelatory plate of *kangkung belacan* I ate while I was writing this book. The renowned Malaysian dish uses a particular style of fermented shrimp paste that's not easy to get hold of. But any fermented shrimp paste adds the uniquely pungent salty-sweet tang I've craved so often since eating that dish; I've used it, boosted by fresh chilli, with numerous wok-fried greens since. Look for Thai or Vietnamese shrimp paste online, or follow your nose if in a shop.

Try to use morning glory (*kangkung* in Malay) if you can get hold of it. The long, thin, hollow stems retain a relatively fresh, grassy bite even when wilted, and there's loads of surface area for the sauce to cling to. But if you struggle to find it, pak choi or pretty much any other green vegetable from an Asian supermarket would take the flavours well. As, by my reckoning, would purple sprouting, tenderstem or normal florets of broccoli, spring greens and probably kale too.

This is the kind of dish that would hold its own alongside a *sticky, dark beef rendang* or a *coconut-based curry*, or otherwise add interest to plainer ingredients such as *soft tofu*, *chicken breast* or a *fried egg*.

Serves 4–6

600g morning glory, or other greens
3 banana shallots
2 medium red chillies
3 tablespoons sunflower or vegetable oil
2 tablespoons dried shrimp paste
2 heaped teaspoons caster sugar

Prepare all the ingredients in advance, as the cooking process is quick. For morning glory, or any other greens with a long stem and fragile leaf, trim off the leafy ends at the point where the stems thicken and set aside. Cut the stems into 5cm lengths – there may be the odd leaf branching out from these. I prefer to keep the stems and leaves separate so as to cook them for the right amount of time.

———

Peel the shallots and chop them roughly into quarters from root to tip; in this dish, they're good left as distinct petals. Chop the chilli into thin rings along its length.

———

Place a wok over a very high heat. Add the oil and allow it to heat up for 30–45 seconds, then add the shallots and stir-fry for 1 minute before adding the fermented shrimp paste. Cook this for 30 seconds, taking care not to let it burn, then add the green stems and sprinkle over the sugar (you may need to add the stems in a couple of batches if your wok isn't huge).

———

Stir-fry for 1–2 minutes, adding about 100ml water to help steam the greens, then remove the wok from the heat just before the stems lose their spark and crispness. Add the leaves and let these wilt in the residual heat for 30 seconds. Transfer to a serving platter, ensuring you pour any sauce from the wok over the greens. Serve immediately.

———

ALONGSIDE: *Courgette and edamame salad* (page 110); *Quick-pickled daikon* (page 210); *Flavoured butter bread* (page 234); *Mustard seed, lemon and thyme rice* (page 288); *Crisp-bottomed Persian rice* (page 302)

Turnip tops with burnt lemon and olive oil

PREPARATION: *on a hob*
TIME NEEDED: *less than 15 minutes*

Although the words translate exactly, we'll have to concede that the Italian *cime di rapa* sounds more appealing than the English 'turnip tops'. I'm sure that's one reason why these greens are not on every family's meal table – another closely linked one being our general apathy about the roots from which they sprout.

Whatever the case, it's a shame. Turnip tops have a hint of mustard in them (worth bearing in mind when deciding what they go with), with little buds and long stems that have similar properties to purple sprouting broccoli, and cook in no time at all. Just dousing them in peppery extra-virgin olive oil and salt is the classic Italian way to season them, though I love the addition here of jammy and slightly bitter charred lemon juices. I can think of few things better than a large plate of these, a *whole baked sea bass or turbot* and a bottle of something cold and white to wash it all down.

Turnip tops are usually available during winter and spring. Outside those seasons, the burnt lemon and olive oil dressing and the sprinkle of toasted sunflower seeds would work well with pretty much any green vegetable.

Serves 4–6

1 large or 2 small lemons
3 tablespoons peppery extra-virgin olive oil
600–750g turnip tops on the stem
25g sunflower seeds, toasted (optional)
Sea salt

Put a ridged grill pan or heavy-bottomed frying pan on the hottest part of your hob. Cut the lemons in half widthways, then trim the knobbly end off each half, so that the lemon can sit flat on either end.

Place the lemons flesh-side down on the smoking-hot pan and cook for 4–5 minutes, or until well charred. Turn over and char the other side for the same amount of time. Remove and allow to cool for a few minutes before squeezing their juices through a sieve (to catch the seeds) into a large mixing bowl. Add a good pinch of salt and the olive oil. Whisk with a fork to emulsify the liquids.

In order that the turnip tops are cooked to their best advantage, you need to divide them into two piles: the leaves and the rest. You can do this in advance of eating, but the cooking should be done at the last minute.

Cut off the bottom 1–2cm (the bit that holds the stems together) and discard it, then trim the leaves from the other end and set aside. You will be left with a tangle of long, thin stems and (if you're lucky) a few sprouting buds, which look similar to purple sprouting broccoli. Trim the buds from the stems, then cut the stems to 4–5cm lengths and add them to the buds.

Bring a large pan of salted water to the boil. Add the turnip-top stems and buds and cook for 60 seconds, then add the leaves and cook

for 45–60 seconds more, pushing them under the water at the beginning. Drain thoroughly, then add to the bowl with the lemon and oil dressing. Toss and stir the leaves in the dressing. Check for seasoning, sprinkle with the sunflower seeds (if using) and serve immediately.

ALONGSIDE: *Celeriac baked in a salt and thyme crust* (page 198); *Baked Jerusalem artichokes with yoghurt and sunflower seeds* (page 206); *White wine and dill carrots* (page 222); *Cheesy polenta* (page 238); *White beans with fennel seeds, chilli and rocket* (page 274)

Wilted spinach with coconut, ginger and pink peppercorns

PREPARATION: *on a hob*
TIME NEEDED: *less than 15 minutes*

I think a very quick, light touch in the cooking is the best way with spinach. Anything else results in shrivelled leaves that have spilled all their moisture and basically become squeaky and boggy. So if you're, say, sautéing spinach, it's preferable to heat the leaves for just a minute or two, then remove the pan from the stove well before its contents are fully cooked through. They'll continue to wilt in the residual heat. I strongly recommend using large spinach leaves rather than baby ones, as they're better both in texture and taste. Look for bunches of spinach still on their stems, as these add bulk and interest.

The coconut, ginger and pink peppercorns add sweetness, spice and life to the spinach. It's really good with *fish dishes*, and also with *beef*.

Serves 4–6

600–750g large-leaf spinach, including stems
4 teaspoons coconut oil
1 onion, sliced into thin crescents
25g fresh ginger, peeled and cut into thin matchsticks
Juice of ½ lemon
30g coconut flakes
2 teaspoons pink peppercorns
Sea salt

Bunched spinach requires a thorough wash: fill the sink or a large bowl with cold water, add the spinach and give it a good fondle. Transfer the leaves to a colander, drain away the water (and mud) and repeat until completely grit and mud free. Trim the leaves off the stems and set the leaves aside. Cut the woody base off the stems and discard it, and cut the stems themselves into 4–5cm lengths. Set aside in a separate pile.

———

Put a wok or large frying pan over a high heat. Add the oil and wait until it has heated. Add the onion and ginger and allow them to colour (for once!) and turn crisp and sticky; don't allow them to burn. This could easily take 2–3 minutes. When the onion is golden, add the spinach stems and cook for 30–60 seconds. Add two thirds of the leaves (probably in a couple of stages unless you have an enormous pan) and let them cook for 45–60 seconds, then use tongs to shuffle the leaves around, ensuring those at the top are exposed to direct heat. Cook for just a few seconds more, then turn off the heat and add the final third of the leaves.

———

Season with salt, squeeze in the lemon juice, toss and quickly transfer to a serving dish. The leaves will continue to wilt, but not as quickly as they would in the pan. Add three quarters of the coconut flakes and peppercorns. Mix well, then sprinkle the rest over the top. Serve immediately.

———

ALONGSIDE: *Aubergine purée* (page 138); *Hasselback potatoes with bay and caraway* (page 172); *Rosemary and chilli roast squash* (page 184); *Carrot, cumin and nigella seed salad* (page 214); *Crisp-bottomed Persian rice* (page 302)

Garlic oil pea shoots

PREPARATION: *on a hob*
TIME NEEDED: *less than 15 minutes*

In Western cuisine, pea shoots are used as a garnish or perhaps sparingly in a mixed salad. What a shame that is. I first saw the light at a dim sum restaurant in Hong Kong, when our order of pea shoots arrived as a huge bowl filled with a tangled mass of glossy, flavourful green tendrils wilting in a garlic-infused oil. For me, this was a game changer, and is now something I regularly enjoy with *five-spiced pork belly, duck or chicken, whole baked white fish* or *tofu*.

Serves 4–6

4 tablespoons sunflower or vegetable oil
3 garlic cloves, crushed
4 tablespoons Shaoxing wine or dry sherry
1 teaspoon golden caster sugar
400–500g pea shoots
Sea salt

This is best cooked in a large wok, although a large frying pan or saucepan would do the trick. Put the oil, garlic and a pinch of salt in the wok and place over a low-medium heat for 3 minutes. Allow the oil to heat up very slowly, so that the garlic softens and infuses its flavour into the oil, but does not become crisp, brown and bitter.

Turn the heat up and wait for 10 seconds until the garlic starts to fry (you might need a little longer if you're not using a wok), then add the Shaoxing wine and sugar. Let the wine bubble, steam and reduce by half (the wok should by now be very hot), then add two thirds of the pea shoots.

Pea shoots wilt very quickly, so move the curly mass of green constantly for 45–60 seconds, exposing most of them to direct heat; this is best done with a pair of tongs. Turn the heat off when most of the shoots have wilted. Add the remaining raw shoots, then tip the contents of the pan (including any juices) into a warmed serving bowl. The residual heat will finish cooking the raw shoots. Serve immediately.

ALONGSIDE: *Courgette and edamame salad* (page 110); *Smacked cucumbers* (page 158); *Quick cucumber and daikon kimchi* (page 160); *Sesame soba noodles* (page 254); *Almond and anise rice* (page 298)

13:36

French-ish peas

PREPARATION: *on a hob*
TIME NEEDED: *less than 15 minutes*

The classic dish *petits pois à la Française* involves cooking peas in chicken stock with shredded lettuce and spring onions. This recipe picks up a similar theme, in that lettuce and spring onions are involved, but it focuses on peas in their pods (sugar snaps and mangetout) and adds cooling mint and refreshing lemon. All of which makes for a clean, fresh and vibrant side dish, ideal for when you were thinking of boiling some peas, but would prefer something with a little, um, *je ne sais quoi*.

You could swap the sugar snaps, mangetout and green beans with normal peas if you wish. Also, in spring and early summer I often use asparagus spears instead of green beans. Whatever you use, don't boil it for too long. This side is meant to be fresh, not dull and without bite. It's especially good with *oily fish such as salmon or trout*, or rich, heavy meat that needs something bright to cut through it, like *slow-cooked lamb shoulder* or *venison casserole.*

Serves 4–6

200g green beans
400g sugar snap peas
200g mangetout
1 little gem lettuce, cut in half and thinly sliced
3 spring onions, thinly sliced
Leaves from 5 or 6 stems mint, finely shredded
3 tablespoons peppery extra-virgin olive oil
Juice of 1 lemon
Sea salt

Fill your largest pan with salted water and bring it to the boil. Meanwhile, cut the woody tops off the green beans. I leave the tails on, but if you want to, trim those off too.

Once the water is at a rapid boil, add the green beans and cook for 2 minutes before adding the sugar snap peas. A minute later, add the mangetout. Another minute after that, add the lettuce and spring onions. Cook for 30 seconds longer, then drain well.

Return the drained greens to the saucepan and add the mint, oil and a good pinch of salt. Gently stir so that the mint and liquids are evenly spread, then serve straight from the pan or decant into a serving dish. Add the lemon juice and send to the table.

ALONGSIDE: *Cauliflower cheese* (page 132); *Boulangère potatoes* (page 168); *Scorched sweet potatoes with sobrasada butter* (page 190); *Butter-glazed turnips with horseradish* (page 204); *Beetroot gratin* (page 224)

Asparagus with cured egg yolk

PREPARATION: *on a hob*
TIME NEEDED: *less than 15 minutes*

Okay, the 'Time needed' entry is slightly misleading: although cooking the asparagus really does take less than 15 minutes, the curing and dehydrating of an egg yolk is a longer undertaking (very little work, but about 30 hours of waiting).

But please try it! Cured and dehydrated egg yolk can be grated on a variety of boiled greens, or used as a seasoning for pasta dishes. It has a similar salty, umami quality to Parmesan or bottarga, although there's also the creamy butteriness of egg yolk that clings to and coats hot vegetables. You'll only need one yolk for this dish, but given the effort it's worth curing 3 at once and using them as a Parmesan substitute for the next week or so.

Asparagus is best when cooked simply: a quick dance in boiling water until the spears just begin to flop. For this particular recipe, the thinner the spears the better, as there's more surface area for the grated egg to cling to.

There's a variety of things I'd serve this with, from *cold cuts of roast beef and ham*, recently carved from the bone, to *crab tarts* or *poached trout*. If English asparagus is out of season, or you'd like more bulk, the asparagus could be substituted or supported by frozen peas; blanched, like the spears, for barely 4 minutes.

Serves 4–6

750g asparagus
5 tablespoons extra-virgin olive oil
Juice and finely grated zest of ½ lemon
Sea salt and freshly ground black pepper

Cured egg yolks
Fine table salt, for curing
Caster sugar, for curing
Leaves from 10–20 sprigs thyme
3 egg yolks (ideally Burford Browns)

To cure the egg yolks, find a small plastic or other non-reactive container that will comfortably hold the yolks with a few centimetres of space around each one. Fill it 1–2cm deep with fine table salt, then add the same amount of caster sugar (you could measure the weight of the salt and replicate with sugar, but by eye is fine). Add the thyme leaves and mix thoroughly. Tip half of the curing mixture into a separate bowl. Break the eggs, reserving the whites for another use (such as Celeriac baked in a salt and thyme crust, page 198), and gently place the egg yolks on the curing mixture in the container, then sprinkle the remaining mixture over the top. Cover with a lid or clingfilm and leave in the fridge for 24 hours.

After 12 hours, check the yolks. The tops might be bare. If so, spoon any excess curing mixture from the sides of the container to cover the yolks and leave for another 12 hours.

Once 24 hours is up, the yolks will be firm to the touch and will look like boiled sweets. Preheat the oven to its very lowest setting – no more than 50°C. Take the yolks out of the curing mixture and gently remove any excess with a clean damp cloth. Put the yolks on a silicone baking mat or non-stick baking sheet and leave in the oven for 6–8 hours, or until they have shrivelled to look like the surface

of the moon. They'll keep in an airtight container at room temperature for at least a week.

To cook the asparagus, bring a large pan two thirds full of heavily salted water to the boil. Bend each spear from tip to base. They will snap at the point where the fleshy stem becomes woody. Discard the woody ends. When the water is at a rapid boil, add the asparagus and cook for 3–4 minutes. Drain the asparagus as soon as the thicker ends are tender, and well before they start to dull in colour and flavour.

Meanwhile, mix together the oil, lemon zest and juice. Put the asparagus on a serving dish or return them to their pan. Coat them with the dressing and season with 10 turns of the pepper mill (remember that the cured yolk will add salt). Finely grate over 1 cured egg yolk using a microplane grater or something similar, and serve immediately.

ALONGSIDE: *Gem lettuce, mint and spring onion* (page 86); *New potatoes with seaweed butter* (page 176); *Cinnamon, chickpea and apricot couscous* (page 242); *Spinach and preserved lemon freekeh* (page 248); *Red rice with beetroot, feta and wild oregano* (page 300)

Agretti with olive oil

PREPARATION: *on a hob*
TIME NEEDED: *less than 15 minutes*

Also known as monk's beard or *barba di frate*, agretti is a relatively specialist ingredient. It's only around at the very end of winter through spring, and I include a 'recipe' here because I suspect that, during those months, most of us would pass over a bunch of these long, noodle-like green strands, thinking that we don't really know what to do with them. In fact, it's all very easy: wash, boil for less than 60 seconds and dress with some peppery olive oil. In other words, next to no effort.

But your sense of adventure is rewarded with a wonderful seasonal side: one that's grassy, fresh and has great texture. In restaurants you often find just a few strands as part of a dish. At home I like generous twirls of it next to *white fish*, *lamb* and *mutton*, *seafood such as scallops and crab*, or even just with *cooling mozzarella or ricotta*.

Serves 4–6

1 large bunch (about 300g) agretti
4–5 tablespoons extra-virgin olive oil
Sea salt and freshly ground black pepper

Cut the tough, woody and stringy root ends off the base of the agretti. Fill a large bowl or sink with cold water and plunge the agretti in. Shake it about to loosen any mud and grit. Transfer to a sieve or colander, empty the sink or bowl and repeat until the agretti is completely clean (probably 4–6 times).

———

Bring a large pan of salted water to the boil. When it's at a rapid rolling boil (and you're about to eat), add the agretti and blanch it for 45–60 seconds. No more. Drain and return it to the pan or put it in a serving bowl. Season with a pinch of salt and black pepper, then dress liberally with the oil. Mix well to ensure the strands are all glossed. Serve immediately.

———

ALONGSIDE: *Radicchio with a smoky blood orange and maple dressing* (page 80); *Anchoïade mashed potatoes* (page 180); *Roast butternut squash purée* (page 188); *Wine-poached salsify with gremolata* (page 200); *White beans with fennel seeds, chilli and rocket* (page 274)

Dijon-dressed green beans

PREPARATION: *on a hob*
TIME NEEDED: *less than 15 minutes*

String beans, green beans, snap beans, fine beans, haricots verts – these names all refer to pretty much the same thing: a green climbing bean, long, thin, slightly waxy to the bite and these days seemingly forever in the shops.

No doubt you'll have your own preferred way of cooking and serving green beans already, but if you want to do something a bit different there are any number of options: sesame and soy, garlic and bacon, almond and brown butter… I could go on, although I think this combination of beans and a Dijon mustard and shallot-heavy dressing is as good as any. Do give it a go.

Warm green beans enjoy the same dressing, though there's just something about it that's particularly good when served cold. *Tuna*, *salmon*, *pork chops* and *chicken* are classic matches.

Serves 4–6

500g green beans
1 tablespoon Dijon mustard
2 tablespoons white wine vinegar
4 tablespoons extra-virgin olive oil
1 teaspoon golden caster sugar
1 garlic clove, crushed
1 banana shallot, very thinly sliced
Sea salt and ground white pepper

Trim the woody tops off the beans. I tend to bunch them together and cut with scissors to save time. I also keep the stringy 'tails' on and leave the beans whole and long.

Bring a large pan of salted water to the boil. When the water is rolling rapidly, add the beans. Return to a gentle simmer and cook for 3–5 minutes. Pull one out to taste every 30 seconds or so from 3 minutes onwards. There's a fine line between slightly waxy and under-flavoured; crisp, verdant and sparky; and soft and dull. It's the middle level that you want. When the beans are ready, drain immediately and plunge into iced water or rinse under cold water until cool.

Whisk or shake together the mustard, vinegar, oil and sugar until the dressing has emulsified. Add a pinch of salt and pepper and the garlic and mix one more time. Pour the dressing into the bottom of a large bowl and add the shallot. Toss in the dressing and leave for 2 minutes or more, then add the cooled green beans and stir well to ensure all the beans are coated.

ALONGSIDE: *Grilled green tomatoes with oregano and chilli* (page 102); *Shaved fennel with tarragon* (page 118); *New potatoes with pickled samphire and sorrel* (page 174); *Celeriac baked in a salt and thyme crust* (page 198); *Red rice with beetroot, feta and wild oregano* (page 300)

Runner beans with bacon and walnuts

PREPARATION: *on a hob*
TIME NEEDED: *less than 15 minutes*

I wonder if runner beans appear a little unapproachable to some, with their hard, almost crocodile-like scaly flat sides, and remarkable length. As it happens, very little needs to be done to turn them into an excellent side: just top and tail and peel the stringy edges, then cut into fork-sized pieces; steam or briefly boil, and serve with butter or oil, salt and pepper.

But perhaps a little more could be done to draw in any remaining doubters. Here, they're sliced finely and accompanied by the fat, salt and smoke of good lardons, and the tang of a hot cider vinegar dressing. It's a versatile side, although *pork*, *veal* and *fish such as hake, skate or cod* are particularly good matches.

Serves 4–6

300–400g runner beans
150g smoked lardons
1 tablespoon sunflower oil
1 banana shallot, finely diced
1 tablespoon cider vinegar
Leaves from 6–8 stems flat-leaf parsley
50g walnut halves, roughly chopped
Freshly ground black pepper

Run a vegetable peeler down the edges of the runner beans, then cut them lengthways into 2–3 long thin strips per bean, like spaghetti. Cut these into 4–5cm lengths and bring a large pan of salted water to the boil. Cook the beans in the boiling water for 3–4 minutes, or until just starting to flop, but still bright green and with bite. Drain and return them to the pan.

Meanwhile, put the lardons in a large heavy-bottomed frying pan with the oil and cook over a medium heat (starting from cold helps render the fat). As the lardons begin to turn golden, add the shallot and cook for 3–4 minutes.

Remove the frying pan from the heat and pour in the cider vinegar. Stir to combine the fats and the vinegar, then scrape and pour the pan's contents over the drained beans. Add the parsley and walnuts and a generous grind of black pepper (the lardons will provide enough salt). Toss well to ensure the beans, bacon and other bits are thoroughly mixed. Serve immediately.

ALONGSIDE: *Grilled green tomatoes with oregano and chilli* (page 102); *Creamed sweetcorn with feta* (page 122); *Boulangère potatoes* (page 168); *Anchoïade mashed potatoes* (page 180); *Carrot-juice carrots* (page 218)

Puttanesca runner beans

PREPARATION: *on a hob*
TIME NEEDED: *30 minutes to an hour*

Runner beans and tomatoes are a pretty classic summer match. Roasting cherry tomatoes and blanched beans at the same time is one way of pairing the two ingredients; dousing the beans with a garlic-infused tomato sauce is another. This takes the latter option a little further by embellishing the red sauce as if it were a puttanesca, with chilli, olives and capers.

You won't need to serve many (if any) things alongside this and whatever it's partnered with, whether that's *pan-fried monkfish*, *cod*, some *gammon* or a *bacon chop*. If you think bulk is required, though, consider a grain, potato or root, but nothing too flash. If it suits your schedule, make the sauce in advance and reheat when you need it; cook the beans at the last moment.

Serves 4–6

1 tablespoon sunflower or vegetable oil
½ onion, finely diced
1 garlic clove, crushed
1 mild red chilli, deseeded and finely diced
400g tinned chopped tomatoes
2 teaspoons golden caster sugar
1 teaspoon dried mixed herbs
1 teaspoon balsamic vinegar
15 basil leaves, torn
3 tablespoons extra-virgin olive oil
15–20 kalamata olives
2 teaspoons capers, roughly chopped
300–400g runner beans
Sea salt

Start by making the sauce. Heat the sunflower oil in a medium saucepan over a medium-high heat. Add the onion with a pinch of salt and cook gently for 4–5 minutes without allowing it to colour, stirring occasionally. Add the garlic and chilli and cook for 2 minutes more before pouring in the chopped tomatoes. Half-fill the tomato tin with water, swill and add to the saucepan. Bring to the boil, add the sugar, dried herbs and balsamic vinegar, then reduce to a gentle simmer and cook for about 25 minutes. Season the sauce with a good pinch of salt, two thirds of the basil leaves and two thirds of the olive oil.

———

Meanwhile, pit the olives by tapping them with the bottom of a cup or mug to crack the flesh, then pushing the stone out. Discard the stones and roughly chop the olives. Add these, along with the capers, to the sauce once it's been cooking for 15 minutes.

———

Use a vegetable peeler to peel the stringy thin edges of the runner beans, then cut them on a slight angle into 5–6cm lengths. Bring a large pan of salted water to the boil. Add the beans and cook for 4–5 minutes, or until tender but not dull or soggy. Drain and set aside. You could mix the beans and sauce together at this point and serve from the pan. However, I prefer it when the two are not fully combined: place a couple of spoonfuls of the puttanesca sauce in the base of a serving bowl, pile the drained beans on top and spoon the rest of the sauce over this. Toss the beans in the sauce just a little, before finishing with the remaining basil and olive oil.

———

ALONGSIDE: *Anchoïade mashed potatoes* (page 180); *Sweet potato and rosemary hash-rösti* (page 192); *Roman rosemary polenta* (page 240); *Chicken stock orzo* (page 282); *Lemon and olive oil fregola* (page 284)

Okra chips with cumin salt

PREPARATION: *in the oven*
TIME NEEDED: *15 to 30 minutes*

Okra, also known as ladies' fingers, has a reputation for being sticky and gloopy (in the West, at least). Don't dismiss it, though. Stewed okra in a tomato sauce is one excellent way to cook and serve it, although I prefer these crisp and ridiculously more-ish 'chips'. They're particularly good if you're also serving rice, and will be a lively side for *relatively plain meat or fish dishes*, or hold their own against *spicy curries*, *dal* or *flavourful sauces*.

Serves 4–6

500g okra
1 tablespoon sunflower or vegetable oil
1 heaped teaspoon cumin seeds
1 teaspoon sea salt
Juice of ¼ lemon

Wash the okra and allow it to drain and dry fully. Spreading it out on kitchen paper will speed things up. Preheat the oven to 220°C/Fan 200°C/Gas 7.

Trim the stalk end off each okra pod and cut it in half lengthways. Spread the halves out over a baking tray large enough to hold the okra in one layer. Drizzle the oil over and mix to ensure all of the little fingers are glossed. Turn them so the cut side is facing up; this seems to help them dry and crisp better. Bake on the top shelf for about 20 minutes, or until browned and relatively crisp at the edges, giving the tray a shake or scrape after 15 minutes (the exact cooking time varies depending on the freshness of the okra).

While the okra is cooking, lightly toast the cumin seeds in a heavy-bottomed pan until they just start to darken a little and the air is fragrant. Tip them immediately into a pestle and mortar. Add the salt, then lightly grind so the cumin seeds are crushed and flattened but not completely powdered.

When the okra is crisp, remove it from the oven and sprinkle with the cumin salt. Mix gently to ensure all the okra are seasoned, then spread them out flat and allow to sit for 2–3 minutes (this helps prevent them from steaming and turning soggy). Squeeze the lemon juice over the top, mix and serve.

ALONGSIDE: *Wilted spinach with coconut, ginger and pink peppercorns* (page 54); *Flavoured butter bread* (page 234); *Chickpeas with garlic oil and spinach* (page 266); *Mustard seed, lemon and thyme rice* (page 288); *Curry leaf, cashew and coconut rice* (page 290)

Butter-braised chicory

PREPARATION: *in the oven*
TIME NEEDED: *more than an hour*

Chicory is a forced, pale green, bitter leaf, also known as Belgian endive or witloof. Its tightly packed leaves are crisp and slightly bitter when eaten raw (see page 78). When gently braised in butter and its own juices (it contains a great deal of water) the natural bitterness remains but there's a sweetness too. It is, perhaps, an acquired taste, but one that's worth gaining, as it is an excellent accompaniment to things like *chicken*, *duck*, *pork* and *white fish*. The soft, yielding texture, much like a slow-cooked onion, also provides a good contrast to anything with crunch or bite.

Though it seems like a small detail, the last instruction in the recipe – to slice the cooked chicory in half lengthways, season with salt, pepper, parsley and lemon, and then add the cooking juices – makes all the difference in the eating. If you've any umami crumbs (see page 40) lying around, sprinkle a handful over the top.

Serves 4

8 heads white chicory (Belgian endive)
150g butter, sliced
Leaves from 6–8 stems flat-leaf parsley
Juice of ½ lemon
Sea salt and freshly ground black pepper

Preheat the oven to 160°C/Fan 140°C/Gas 3. Wipe the chicory with a slightly damp cloth to remove any dirt (washing it more thoroughly will make things too soggy).

Put a few slices of butter in the base of an ovenproof dish (preferably one with a lid). Pack the chicory in 1–2 layers, pushing butter in, around and over it. Take a piece of greaseproof paper big enough to cover the dish, butter one side and place it, buttered-side down, over the chicory. Tuck it in at the sides, put the lid on and bake for 60 minutes.

When that time is up, uncover the chicory and shuffle it around so that any that was sitting on top is now underneath, and vice versa. Replace the paper and lid and cook for another 45–60 minutes, until golden and soft. Meanwhile, roll the parsley leaves together and chop very finely.

Once cooked, remove the chicory heads one at a time from the pan, cut them in half lengthways and lay them on a serving plate or platter, cut-side up. Squeeze the lemon juice over, then season with a generous grind of black pepper, a good pinch of salt and the parsley. Finish by giving the buttery braising juices a quick whisk to emulsify them, then pour over the chicory halves.

ALONGSIDE: *Purple sprouting broccoli with tarragon* (page 42); *Boulangère potatoes* (page 168); *Hasselback potatoes with bay and caraway* (page 172); *Wine-poached salsify with gremolata* (page 200); *Baked Jerusalem artichokes with yoghurt and sunflower seeds* (page 206)

PX radicchio Trevisano

PREPARATION: *in the oven*
TIME NEEDED: *30 minutes to an hour*

Radicchio Trevisano is a long, tear-shaped purple radicchio. It's thicker, hardier and more bitter than the round Chioggia variety, which I tend to see more often and enjoy raw in a salad (see page 80). But the Trevisano holds up particularly well to being cooked in a sticky, grown-up fortified wine and butter sauce.

Those glorious burgundy leaves wilt and turn brown. More appealingly, though, they also soften in texture, mellow in flavour and yield some of their own juices while soaking up the Pedro Ximenez, or PX (an intense sweet, dark sherry – you could use a sweet oloroso or Madeira to similar, though not quite as thrilling, effect). There's toffee, coffee, chocolate and all sorts of irresistible flavours here, in part thanks to the PX. I suppose using it is a little bit naughty and a touch lavish but, like all things with these qualities, very desirable.

If you can't find Trevisano, curly radicchio Tardivo works really well. The more fragile red radicchio di Verona, Chioggia, or even red chicory could be used too, but cook them for slightly less time. I think this is particularly grand next to *game birds*, *pigeon* and *rich beef dishes*, but I suspect you'll enjoy it with *white fish* and *wild mushrooms* as well.

Serves 4–6

1–2 heads (about 500g) radicchio Trevisano
70ml Pedro Ximenez sherry
50g butter
Sea salt and freshly ground black pepper

Preheat the oven to 200°C/Fan 180°C/Gas 6. Separate the radicchio leaves by cutting off the base to loosen them. Wash them in cold water and drain briefly, leaving a little water clinging to the leaves. Put them in a small roasting tin, making sure they're no more than 2 or 3 leaves deep.

Pour the Pedro Ximenez and 50ml water over the top, mixing to ensure all the leaves are coated. Sprinkle with a generous pinch of salt and a grind or two of black pepper, then dot the butter on top of the leaves. Make a cartouche by wetting a piece of greaseproof paper a touch bigger than the roasting tin, scrunching it up, then unravelling it, placing it over the leaves and tucking it in around the edge.

Bake in the middle of the oven for 30 minutes, stirring the leaves and replacing the cartouche every 10 minutes, to make sure none of the leaves dry out. The leaves will brown and soften and start giving off a coffee smell. When that's happened, remove them from the oven and transfer to a serving dish. Pour the cooking juices over the top and let the leaves absorb their bath for 5 minutes before serving. Make sure everyone takes both leaves and sauce when helping themselves.

ALONGSIDE: *Rosemary and chilli roast squash* (page 184); *Cheesy polenta* (page 238); *Buckwheat with celery and walnuts* (page 252); *Spelt grains with wild mushrooms* (page 256); *Chicken stock orzo* (page 282)

Wilted bitter leaves with blue cheese dressing

PREPARATION: *in the oven*
TIME NEEDED: *less than 15 minutes*

Here, a tray of mixed bitter leaves is grilled and scorched in wedges, which means the outer edges catch and wilt a little, but the inner cores retain colour and bite. The blue cheese dressing will not suit every meat, and fish rarely, but things like *chicken*, *pork*, *beef*, *veal* and many *roast vegetables* will get along with it nicely, particularly if you've got another, sweeter side nearby to cut through the cheesiness.

A few crumbled walnuts and/or thin slices of sharp apple such as Granny Smith thrown in at the end could be a welcome addition, depending on what the leaves are to be served with.

Serves 4–6

1 round Chioggia radicchio or 3 heads (300–400g) red chicory
2 large heads (about 300g) white chicory (Belgian endive)
3 tablespoons sunflower oil
40g soft, creamy blue cheese such as Gorgonzola, Cambozola, Saint Agur or Danish blue
2 tablespoons extra-virgin olive oil
2 tablespoons white wine vinegar
Freshly ground black pepper

Preheat the grill to medium. Cut the radicchio into quarters and the chicory in half, leaving the hardest part of each core intact. Pour 1 tablespoon sunflower oil into a baking tray. Roll the radicchio and chicory segments in the oil so that they're slightly glossed. Arrange them, cut-side upwards, on the tray and place under the grill about 6cm or so from the heat. Grill for 6 minutes, or until browned and wilted a bit, but not too much.

———

Make the dressing in a large bowl by mixing the remaining sunflower oil and two thirds of the cheese with the back of a fork. When the cheese is soft and the sunflower oil has emulsified with the cheese, add the olive oil. Mash and mix again, then add the vinegar and a pinch of black pepper, whisking until all the components have come together.

———

Remove the leaves from under the grill. Cut out and discard the hard cores so that the leaves separate. Toss them in the dressing, dot the remaining cheese over the top and serve immediately.

———

ALONGSIDE: *Roast Romano peppers* (page 104); *Aubergine purée* (page 138); *Vermouth-braised red onions* (page 146); *Portobello mushrooms baked with oregano* (page 152); *Sweet potato and rosemary hash-rösti* (page 192); *Warm radishes with anise* (page 212); *Roman rosemary polenta* (page 240)

Anchovy-dressed chicory

PREPARATION: *on the counter*
TIME NEEDED: *less than 15 minutes*

Bitter leaves and an anchovy-heavy dressing... there aren't many things that I wouldn't serve this with, although *lamb*, *beef* or *offal dishes* are very good, particularly if they've got a nice char to them.

The anchovies are chopped finely, rather than mashed and emulsified with oil, so there's an intense burst of savouriness with each bite, while the red wine vinegar ensures the dressing is piquant enough to lift the leaves and the salty fish. I know some will recoil at all this, but also that others will find it hugely addictive.

Serves 4–6

1 large or 2 small heads (about 200g) white chicory (Belgian endive)
2 heads (about 300g) red chicory or small red radicchio
Leaves from 6–8 stems flat-leaf parsley, roughly chopped
50g tinned anchovies in oil, finely chopped
¼ garlic clove, crushed
1 tablespoon red wine vinegar
1 teaspoon fish sauce
4 tablespoons extra-virgin olive oil
1 teaspoon golden caster sugar
Sea salt and freshly ground black pepper

Separate the chicory leaves, trimming the bases as needed. Cut the largest 5 or 6 outer leaves in half lengthways and keep the remaining leaves whole. Chop the tightly packed cores finely.

Fill a large bowl or sink with cold water and put the leaves in for a few minutes (this ensures they are crisp and refreshing). Remove from the water and spread out to drain and dry fully on a clean tea towel. Fill a salad bowl or platter with the leaves and sprinkle the parsley leaves over the top.

Make the dressing by whisking the remaining ingredients together (including the oil the anchovies came in) until emulsified. When ready to eat, dress the salad, ensuring all the leaves are well coated.

ALONGSIDE: *Kale, Romanesco, Parmesan and pine nut salad* (page 28); *Mangal chopped salad* (page 108); *Chicken stock and orange-braised fennel* (page 120); *Caponata* (page 140); *New potatoes with seaweed butter* (page 176)

Radicchio with a smoky blood orange and maple dressing

PREPARATION: *on the counter*
TIME NEEDED: *less than 15 minutes*

Orange and maple syrup work brilliantly as a dressing for radicchio, and capers are great at punctuating the sweet flavours. But the use of nutty rapeseed oil and smoked water (easily available online and in good supermarkets) takes things up a notch or two. It's a finger-licking-good salad, as suited to a cool summer lunch based around a simple round of *mozzarella* or a *quiche* as it is to *rich and fatty things like duck, pork belly or mackerel*. If blood oranges are out of season, ordinary oranges work perfectly well.

Serves 4–6

1 medium, tightly packed round red Chioggia radicchio (about 350g)
1 heaped tablespoon mayonnaise
3 tablespoons maple syrup
3 tablespoons cold-pressed rapeseed oil
2 teaspoons sherry vinegar
1 teaspoon smoked water
2 blood oranges
2 tablespoons capers, drained
Sea salt and freshly ground black pepper

Slice the radicchio in half from top to base. Cut out and discard the triangular core from both halves, and separate the leaves. You could cut the largest in half lengthways, but I prefer to leave most of them whole.

Put the mayonnaise and maple syrup in a large bowl and stir or whisk to combine. Add the oil and stir or whisk until the liquids have emulsified, then add the sherry vinegar and smoked water and do the same.

Finely grate the orange zest into the dressing, then slice the ends off each orange so they sit flat on a chopping board. Using a sharp knife, cut down and around the oranges, carefully removing the peel and white pith. Slice the orange flesh in half, then cut it into segments. Set the segments aside and squeeze any juice from the peel you've removed into the dressing bowl. Scrape any other juices from your chopping board into the bowl too. Whisk or stir the dressing, season with salt and pepper and add the capers.

When ready to eat, add the radicchio to the bowl and toss well, ensuring each of the leaves is well coated and the oranges are evenly distributed. Transfer to a serving bowl or platter if you wish.

ALONGSIDE: *Rosemary and chilli roast squash* (page 184); *Sweet potato, celeriac and porcini bake* (page 194); *Green pearl barley* (page 260); *Haricot beans with tomato and persillade* (page 278); *Lemon and olive oil fregola* (page 284)

Pink radicchio with pear and almonds

PREPARATION: *on the counter*
TIME NEEDED: *less than 15 minutes*

The prettiest radicchios – the baby-pink Verona and the yellowy-green, red-flecked Castelfranco – are also the mildest and sweetest. They are, perhaps, a starting point for people unconvinced by bitter leaves as a side salad (or bitter things generally), but you'll only see them in winter and spring, so take advantage when you can.

Make this basic salad with whichever one you can get your hands on, though it's a real treat if you find both. Their leaves need just a simple, sharp dressing: sherry vinegar and a touch of olive oil is ideal. Slivers of sweet, juicy pear and creamy almonds add texture, sweetness and interest, but you could do without them if you're just throwing things together. Like the redder radicchios, these happily accompany hot or cold dishes. Definitely consider the side as a partner for *smoked fish* and for *cheese-themed meals*, whether the dairy is in the form of *feta*, *burrata*, *quiche* or *soufflé*.

Serves 4–6

300g Castelfranco radicchio and/or pink Verona radicchio
1 Comice pear, thinly sliced
A handful of almonds, skin on
1 tablespoon sherry vinegar
2 tablespoons extra-virgin olive oil
Sea salt

Separate the radicchio leaves, cutting them off the core at the bottom. Cut the largest 5 or 6 outer leaves in half lengthways, but leave the rest whole. Fill a large bowl or sink with cold water and put the leaves in for a few minutes to 'shock' them so that they're crisp and refreshed (and refreshing). Remove and drain, then spread out to dry completely on a clean tea towel. Fill a salad bowl or platter with the leaves and add the pear slices and almonds.

Put the vinegar, oil and salt in a small bowl or jar with a lid and whisk or shake until emulsified. When ready to eat, dress the salad and mix well to ensure all the leaves are glossy.

ALONGSIDE: *Green tomato, salted celery and chervil salad* (page 100); *New potatoes with pickled samphire and sorrel* (page 174); *Mixed quinoa with radish and pea shoots* (page 246); *Butter beans with courgettes and tapenade* (page 270); *Lemon and olive oil fregola* (page 284)

Watercress with pickled walnuts

PREPARATION: *on the counter*
TIME NEEDED: *less than 15 minutes*

I really like using watercress as a side dish: it's refreshing, powerfully peppery and robust enough to suit both hot and cold food. Generally it's fine just picked and served plain to take on the juices of whatever you're eating it with, but sometimes you need a little extra, and the pickled walnuts and mustard in this dressing do exactly that.

This is brilliant alongside *beef (particularly roast joints or well-aged steaks)*, *cooked ham* and *game birds*. Make sure you buy good watercress, though. Just like rocket, you get what you pay for.

Serves 4–6

250g watercress
3 pickled walnuts
2 teaspoons juice from the pickled walnut jar
1 heaped tablespoon Dijon mustard
1 teaspoon maple syrup
1 tablespoon extra-virgin olive oil
Sea salt

Pick the watercress stems at the point where the last leaf on each branch meets the stem, then cut any leafless stems into 4–5cm lengths. Mix the leaves and stems together in a bowl. Roughly chop the pickled walnuts and add them to the watercress.

Put the remaining ingredients into a small bowl and whisk until emulsified. When ready to eat, dress the watercress and mix thoroughly to ensure all the leaves and stems are well glossed. I tend to get my hands dirty with this one.

ALONGSIDE: *Sherry cherry tomatoes* (page 98); *Chorizo roast potatoes* (page 170); *Honey and Marmite-glazed parsnips* (page 182); *Bread sauce and parsnip crisps* (page 236); *Spelt grains with wild mushrooms* (page 256)

Gem lettuce, mint and spring onion

PREPARATION: *on the counter*
TIME NEEDED: *less than 15 minutes*

A crisp lettuce, mint, spring onion and lemon ensemble is my go-to side salad. It's refreshing, more than the sum of its parts and deceptively robust alongside warm centrepiece dishes. If I was having a *roast chicken* in the summer, I'd much rather have this and a grain or pulse side than the winter staples of spuds, roots, carrots and boiled greens.

Serves 4–6

3 heads little gem or baby Romaine lettuce, or 1 butterhead lettuce
Leaves picked from 8–10 stems mint, finely chopped
Juice of ½ lemon
3 tablespoons extra-virgin olive oil
1 spring onion, finely chopped
Sea salt and freshly ground black pepper

Separate the lettuce leaves, leaving most of them intact but chopping the inner yellow tightly packed core finely. Wash and dry them if necessary. Fill a salad bowl or serving platter with the lettuce and sprinkle the mint leaves over the top.

Mix the remaining ingredients together to make a dressing and season with a good pinch of salt and pepper. When ready to eat, dress the salad and mix thoroughly to ensure the leaves are well coated.

ALONGSIDE: *Tomato tonnato* (page 96); *Smoky ratatouille* (page 114); *Roast cauliflower with chickpeas and lemon tahini* (page 128); *Mandolin salad* (page 134); *Leeks vinaigrette with crisp-fried leeks* (page 142)

Buttermilk, dill and soy-seed wedge salad

PREPARATION: *on the counter*
TIME NEEDED: *less than 15 minutes*

Was it the invention of the fancy salad bag or its relatively watery, tasteless leaves that consigned iceberg lettuce to the unfashionable ingredient pile? Whatever the cause, there's actually something in the crunch and coolness of an iceberg that remains covertly attractive, and a wedge salad that makes the most of this quality is a fantastically refreshing thing. It's an awesome accompaniment for *chicken wings and legs*, *sweet and rich meats from the barbecue*, and also as part of a *cold buffet*.

Traditional ranch dressings involve sour cream and mayonnaise, but I prefer to cut buttermilk with Greek yoghurt as it feels lighter and fresher. There's loads of dill for interest and quick-pickled radish for the occasional peppery and sour bite. But the icing on the cake – or the sprinkle on the wedge of iceberg – are the soy-sauce glazed pumpkin seeds and toasted quinoa. These add crunch, saltiness and umami, much like fried bacon would in the more traditional version.

Serves 4–6

35g pumpkin seeds
20g sunflower seeds
1 tablespoon light soy sauce
30g quinoa
100g radishes, ideally the French breakfast variety
2 teaspoons white wine vinegar
1 iceberg lettuce

Buttermilk dressing
65g buttermilk
80g Greek yoghurt
1 teaspoon Dijon mustard
1 small garlic clove, crushed
Juice of ½ lemon
Fronds from 5 dill stems, chopped finely
Sea salt

First, toast the pumpkin and sunflower seeds in a heavy-bottomed saucepan over a medium heat, stirring occasionally until two thirds of the seeds are golden brown. Remove from the heat and quickly add the soy sauce. It will bubble and evaporate almost instantly. Stir the seeds so that they are coated by the soy as it steams away. Spread the seeds out so they don't stick together on a large plate to cool.

Wash and dry the pan, then put it back over a medium heat. Let it heat for 2 minutes, then add the quinoa and cover with a lid. After a minute or so, you'll hear the quinoa popping. Let this continue for another minute, shaking the pan once or twice. Then remove from the heat, check the quinoa isn't burning, and (assuming not) put the lid back on and let the quinoa pop away in the residual heat. Once it's stopped popping, add it to the soy-sauce seeds.

Slice the radishes as thinly as you can, preferably using a mandolin. Put in a small bowl or plastic container, add a pinch of salt, the vinegar and 1 teaspoon cold water, and leave to soften while you make the dressing.

Combine the dressing ingredients in a small bowl or jar with a lid and whisk or shake until emulsified. Taste and add more lemon juice,

mustard or dill if you wish. Cut the iceberg into six: cut in half through the stem, then slice each of those halves into three, at all times cutting through the thick stem so that the lettuce holds together in a wedge.

Find a plate or shallow bowl to serve the salad on. Drain the radishes. Spoon a little dressing onto the plate and sprinkle over a handful of radishes. Arrange the wedges on top in one layer. Spoon the dressing all over the lettuce, then top with the remaining radishes and a few more dill fronds if you have them. Finally, sprinkle the seeds generously over the top.

ALONGSIDE: *Gochujang mayo and coconut corn on the cob* (page 126); *Mandolin salad* (page 134); *Fish sauce watermelon salad* (page 156); *Scorched sweet potatoes with sobrasada butter* (page 190); *Mum's bulgar wheat salad* (page 244)

VEGETABLES, FRUITS, FLOWERS & BULBS

At first glance, the collection of vegetables, fruits, flowers and bulbs in this chapter looks like a convenient miscellany of things that don't fit elsewhere in the book. 'Come on, seriously, what links watermelons, aubergines, cauliflowers and onions?' you ask. Fair cop. I don't think there's any useful universal advice to give in respect of cooking or garnishing them.

Except... except that what they have in common – whether mushrooms, cucumbers or corn on the cobs – is the very fact that each one is different, and has a special role to play on our plates. They're the sides you need to lighten up a meal or cool it down. They're the interesting bits that bring blasts of flavour, unusual textures and riots of colour. Often, they're what we rely on to add essential sweetness or an intensity that cuts through the savoury, rich or bland.

These apparent odd ones out are united by the fact that they're often key to the overall success of a meal. What better way to punctuate the monotony of brown food than the sharp flavour and bold colour of a tomato? If you've fennel on your mind, can anything else compare? What would substitute for a side of sweetcorn, when you just know that pop of yellow would be perfect? They're show-offs and need to be used judiciously, either as the thing to build the meal around, or a small but bold extra side to lift proceedings. Either way, give some thought as to whether the other sides will match them; there's rarely much point combining too many at the same time in case they cancel each other out.

Ingredients like peppers, fennel, corn, mushrooms, leeks and watermelons don't require any tinkering for them to have an impact. They're naturally flavourful and, quite possibly, just need to be boiled, steamed, roasted or left raw, without further fuss or flourish, with the caveat that they are generally most effective when perfectly ripe and in season. The difference between a simple tomato salad in late summer and one in winter is immeasurable.

That said, there are ideas and cooking suggestions here that I think make these ingredients even more appealing and effective, for example dressing blackened courgettes with soy sauce, sesame oil and mint (page 112); adding texture to leeks vinaigrette by sprinkling curls of deep-fried leeks on top (page 142); and braising spring onions in the heady anise flavours of Pernod (page 148).

Roasted, fried, braised, boiled, stewed, puréed; baked in a cheesy sauce; dressed with sharp, hot or salty dressings; laced with complementary herbs and spices – depending what you're after, vegetables, fruits, flowers or bulbs can be the side that subtly brings your meal together, or the life and soul of the party.

Tomato tonnato

PREPARATION: *on the counter*
TIME NEEDED: *30 minutes to an hour*

This might seem a surprising combination, but a fishy, umami-rich tonnato (an Italian sauce usually served with cold veal) balances tomato's natural acidity beautifully, punctuated by a sprinkling of salty and sour capers. I've enjoyed this with *veal chops*, *pork belly*, *monkfish* and *cod*, and I'm sure there are many other fine matches.

You're likely to have some tonnato sauce left over, but it's not efficient to make it in a smaller quantity. Happily, it keeps well for 2–3 days if covered and refrigerated. Use it to lubricate cold meats or roast lamb or as a flavoured mayonnaise in sandwiches. The tomatoes must be at room temperature and sliced thinly so that there's plenty of cut surface area for the sauce to cling to.

Serves 6

6 medium (about 500g) tomatoes
2 tablespoons capers
Sea salt and freshly ground black pepper

Tonnato sauce
50g tinned anchovies in oil
160g tinned tuna, drained (120g drained weight)
2 teaspoons fish sauce
1 garlic clove, chopped
2 teaspoons red wine vinegar
3 egg yolks
1 teaspoon Dijon mustard
100g light olive oil

First, make the tonnato sauce. Put the anchovies with their oil, along with all the other sauce ingredients except the olive oil, in a blender or small food processor. Pulse, then blitz for about 1 minute, or until smooth. Add the olive oil in a steady drizzle until the mixture has completely emulsified and is smooth and glossy. Transfer it to a bowl and leave it in the fridge for 30 minutes to an hour. It will firm up a little in that time – not essential, but nice.

Spoon 4–5 tablespoons of the tonnato sauce over a large serving plate. Slice the tomatoes thinly and layer them on top of the sauce. Add a good grind or three of black pepper, and just a little salt (the sauce and capers are themselves quite salty). Sprinkle the capers over the top and serve.

ALONGSIDE: *Purple sprouting broccoli with tarragon* (page 42); *Charred Romanesco* (page 46); *Agretti with olive oil* (page 62); *Pink radicchio with pear and almonds* (page 82); *Hasselback potatoes with bay and caraway* (page 172)

Sherry cherry tomatoes

PREPARATION: *in the oven*
TIME NEEDED: *15 to 30 minutes*

The idea with this recipe is to cook the tomatoes aggressively so that they blister, shrivel, intensify and sweeten, but not for so long that they turn to a mush. The oloroso sherry adds a soft, rounded toffee sweetness to counter tomato's natural acidity, and a dash of sherry vinegar at the end adds a different layer of sharpness. A couple of spoonfuls of these make an excellent hands-off side dish that adds a burst of interest to plainer foods like *white fish* or *chicken*, or cuts through rich flavours such as a *chorizo sausage bake* or a *cheese-heavy sauce*.

Serves 4–6

500–600g cherry tomatoes
2–3 tablespoons olive oil
50ml oloroso sherry
1 teaspoon sherry vinegar
Sea salt and freshly ground black pepper

Preheat the oven to 230°C/Fan 210°C/Gas 8. Remove the tomatoes from their vine and/or pull off any green tops. (They may look pretty but they add nothing once you're cooking and eating.) Put the tomatoes on a small baking tray and drizzle over the oil and a good pinch of salt and freshly ground black pepper. Mix to ensure all the tomatoes have a good sheen, then bake for 12 minutes, or until they blister and darken in places.

After 12 minutes, add the sherry to the roasting tin (be careful; it'll bubble and spit) and give the tray a shake. Return to the oven and bake for 8–10 minutes more. The tomatoes will be close to collapsing but should still hold their own.

When fresh from the oven, they'll be hotter than the sun, so you've got a few minutes spare before eating. Spoon the tomatoes into a serving bowl, leaving any juices in the roasting tin. Add the sherry vinegar to the juices, stir to combine the liquids then pour over the tomatoes, leaving them for at least 5 minutes to cool and soak up the flavours.

ALONGSIDE: *Charred Romanesco* (page 46); *Dijon-dressed green beans* (page 64); *Butter-braised chicory* (page 72); *Cauliflower cheese* (page 132); *Za'atar mushrooms with curd* (page 154)

Green tomato, salted celery and chervil salad

PREPARATION: *on the counter*
TIME NEEDED: *30 minutes to an hour*

There isn't a classic tomato salad in this book. Not because it's not worthy; it's one of the best, most versatile and popular sides there is, and I make it all the time. Rather, you've seen tomato, salt, olive oil and basil a million times, and don't need to see it again here.

This green tomato salad, however, is a legitimate alternative: it's cooling, refreshing, a little bit sharp and grassy. The salted celery helps season the tomatoes and adds texture, and chervil – in flavour a cross between parsley and tarragon – is a herb we should all use more. At any event, it adheres to the same principles I follow with the traditional red varieties: use the best tomatoes you can get hold of and only when in season; keep and serve tomatoes at room temperature; season liberally with good salt and let them sit for a while before eating. Plus lots of good extra-virgin olive oil.

This side goes with many things, but particularly *oily and pink fish* and *cold cuts of meat*. I tend to use green heirloom tomatoes – which are meant to be green – when making it. You could use unripe green tomatoes instead; just be sure to slice them thinly, rather than cut into wedges. If neither are to hand, the salted celery and chervil combination is good with red varieties too.

Serves 4–6

2 celery stalks
1 teaspoon sea salt
4–6 green heirloom tomatoes, at room temperature
A handful of celery leaves, roughly chopped
Leaves from 8–10 stems chervil
3 tablespoons extra-virgin olive oil

Slice the celery into 4 or 5 thin lengths about 2mm wide, then cut across them to create 2mm dice. Put them in a mixing bowl with the salt. Toss, then leave for about 30 minutes. The salt will extract moisture and season the celery.

Cut the tomatoes into wedges, chunks and slices (I think a mix of shapes works well here). Layer half of them on a medium serving plate. Spoon half the salted celery over the top, sprinkle with half the celery leaves and chervil, then place the remaining tomatoes over the top and spoon over the remaining celery bits and juice. Finish with the remaining herbs and drizzle over the oil. Let this sit for a further 30 minutes – the salt in the celery will draw out the tomato juices, softening and seasoning them.

ALONGSIDE: *Purple sprouting broccoli with ricotta and orzo* (page 44); *Mandolin salad* (page 134); *Mum's bulgar wheat salad* (page 244); *Mixed quinoa with radish and pea shoots* (page 246); *Butter beans with courgettes and tapenade* (page 270)

Grilled green tomatoes with oregano and chilli

PREPARATION: *in the oven*
TIME NEEDED: *15 to 30 minutes*

Although I enjoy roast or pan-fried cherry tomatoes, to my mind (and I think the minds of others too), large red tomatoes are only acceptable if cooked to absolute perfection (caramelised, blistered, fully soft) and placed next to bacon, sausage and black pudding; but otherwise: no thanks.

Green tomatoes are a better option. You'll find sharp, hard, unripe green tomatoes as well as softer, more subtle heirloom varieties in the shops. Both seem to enjoy a little heat from a grill, as well as the complementary seasonings of dried oregano, chilli and nutty rapeseed oil suggested in this recipe.

I like to eat warm, yielding green tomatoes with things like *grilled fish (salmon, mackerel, sardines, cod)* and *cheeses like ricotta and halloumi*; basically, they're juicy and luscious and are effective at cutting through savoury and salty foods without hogging the limelight.

Serves 4–6

4–6 large green tomatoes (either unripe or intentionally green)
3–4 tablespoons cold-pressed rapeseed oil
2 teaspoons dried oregano
1 medium mild red chilli, finely diced
Sea salt and ground white pepper

Preheat the grill to medium-high. Cut the tomatoes in half widthways (rather than from stem to tip). Place each of the halves on a small baking tray into which they all fit snugly, cut-side up. If they don't sit flat, slice a tiny bit off the other end so that they do. Drizzle and slick the tomatoes with 2 tablespoons oil. Sprinkle them with a little pinch of white pepper, a bigger pinch of salt and a scattering of dried oregano.

Place under the grill about 8–10cm from the heat with the oven door ajar. Cook for 8–12 minutes, during which time they'll sizzle and spit, soften and sink a little (but not totally), and dry out a touch on top. Soft, ripe tomatoes will take less time than harder, unripe green tomatoes; you're looking for the flesh to sink a little, the outer skin to start slipping and the tomato to be tender but still hold its shape. Remove from the oven, drizzle each with more oil, add another sprinkle of salt and top with the diced red chilli.

ALONGSIDE: *Purple sprouting broccoli with ricotta and orzo* (page 44); *Spinach and preserved lemon freekeh* (page 248); *Buckwheat with celery and walnuts* (page 252); *Butter beans with sage* (page 272); *Chicken stock orzo* (page 282)

Roast Romano peppers

PREPARATION: *in the oven*
TIME NEEDED: *15 to 30 minutes*

Romano peppers are the long, thin, dark red peppers that are usually sold in twos or threes at supermarkets. They're sweeter and more luxuriously flavoured than bell peppers, and need no more encouragement than a drizzle of olive oil and a ferociously hot oven to turn them into a pretty satisfactory bit on the side. Here, though, they're embellished with cherry tomatoes, garlic and fresh thyme, before being sharpened with a dash of vinegar and a few capers.

They are great as a foil to *rich, hearty meat dishes*, whether that's a *roast joint of beef* or *spicy lamb stew*, and also as a way to liven up more subtle things like *herb-crusted fish fillets*, *grilled halloumi* or *baked mushrooms*.

Serves 4–6

6 Romano peppers
Leaves from 6–8 sprigs thyme
2 garlic cloves, very thinly sliced
3 tablespoons extra-virgin olive oil
24 cherry tomatoes
1 tablespoon red wine vinegar
2 teaspoons capers, roughly chopped
Leaves from 4–5 stems flat-leaf parsley
Sea salt and freshly ground black pepper

Preheat the oven to 220°C/Fan 200°C/Gas 7. Cut the peppers in half lengthways and trim out the seeds. You could cut the stems off too, but there's no pressing need to do so. Put the halves on a baking or a shallow roasting tray, cut-side up; ideally, the peppers will fit snugly in one layer. Season with a good pinch of salt and pepper and scatter the thyme leaves over each half, along with the slices of garlic. Drizzle with the oil, then place 2 cherry tomatoes in each pepper half.

Roast in the top half of the oven for about 25 minutes, or until the peppers have shrunk a little, are soft, sweet and charring at the edges and the tomatoes have blistered. Keep an eye on them, though, and remove them before they dry out. Add a drop or two of red wine vinegar to each pepper and sprinkle with capers and parsley (more olive oil wouldn't hurt). Serve immediately.

ALONGSIDE: *Grilled hispi cabbage with anchovy and crème fraîche* (page 10); *Hasselback potatoes with bay and caraway* (page 172); *Colcannon* (page 178); *Borlotti beans and cavolo nero with basil and hazelnut smash* (page 268); *Mac 'n' cheese* (page 286)

Quick romesco

PREPARATION: *on the counter*
TIME NEEDED: *less than 15 minutes*

Romesco is more than a sauce. To me, it's something that, when served liberally, binds and invigorates a meal. It's bold, bright and perky in both looks and taste, but the blitzed almonds add heft and substance.

If you've grilled, roasted or pan-fried a *light-fleshed meat such as quail or chicken thighs*, or a *sturdy white fish like monkfish, cod or pollock*, then a generous spoonful or two of smoky, nutty and sweet puréed roast peppers is a real party starter, particularly when joined by some boiled or steamed seasonal greens. It can handle punchy flavours too: *chorizo sausages* or *calves' liver*, for example.

This version takes barely 5 minutes to put together. No need to roast peppers when jars of cooked and skinned ones are readily available and actually pretty economical.

Serves 4–6

1 jar roasted peppers in brine, drained (300–400g drained weight)
70g blanched whole almonds
1 teaspoon Spanish sweet smoked paprika
1 teaspoon sherry vinegar
2 tablespoons extra-virgin olive oil
Sea salt

Drain and roughly chop the peppers. Place all the ingredients in a blender or food processor and blitz until smooth. Add a pinch or two of salt.

The romesco will store well in the fridge for 2–3 days if covered. If it separates, just give it a stir. It can be warmed gently in a pan or served cold.

ALONGSIDE: *Purple sprouting broccoli with tarragon* (page 42); *Asparagus with cured egg yolk* (page 60); *Anchovy-dressed chicory* (page 78); *Chorizo roast potatoes* (page 170); *Roman rosemary polenta* (page 240)

Mangal chopped salad

PREPARATION: *in the oven*
TIME NEEDED: *15 to 30 minutes*

This warm chopped salad is inspired by two types of side dish served at the Turkish *ocakbaşı* restaurants near where I live in northeast London: sweet onions charred over a *mangal* (charcoal grill) yet still a little raw, which are drenched in lip-puckering pomegranate molasses and sprinkled with Aleppo chilli flakes; and light green Turkish peppers, which are grilled and sometimes served whole, or otherwise chopped into a salad with raw tomatoes and cooked red peppers.

Few of us have the charcoal grill, let alone the extraction facilities of one of these restaurants, but you can get a similar black-edged but still crunchy effect in a blisteringly hot oven. Once charred, all the ingredients get roughly chopped and tossed together with a sharp and deliberately aggressive helping of the molasses.

This has become an essential side when I'm cooking a *roast leg of lamb* in the summer, along with a couscous or bulgar wheat dish and some crisp, perhaps bitter salad leaves. It's excellent with *falafel*, *grilled chicken skewers*, *fish* and *offal-heavy dishes* too.

Serves 4–6

4 onions
2 medium-large red bell peppers
6 long green Turkish peppers
2 mild red chillies
2 tablespoons sunflower or vegetable oil
3 large tomatoes
5 tablespoons pomegranate molasses
1 teaspoon Aleppo chilli flakes (pul biber)
Leaves from 7–8 stems flat-leaf parsley, roughly chopped
Sea salt

Preheat the oven to its highest temperature (about 250°C/Fan 250°C/Gas 10). Peel and quarter the onions. Cut the red peppers in half and remove the seeds, then cut each half into quarters and put them in a roasting tin with the onions, whole Turkish peppers and whole chillies. Add the oil and toss to ensure all the vegetables are well glossed. Sprinkle with a few heavy pinches of salt. Roast on the top shelf for 15–20 minutes, shaking the tin after 10 minutes, until the vegetables are charred at the edges but not soft (the onions, in particular, should retain some crunch).

Transfer the vegetables to a chopping board and very roughly chop them, then scrape them into a large bowl or serving dish. You'll need to do this in stages. I like to do it one vegetable type at a time, but I suspect that's a personal thing. Try to keep any juices and seeds that burst out, transferring them to the bowl as you go.

Chop the tomatoes into large chunks and gently stir them into the warm vegetables along with the pomegranate molasses, chilli flakes and parsley. Taste and add more salt, chilli flakes or molasses if you wish. Sprinkle another pinch of chilli flakes over the top and serve warm or at room temperature.

ALONGSIDE: *Anchovy-dressed chicory* (page 78); *Roast cauliflower with chickpeas and lemon tahini* (page 128); *Aubergine purée* (page 138); *Flavoured butter bread* (page 234); *Mum's bulgar wheat salad* (page 244)

Courgette and edamame salad

PREPARATION: *on the counter*
TIME NEEDED: *less than 15 minutes*

Although I think the trend of substituting spiralised courgettes for pasta is a waste of time and energy, when they're still raw and used as a salad, thin strips (either curled or straight) bring freshness and crunch and are an excellent carrier of a good dressing. They're a cooling, versatile side salad that I'd happily eat with pretty much any *fish*, *pork* or *tofu* (and probably a great deal more).

The dressing for this side is made from Japanese condiments: sweet mirin, sour rice vinegar and savoury sesame oil. Frozen, ready-podded edamame (soya) beans fit the theme and are widely available, but use broad beans or peas if you can't find them.

Serves 4–6

500g courgettes, ideally a mixture of yellow and green
2 tablespoons sesame oil
2 tablespoons mirin
3 tablespoons rice vinegar
150g podded edamame beans, defrosted
10–15 mint leaves, finely chopped

Cut a quarter of the courgettes into 2–3cm thick wedges. Use a handheld julienne peeler to create long, thin strips down the remaining courgettes. When doing this, imagine the courgette has four sides, peel until you reach the floury, seeded middle, then turn to peel the next side and repeat all the way round. You could use a spiraliser or a mandolin to create the same effect.

Combine the sesame oil, mirin and rice vinegar by putting them in a jar or dressing bottle or bowl and shaking or whisking them together until emulsified.

Put the edamame and courgette wedges and ribbons in a serving bowl, add the mint and toss. About 5 minutes before eating, mix in the dressing and ensure all surfaces are coated.

ALONGSIDE: *Spring greens in shiitake dashi* (page 14); *Baby pak choi with sticky garlic and ginger* (page 48); *Mixed quinoa with radish and pea shoots* (page 246); *Buckwheat with celery and walnuts* (page 252); *Three pepper rice* (page 294)

Courgettes with soy, sesame, mint and chilli

PREPARATION: *on a hob*
TIME NEEDED: *less than 15 minutes*

After a childhood of being served watery, overcooked courgettes (sorry, Mum), it was a bit of a surprise to discover how good they can be when they've retained a bit of crunch, whether served raw and doused in a dressing at the last minute (see page 110) or cooked very quickly over a high heat. The aim in the latter method, used here, is to char the edges before the flesh softens too much.

Simple charred courgettes are a good side for many meals – just dress them with lemon and olive oil. However, if, as here, you add ginger, sesame oil, sesame seeds and soy sauce too, then turn the heat off, throw in some hastily chopped chilli and garnish with fresh mint, the result moves from merely good to really fantastic. Great as a week-night stir-fry supper with a *fried egg* or perhaps some *salmon*, *rice* or *noodles*; or as part of a banquet with, say, *crispy pork belly* or a *whole baked bream*.

Serves 4–6

1–2 green courgettes (about 200g)
1–2 yellow courgettes (about 200g)
1 round green courgette (about 100g), or 1 additional ordinary one
1 tablespoon sunflower oil or vegetable oil
1 tablespoon sesame oil
2 tablespoons light soy sauce
5–6cm ginger, peeled and thinly sliced
1 tablespoon sesame seeds
1 medium red chilli, finely chopped
Leaves from 6–8 stems mint, finely chopped
Juice of 1 lime

Cut the long courgettes into chunky triangles (the best way to do this is to cut them diagonally widthways, rolling the courgette a half-turn in between each cut). Cut the round courgette in half, then each of those halves into four segments.

Set a wok over a very high heat. Add the sunflower oil and heat for 30–60 seconds until smoking hot. Add the larger pieces of round courgette (if using), flat-side down. Don't move them around – we want colour.

After about 1 minute, or once they've browned a bit, remove them from the wok and add the long courgettes, adding a little more oil if you think it's required. Again, cook flat-side down until charred, then turn them over and char for 45–60 seconds more, making sure they've still got a bit of bite. Don't let them turn translucent.

Return the round courgette pieces to the pan and add the sesame oil, soy, ginger and most of the sesame seeds. Quickly stir once, then turn the heat off. Add half the chilli, half the mint and all the lime juice. Stir again, then transfer to a serving bowl. Garnish with the remaining sesame seeds, chilli and mint.

ALONGSIDE: *Fish sauce watermelon salad* (page 156); *Quick-pickled daikon* (page 210); *Sesame soba noodles* (page 254); *Coconut jasmine rice* (page 296); *Crisp-bottomed Persian rice* (page 302)

Smoky ratatouille

PREPARATION: *on a hob and in the oven*
TIME NEEDED: *more than an hour*

The most elevated form of ratatouille is legendary French chef Michel Guérard's *confit byaldi*: a tian of thinly sliced yellow and green courgette, aubergine and tomato, laboriously layered over a reduced pepper and tomato sauce, then baked until soft and intensely flavoured. At the other end of the spectrum are the same vegetables stewed together until mushy and indistinguishable. Fortunately, the happy medium of a bit of effort and thought – but not too much – makes the best ratatouille of them all.

Cooking each of the vegetables separately to suit their individual characteristics before gently baking and resting them, so that the flavours mingle just enough, ticks all the taste boxes, although I like adding a further twist of smoked water and salt, two ingredients that add an incredible flavour and I think should become as commonplace as pomegranate molasses and tahini. You can easily buy them online and in some supermarkets. There may well be leftovers, but that's not a bad thing; ratatouille keeps very well in the fridge for 2–3 days and is as suited to *confit duck legs* as it is to some *quality sausages* or a *cold slice of quiche*.

Serves 6

1kg aubergines
3 large red peppers
Extra-virgin olive oil, for frying
1 onion, finely diced
3 garlic cloves, thinly sliced
500g tomatoes, roughly chopped
3 tablespoons smoked water
800g courgettes, a mix of green and yellow if possible
Sunflower oil or vegetable oil, for frying
350g cherry tomatoes, left whole
Leaves from 1 small bunch (25g) basil
Smoked sea salt flakes
Sea salt and freshly ground black pepper

Cut the aubergines into four lengthways, then slice each quarter into 4cm-wide chunks.

———

Preheat the oven to its highest temperature (about 250°C/Fan 250°C/Gas 10). Quarter the peppers lengthways, removing the seeds and stalks. Put them on a baking tray, skin-side up, and roast on the top shelf for 15 minutes, or until the skins are blackening and the flesh is soft. Tip them into a bowl, cover with clingfilm and leave to sweat for 10 minutes. You should then be able to push the skins off the peppers with ease. Discard the skins and reduce the oven temperature to 170°C/Fan 150°C/Gas 3½.

———

While the peppers are doing their thing, make a smoky tomato sauce. Heat a little olive oil in a pan over a medium-low heat, add the onion and a pinch of salt and cook gently for 4–5 minutes. Add the garlic and soften it for 2 more minutes, then add the chopped tomatoes and smoked water and simmer gently for 15–20 minutes. Add a good pinch of smoked salt, then decant the sauce into a small roasting tin. Put the skinned peppers on top.

———

Meanwhile, cut the courgettes into discs 2–3cm thick. Heat a frying pan or wok over a high heat, add 1 tablespoon vegetable or sunflower oil and char the courgettes on each side – you'll need to work in batches to quickly

colour and blister the cut sides while keeping the flesh relatively firm. Each batch takes only 2–3 minutes if your pan is hot enough (put the extractor fan on). When coloured but still firm, tip them into the tin with the peppers.

———

Finally, brown the aubergines over a medium-high heat in the same frying pan or wok. Use just a little sunflower oil and turn each piece only when it's starting to become translucent. Any charring is good – desirable, in fact. Transfer them to the roasting tin once done.

———

Carefully redistribute the top layers of vegetables (but not the sauce) so they're evenly mixed and season generously with smoked salt and black pepper. Bake for 30 minutes, then turn the vegetables, again without disturbing the sauce, and add the cherry tomatoes. Return to the oven for 30 minutes more, by which time the tomatoes will be blistered and the vegetables tender but not mushy.

———

Remove the ratatouille from the oven, sprinkle three quarters of the basil over the top and gently coerce the sauce from the bottom of the tray over and around the vegetables. Taste to check the seasoning and add pepper and salt if you wish. Dot with the remaining basil leaves. I think it's best about 20–30 minutes after leaving the oven, when lukewarm, once the flavours have had time to soften and get to know each other.

———

ALONGSIDE: *Grilled tenderstem broccoli with umami crumbs* (page 40); *New potatoes with seaweed butter* (page 176); *Wheat berries with capers and tomatoes* (page 250); *Herb-loaded lentils* (page 262); *Haricot beans with tomato and persillade* (page 278)

Steamed marinated fennel

PREPARATION: *on a hob*
TIME NEEDED: *30 minutes to an hour*

I really like fennel when it's been steamed. Its flesh quite quickly becomes soft and juicy, and though the aniseed flavour remains, it's more subtle than when raw. I also find the cooking process makes the fennel particularly receptive to other flavours. Dressing it while still warm with peppery olive oil, diced chilli and the zest and juice of a lemon is extremely effective; the flavours are soaked up as the fennel cools, with the later addition of feta and almonds adding sharpness and savoury crunch respectively. You'll reap the benefits of buying good peppery extra-virgin olive oil if you use it here.

This is a versatile side dish that requires very little hands-on cooking time, and can be left to sit for as long as you can resist it. Great when you're looking for a *mix of cold salads*, or with *salmon*, *trout* and *chicken*.

Serves 4–6

800g fennel bulbs
Juice and finely grated zest of ½ lemon
1 mild red chilli, deseeded and finely diced
4 tablespoons peppery extra-virgin olive oil
20g almonds, skin on, lightly crushed
75g feta cheese
Sea salt

Trim the base and tops off the fennel bulbs, reserving any feathery fronds for later, then separate the layers of fennel. Cut each of these in half or thirds from root to tip, so that they're never wider than 4–5cm. Spread the fennel segments over the base of a steaming basket, preferably in one layer (if you have stacking baskets, that's ideal). Set it over a pan of boiling water and steam for around 5–6 minutes, or until the fennel is tender and translucent.

———

Tip the cooked fennel into a fairly flat serving dish or bowl. Immediately sprinkle it with the lemon zest, chilli and a good pinch of salt. Add the lemon juice and oil and mix well, then let it sit and cool to room temperature for 30 minutes, during which time the fennel will soak up some of the dressing and the flavours will mingle.

———

Later, add half the reserved fennel fronds, half the crushed almonds and crumble in half of the feta. Mix, then sprinkle the remaining fronds, almonds and feta over the top. Ensure everyone takes a spoonful or two of dressing from the bottom of the bowl.

———

ALONGSIDE: *Kale, Romanesco, Parmesan and pine nut salad* (page 28); *Gem lettuce, mint and spring onion* (page 86); *Scorched sweet potatoes with sobrasada butter* (page 190); *Beetroot gratin* (page 224); *Green pearl barley* (page 260)

Shaved fennel with tarragon

PREPARATION: *on the counter*
TIME NEEDED: *15 to 30 minutes*

This tangle of lightly and simply dressed fennel shavings is my go-to side for almost *any white fish dish*. I can't think of many better meals than a *whole roast or barbecued turbot* served simply with this salad and perhaps a few chunks of good bread to mop things up. That said, the anise flavours suit plenty of other seafood and meat mains too, whether that's a *skate wing drowning in brown butter, poached salmon or chicken* or *rich, sizzling lamb chops*.

It takes just a few minutes to put together, and somehow manages to be cooling and invigorating as well as comforting, and a surprisingly good carrier of warm cooking juices. If it becomes a staple for you too, a cute variation is to swap the lemon juice for the same quantity of orange and a little finely grated zest.

The recipe includes the process of plunging just-shaved fennel into iced water for 15–30 minutes. This has the double benefit of 'shocking' the fennel so it curls and is super crunchy, and prevents it from oxidising. But it's not essential, so skip it if you've only got 5 minutes.

Serves 4–6

400g fennel
Juice of ½ lemon
1 tablespoon extra-virgin olive oil
Leaves from 8–10 stems tarragon, roughly chopped
Sea salt

Fill a large bowl three-quarters full with cold water and add a pinch of salt and a handful of ice cubes. Cut the top stems of the fennel off, reserving any herby fronds. Neatly trim any brown or tired-looking bits from the base of the bulb, but ensure the bulb stays in one piece.

———

Use a mandolin to shave the fennel to almost paper-thin lengths from root to tip. It takes only a few seconds; just make sure you use the guard for the last few centimetres. Drop the fennel shavings into the iced water and leave for 15 minutes to curl and crisp.

———

Drain the fennel and pat it dry with a clean tea towel. Put it back in the bowl along with the lemon juice, oil, a generous pinch of salt, the tarragon and any reserved fennel fronds. Mix and serve within 10 minutes, so that the fennel is still crunchy.

———

ALONGSIDE: *Za'atar mushrooms with curd* (page 154); *New potatoes with seaweed butter* (page 176); *Seeded rye and honey soda bread* (page 232); *Cinnamon, chickpea and apricot couscous* (page 242); *Haricot beans with tomato and persillade* (page 278)

Chicken stock and orange-braised fennel

PREPARATION: *in the oven*
TIME NEEDED: *more than an hour*

This fennel braised in chicken stock and a squeeze of orange juice is the result of a Monday evening spent hastily scrabbling through the fridge, freezer and veg box for anything I could find to bolster my roast chicken leftovers. But it's since been repeated many times. As it cooks, the fennel is infused with the flavour of an ever-reducing, ever-intensifying chicken stock, the remaining juices of which can double as gravy. By the time it's done, the fibrous vegetable has turned soft, sweet and tender, and the citrus lifts the dish and makes it sing.

This side is particularly good with *roast pork* or, indeed, *chicken* – from which you can make more stock. It's very tolerant of being reheated or kept warm while the rest of your meal comes together.

Serves 4–6

500ml chicken stock, preferably proper stock, rather than from powder
3 medium-large fennel bulbs
50g butter
1 orange
3 sprigs thyme
Sea salt and freshly ground black pepper

Preheat the oven to 160°C/Fan 140°C/Gas 3. Put the stock in a small pan over a medium-high heat and simmer to reduce by a quarter, concentrate the flavours and thicken it a little.

Meanwhile, trim the tough tops off the fennel bulbs, leaving just a centimetre or two still attached, and reserving any herby fronds for later. Neatly trim off any brown or tired-looking bits, ensuring the bulb stays in one piece. Cut the bulbs in half from top to bottom, then cut each half into three wedges lengthways.

Melt the butter in a heavy-bottomed frying pan, add the fennel wedges cut-side down and cook for 1–2 minutes on each side. Arrange the fennel in an ovenproof dish that holds it snugly. Use a vegetable peeler to remove the zest of the orange in strips. Arrange these and the sprigs of thyme under and around the fennel, and season with salt and black pepper. Juice the orange and add the juice to the dish, then pour in enough stock to come two thirds of the way up the vegetables.

Take a piece of greaseproof paper or baking parchment that's slightly bigger than your dish. Wet it under running water, crumple it and then open it up again. Place this over the fennel, tucking the edge in like a blanket. Bake for about 40 minutes, turning the wedges over after 25 minutes. Remove the paper for the final 10 minutes to give the fennel a little colour and help reduce the liquid. It's ready when a fork easily slides into the fennel and the cooking juices are thick and glossy.

ALONGSIDE: *Flower sprouts with lemon and anchovy butter* (page 30); *Anchoïade mashed potatoes* (page 180); *Sweet potato and rosemary hash-rösti* (page 192); *'Young Turk' celeriac* (page 196); *Wine-poached salsify with gremolata* (page 200)

Creamed sweetcorn with feta

PREPARATION: *on a hob*
TIME NEEDED: *30 minutes to an hour*

Creamed corn hails from the Midwest and Deep South of America; forget modern 'dude' food, think hearty, comforting country cooking. Although there's a natural creaminess to sweetcorn kernels when they're puréed, many recipes still involve dairy. Some add cream, but I find that too heavy, preferring to add milk and, in this case, a slab of totally un-American tangy and salty feta at the end, which seems to perk things up.

Unusually, I'm happy to advocate a second sweet side dish to go alongside this. Rather than sugary overkill, peas, carrots, sweet potatoes or pumpkin are helpful alongside puréed sweetcorn because they add the bite and texture it lacks. That said, definitely have another, plainer and more savoury side too, to balance things. I'm assuming, by the way, that all of these things are supporting *something rich and savoury like steak, beef brisket or beef ribs*, or perhaps *roast chicken* or *guinea fowl*.

Serves 4–6

300ml milk
4 sprigs thyme
1 bay leaf
10g butter
½ large onion, finely diced
1 garlic clove, thinly sliced
500g drained tinned sweetcorn
100g feta, roughly cubed
Sea salt and freshly ground black pepper

Bring the milk to a gentle simmer in a small pan. Add the thyme and bay leaf, remove the pan from the heat and allow the herbs to infuse for 15 minutes, or more.

Melt the butter in a medium saucepan. Add the onion and a pinch of salt and cook gently for 3–5 minutes, or until softened and sweetened. Add the garlic and sweetcorn and cook for a further 2–3 minutes, stirring occasionally. Add the milk, thyme and bay to the corn, bring to a gentle simmer and cook for 15 minutes.

Remove the herbs, pour the corn and its liquid into a blender and blitz for 30 seconds. Add the feta and blitz for a further 30–60 seconds until you have a smooth and consistent texture. You could reserve about a quarter of the kernels and return them to the mix once the rest has been blitzed. But I prefer creamed corn to be fully, well, creamed. Add a few grinds of black pepper and taste to check for seasoning. Be careful with the salt, as feta contains plenty of its own.

ALONGSIDE: *Bacon and buttermilk cabbage* (page 18); *Sprout tops with Jerusalem artichokes and apple* (page 36); *Runner beans with bacon and walnuts* (page 66); *Chorizo roast potatoes* (page 170); *Scorched sweet potatoes with sobrasada butter* (page 190)

Honey, thyme and lime butter corn

PREPARATION: *on a hob*
TIME NEEDED: *less than 15 minutes*

This is a quick way of pimping tinned or frozen sweetcorn, with each of the elements adding a layer of sweetness and aromatics to the corn kernels. The result is remarkably uplifting. Try the same flavours with corn on the cob, too – just gently melt the ingredients in a pan before painting them over the cooked (boiled and/or grilled) cobs.

What would you eat it with? Absolutely *any pork dish*, *chicken*, *white fish*, *oily fish such as salmon and trout*, *tofu*, *fried eggs*, *rich beef dishes*... Perhaps a better question to ask would be what wouldn't work?

Serves 4–6

400g drained tinned or defrosted frozen sweetcorn
Leaves from 8–10 sprigs thyme
25g butter
3 teaspoons runny honey
Juice and finely grated zest of ½ lime
Sea salt and freshly ground black pepper

Heat the sweetcorn: cook frozen in boiling water for 3–4 minutes, or tinned with 2–3 tablespoons water over a medium-high heat for 4 minutes, stirring occasionally. Drain the corn and return it to the saucepan. Place over a low heat and add the thyme leaves, butter and honey. Cook for 1–2 minutes, stirring to aid the melting and mingling of the butter and honey.

Remove from the heat, add a generous pinch of salt and many grinds of black pepper, plus the lime zest and juice. Stir and serve up.

ALONGSIDE: *Charred fermented cabbage* (page 12); *Okra chips with cumin salt* (page 70); *Colcannon* (page 178); *Butter-glazed turnips with horseradish* (page 204); *Carrots with brown butter and hazelnuts* (page 220)

Gochujang mayo and coconut corn on the cob

PREPARATION: *on a hob*
TIME NEEDED: *less than 15 minutes*

Corn on the cob makes for a slightly unwieldy side dish; it's arguably only really suitable when the rest of your meal is also to be eaten by hand. And yet it does work, particularly in barbecue season. If you're already getting your fingers dirty with *sticky chicken thighs*, *racks of pork ribs* and so on, why not carry on? Alternatively, *Asian-inspired meals involving pork, tofu or white fish* would suit these lip-smacking cobs too.

Gochujang is a Korean condiment made from red pepper, chilli, rice and fermented soybeans. It's readily available in Asian supermarkets and online and adds a complex but irresistible mix of heat, sweetness and umami. This combines to great effect with the coconut and corn, but if it sounds too fiery, see page 124 for a more subtle lime, honey and thyme alternative.

Serves 6

3 tablespoons gochujang
5 tablespoons mayonnaise
40g desiccated coconut
4 corn cobs

Make the gochujang mayo by mixing the gochujang and mayonnaise in a bowl until fully combined. Spoon this onto a small plate. Put the coconut on another plate, and bring a pan of salted water to the boil.

Cut the corn cobs into 2 or 3 pieces to shorten them. Put them in the boiling water and cook for 4 minutes, then remove and drain. Then, holding the flat ends (not the kernels), roll a cob in the mayonnaise until fully covered, then roll it in the coconut until completely coated. Repeat with the remaining cobs.

ALONGSIDE: *Garlic oil pea shoots* (page 56); *Fish sauce watermelon salad* (page 156); *Flavoured butter bread* (page 234); *Black bean, coriander and lime rice* (page 292); *Three pepper rice* (page 294)

Roast cauliflower with chickpeas and lemon tahini

PREPARATION: *in the oven*
TIME NEEDED: *more than an hour*

It's no longer a secret that roast cauliflower is a very fine thing. Once it's lost most of its water content it turns nutty, sweet and moreish. This dish takes those nuggety golden-brown bits of cauliflower and mixes them with spiced chickpeas and crunchy, fresh cauliflower leaves. The sharp lemon tahini yoghurt brings everything together. You could use it to inspire your meal (I'm thinking *Middle Eastern spiced meats* and *slow-cooked stews*) or include it as part of any large buffet.

As an aside, many recipes seem to underestimate how long it takes to roast a cauliflower. In my experience it's very definitely 50–60 minutes, not, say, 20. Which means it needs to fit neatly with the timings of the rest of your meal. If your oven is going to be full, note that you can make this well in advance, serving it at room temperature and adding the dressing just before eating.

Serves 4–6

2 medium cauliflowers, with plenty of green leaves
6 tablespoons cold-pressed rapeseed oil
1 tablespoon cumin seeds
400g cooked chickpeas, drained
Sea salt

Tahini dressing
1 tablespoon tahini
Juice of 1 lemon
2 tablespoons Greek yoghurt
1 heaped teaspoon sumac

Preheat the oven to 200°C/Fan 180°C/Gas 6. Trim the green leaves from the cauliflowers and set them aside. Cut each cauliflower into florets, then cut the largest florets in half. Cut the stalk and core into 3–4 cm chunks and put all the florets, stalks and core in a roasting tin. Spoon 4 tablespoons oil over the top and mix well. Roast on the top shelf for about an hour, turning occasionally, until it is nutty brown. After 25 minutes, lightly crush the cumin seeds in a pestle and mortar and sprinkle them, with a pinch or two of salt, over the cauliflower, before returning it to the oven.

Meanwhile, spread the chickpeas out on a small baking tray. Add 1 tablespoon oil, toss and sprinkle with a pinch of salt. Roast below the cauliflower for 20 minutes. When the chickpeas and cauliflower are done, remove them from the oven and allow to cool.

Wash and drain the cauliflower greens. Set the small, bright green-yellow ones to one side. Cut the largest and thickest stems in half lengthways down the middle of the stem so they cook quickly. Trim any woody or brown ends from the middle third before placing them in a colander. Bring a pan of water to the boil and blanch the large leaves for 30 seconds, then immediately drain them over the medium leaves in the colander. Rinse until cool under cold running water, then leave them to drain.

Make a dressing by mixing the tahini with the lemon juice until you have a smooth paste. Add the yoghurt and mix well.

To serve, toss the chickpeas and all the cauliflower greens with the cooled roast cauliflower. Spoon half the dressing over a large serving platter, sprinkle half the sumac over that, top with the cauliflower and chickpea mixture, then spoon the remaining dressing over the top of that, finishing with a generous sprinkling of sumac.

ALONGSIDE: *Radicchio with a smoky blood orange and maple dressing* (page 80); *Mangal chopped salad* (page 108); *Flavoured butter bread* (page 234); *Wheat berries with capers and tomatoes* (page 250); *Crisp-bottomed Persian rice* (page 302)

Yeasted cauliflower purée

PREPARATION: *on a hob*
TIME NEEDED: *15 to 30 minutes*

In the same vein as the recipes on pages 106, 138 and 188, this light and velvety cauliflower purée is a high-impact side rather than an alternative to the bulk of mashed potato. That said, it does have a relatively subtle flavour, so you might serve it in greater quantity than the naturally sweeter squash, pepper or aubergine purées. The dried yeast adds an (enjoyably) cheesy mustiness and depth to the pure, milky-white cauliflower – consider it a seasoning or condiment worth experimenting with.

You can make this well in advance of eating it – just heat it up gently with a tablespoon or two more milk. Taste and season it again before serving. It's a really good foil to *rich and fatty meats such as lamb chops*, as well as *pan-fried scallops*.

Serves 4–6

1 medium cauliflower
1 garlic clove, peeled
1 bay leaf
15g dried active yeast
300ml milk
½ teaspoon sea salt
Juice of ¼ lemon

Remove the leaves from the cauliflower and reserve them for another occasion (see page 38). Cut the florets off, then chop the remaining head, core and stalk into 5cm cubes. Put the cauliflower, garlic and bay leaf in a medium saucepan, sprinkle with the dried yeast and add the milk (it won't cover the cauliflower completely). Bring to the boil, then simmer for 20 minutes. Be careful not to let the milk boil over and stir occasionally so the cauliflower at the top cooks through fully.

Drain the cauliflower, reserving the milk, and discard the bay leaf. Weigh the drained cauliflower. Calculate 40 per cent of the weight of the cauliflower and measure that amount of warm milk. Put the cauliflower in a blender and add the measured amount of milk, then pulse and blend until smooth and silky. Add a little more milk to loosen it further if you wish. Taste, then add the salt and lemon juice to season.

ALONGSIDE: *Chard with chilli, shallot and cider vinaigrette* (page 6); *Cavolo nero with garlic, chilli and orange* (page 24); *Purple sprouting broccoli with tarragon* (page 42); *Hasselback potatoes with bay and caraway* (page 172); *Rosemary and chilli roast squash* (page 184)

Cauliflower cheese

PREPARATION: *on a hob and in the oven*
TIME NEEDED: *30 minutes to an hour*

Some observations as to what makes a good cauliflower cheese: a number of recipes leave the cauliflower whole or halved, which is visually appealing but flawed, as it leaves too little surface area for the sauce to cling to; the cauliflower should be parboiled, but not so much that it turns soggy; the white sauce should be boldly flavoured by strong farmhouse Cheddar; a shallow dish is better than a deep one (again, a question of surface area); and a crumbed top can be good, but there's something to be said for keeping things pure and simple.

Other than that, you know the drill: it's essential with *roast beef* and very welcome next to *roast lamb*, *cooked ham* or *braised leeks*.

Serves 4–6

1 litre milk
5 black peppercorns
1 garlic clove, flattened
½ onion, peeled
1 sprig rosemary
2 bay leaves
60g butter
60g plain flour
140g strong farmhouse Cheddar, grated
2 teaspoons Dijon mustard
⅙ nutmeg, freshly grated
½ teaspoon ground white pepper
2 medium-large cauliflowers
Sea salt

Make the cheese sauce. Put the milk in a heavy-bottomed saucepan with the peppercorns, garlic, onion, rosemary and bay leaves. Bring to the boil, then remove from the heat and allow the aromatics to infuse for 30 minutes. Discard the aromatics, then keep the milk warm over a very low heat.

———

In a separate pan (large enough to hold all the milk and cheese), make a roux by melting the butter over a medium heat, then adding the flour. Stir the flour into the butter and keep stirring until the initially rather stiff mixture loosens – about 2–3 minutes. Add 1 ladle of warm milk and stir until it is fully incorporated before adding another. Continue until all the milk has been added, then cook for 10 minutes over a low heat until the sauce has thickened and it no longer tastes of raw flour. Stir in the cheese, mustard, nutmeg and pepper. Check the seasoning and add salt if you wish (if the cheese is strong enough, this shouldn't be necessary). Set aside.

———

Preheat the oven to 220°C/Fan 200°C/Gas 7. Bring a large pan of salted water to a rolling boil. Cut the cauliflowers into 7 or 8 fairly large florets and slice the core and stalk into 2cm discs. Add the cauliflower to the pan and cook for 4–5 minutes, or until just tender. Drain, then tip into an ovenproof dish that will hold it snugly in no more than two layers. Pour the cheese sauce over the top – it should be thick enough to hug the florets. Put the cauliflower dish on a baking tray to catch any overspill and bake on the top shelf for 15 minutes, or until the top is burnished and bubbling.

———

ALONGSIDE: *Braised red cabbage and beetroot* (page 22); *Deep-fried Brussels sprouts* (page 32); *French-ish peas* (page 58); *Chorizo roast potatoes* (page 170); *Carrot-juice carrots* (page 218)

Mandolin salad

PREPARATION: *on the counter*
TIME NEEDED: *less than 15 minutes*

The mandolin is an incredibly useful kitchen tool that transforms tough root veg and fibrous bulbs into fresh, crunchy salads in a matter of seconds. Indeed, whenever I look at a kohlrabi, fennel, cauliflower, cucumber or radish (whether it's Japanese black, heirloom, watermelon, French breakfast or the totally normal but still excellent type) sitting unloved in my salad drawer, slicing it thinly is always one of the first options that springs to mind.

The vegetable types, quantities and ratios below are just a guide. Really, you should just use whatever veg you fancy or have to hand. But if you do make a mandolin salad like this one, which contains peppery radishes, anise from fennel, the cooling crunch of kohlrabi and cauliflower, and the juiciness of a cucumber, you'll find it particularly suited to *grilled oily fish like mackerel* or a *buttery pastry tart,* or as a deceptively impressive salad as part of a summer buffet.

Please use the safety guard. The time it takes to make this dish is significantly increased if you also have to take cursing and first aid into account.

Serves 4–6

½ kohlrabi (about 200g)
½ bulb (about 150g) fennel and its fronds
⅓ cucumber (about 100g), peeled
5 French breakfast radishes
⅓ head cauliflower
2 teaspoons extra-virgin olive oil
1 teaspoon moscatel or sherry vinegar
Sea salt

Use a mandolin to slice the vegetables to 1–2mm thick as follows. Do the kohlrabi first and sprinkle a pinch of salt over the slices so that they soften just a little. Trim the base off the fennel, cut the stalks off the top and save any fronds, then slice it thinly from root to tip and transfer it to a bowl of iced water so that it curls and remains fresh. Slice the cucumber into rounds and the radishes lengthways and add these to the iced water. For the cauliflower, break it into florets and carefully slice them lengthways. (This is a bit of a fiddle, but don't worry about it crumbling – that'll add texture.)

When everything is ready, drain the fennel, radish and cucumber and mix the components together. Dress with oil and vinegar, mix, add as many fennel fronds as you can pick, and serve immediately (the vinegar and salt will cause the vegetables to wilt).

ALONGSIDE: *Tomato tonnato* (page 96); *Sherry cherry tomatoes* (page 98); *Flavoured butter bread* (page 234); *Cinnamon, chickpea and apricot couscous* (page 242); *Red wine, anise and orange lentils* (page 264)

Baby aubergine, oregano and chilli bake

PREPARATION: *in the oven*
TIME NEEDED: *30 minutes to an hour*

Aubergine is often described as requiring a lot of oil and plenty of time in a hot pan or deep fryer, but I think this relatively dry oven-roasted method achieves a perfectly satisfying result. Actually, the result is more than satisfying: it's utterly luxurious (though that may be on account of the cream and cheese).

If you can't find baby aubergines, it's okay to use ordinary ones cut in half lengthways, then into 2–3cm half moons. However, I have a particular fondness for the texture that the baby variety provides; the ratio of skin to flesh is higher, which adds a pleasing chewiness to what are otherwise decadently silky mouthfuls. This dish + *a roast rib of beef* + some crisp potatoes + a mound of brassica leaves = heaven.

Serves 4–6

3 tablespoons sunflower or vegetable oil
About 750g baby aubergines
2 red onions, halved and thinly sliced
300ml double cream
130ml milk
1 garlic clove, thinly sliced
Leaves from 4 stems oregano, or 1 heaped teaspoon dried oregano
1 mild chilli, finely diced
35g Parmesan, grated
Juice and finely grated zest of ¼ lemon
Sea salt and freshly ground black pepper

Preheat the oven to its highest temperature (about 250°C/Fan 250°C/Gas 10). Pour the oil into a large roasting tin that will easily fit the aubergines in one layer. Wash and dry the aubergines, slice the stalk tips off, then cut each one in half. Add them to the tin and mix well so that every piece is glossed. Roast on the top shelf for 15 minutes, or until they colour and shrivel. Remove from the oven, add the onions, toss well and set aside (this is so that the onions receive a little of the residual heat before the next stage). Turn the oven down to 170°C/Fan 150°C/Gas 3½.

Meanwhile, put the cream, milk, garlic, oregano and chilli in a saucepan and place over a medium heat. When it's nearly simmering, add the Parmesan and stir until melted and fully incorporated. Remove from the heat.

Tip the aubergine and onions into a smaller ovenproof dish so that they fit in 1–2 layers. Pour the cream mixture over the top and gently stir it in. Bake for 20 minutes or so, or until the aubergines are soft and yielding and the cream is thick and lightly golden on top. Finish with a squeeze of lemon and a sprinkle of zest as a seasoning to lift and refresh the dish, rather than to make it taste of lemon.

You could prepare this in advance, stopping once you've mixed the aubergines and cream. If you do that, add another 5–10 minutes to the final cooking stage and don't add the lemon until just before serving.

ALONGSIDE: *Flower sprouts with lemon and anchovy butter* (page 30); *Rosemary and chestnut sprouts* (page 34); *Sweet cauliflower greens* (page 38); *Purple sprouting broccoli with tarragon* (page 42); *Hasselback potatoes with bay and caraway* (page 172)

Aubergine purée

PREPARATION: *in the oven*
TIME NEEDED: *30 minutes to an hour*

When aubergines are aggressively roasted or grilled, their subtle earthiness is replaced by more intense savoury, caramel and smoky notes. Yet the texture of roasted aubergine is a little odd: the skin, still full of flavour, takes some chewing (if you attack it at all), and the inside turns to watery, lumpy pulp. By far the best thing to do, in my opinion, is blitz the lot, leaving you with a silky-smooth and powerful purée. The cumin and pomegranate molasses in this recipe ramp up the flavour further; it's intense.

Consider this next time you're cooking *lamb*, *hogget* or *mutton*, *venison*, *sea bass*, *monkfish* or *roast vegetables*, although make sure any other dishes you serve alongside have some bite or crunch.

Serves 4–6

3 medium aubergines (around 300g each)
½ tablespoon sunflower or vegetable oil
5 tablespoons light olive oil
1 tablespoon extra-virgin olive oil
4 tablespoons pomegranate molasses
1½ teaspoons cumin seeds, toasted and ground
Juice of ¼ lemon
Sea salt and ground white pepper

Preheat the oven to 250°C/Fan 230°C/Gas 10. Prick the aubergines and put them on a small baking or roasting tray. Rub them with the sunflower oil and roast for 40–45 minutes, until they're sunken and a little blackened. Turn them over halfway through.

Once cooked, cut the aubergines in half lengthways, then into rough chunks and put them in a blender or food processor, skin and all. Scrape the juices from your chopping board in too. Add the olive oils, pomegranate molasses, cumin, ½ teaspoon salt and a pinch of white pepper. Blitz and blend for a couple of minutes until very smooth and glossy and any black flecks of skin are obliterated. Add the lemon juice. Taste and add more salt or lemon juice if needed (it's not supposed to taste lemony, but as a seasoning it lifts it).

You can (and probably should) make this in advance. Gently warm it in a saucepan when required. Add 1 tablespoon water or a dash more oil if you keep it warm for a while, as some liquid will evaporate. Taste and check for seasoning again before serving.

ALONGSIDE: *Cabbage with juniper butter* (page 20); *Charred Romanesco* (page 46); *Anchovy-dressed chicory* (page 78); *Vermouth-braised red onions* (page 146); *Rosemary and chilli roast squash* (page 184)

Caponata

PREPARATION: *on a hob and in the oven*
TIME NEEDED: *more than an hour*

Caponata is one of my Death Row side dishes. This version is an amalgamation of numerous different recipes and methods I've read, tried and adapted over the years rather than one passed down from an Italian *nonna*. So it's probably totally inauthentic. The charge sheet starts with the roasting (rather than frying) of aubergines, continues with the use of Romano peppers in a traditionally Sicilian dish, and carries on in the method.

But it does have an awesome balance of sweet and sour and works well with rich, oily foods as well as softer and more subtle ingredients, such as *slow-roast lamb shoulder*, *grilled mackerel and sardines*, *tuna steaks* or *baked white fish*. It takes a little time, although it's mostly hands-off and is well worth the wait.

The recipe says it serves 6, and it does. But that's with generous helpings – fingers crossed the cook gets lucky and has leftovers for lunch the next day, when it will taste even better.

Serves 6

1kg aubergines
3 tablespoons sunflower oil
3 tablespoons olive oil
350–400g red onions, quartered
4 Romano peppers, halved then cut into 4–5cm chunks
400g (5–6 sticks) celery, cut into 3cm lengths
3 garlic cloves, thinly sliced
50g tinned anchovies in their oil
50g capers, drained
1 teaspoon dried thyme
1 teaspoon dried oregano
700g plum tomatoes, cut into 4–5cm wedges
3 tablespoons red wine vinegar
30g demerara sugar
16–20 basil leaves
20g toasted pine nuts (optional)
Sea salt and freshly ground black pepper

Preheat the oven to its highest temperature (about 250°C/Fan 250°C/Gas 10). Quarter the aubergines lengthways, then cut across the lengths into 3–4cm widths. Pour the sunflower oil into a medium-large roasting tin and put it in the oven for 5 minutes to heat up. Remove the tin and add the aubergine pieces, carefully shuffling them to coat with hot oil, then roast for 15–20 minutes, or until they brown and shrivel a bit.

In the meantime, heat the olive oil in a large frying pan over a medium heat. Add the onions and fry for 3–4 minutes, allowing the cut edges to brown just a little. Add the peppers and celery and cook for a further 10 minutes, or until softened and sweetened. Turn the heat down to low, add the garlic and cook gently for 3 minutes more. Roughly chop the anchovies and add them to the pan with their oil, along with the drained capers and herbs. Remove from the heat.

Remove the aubergines from the oven and tip them into a bowl, then turn the oven down to 160°C/Fan 140°C/Gas 3. Transfer the contents of the frying pan to the roasting tin. Layer the aubergines on top and the tomatoes on top of them, then drizzle with the vinegar and

sprinkle with sugar so it coats the tomatoes. Return to the bottom shelf of the oven and bake for 1 hour. The tomatoes will dry and intensify and the other vegetables will soften and sweeten.

Remove from the oven, gently stir the vegetables and let them sit and absorb the sweet-and-sour juices for at least an hour, if not overnight (they will soften further over that time). Patience is a virtue here.

Add the basil and the pine nuts, if using, just before serving. I like to eat this at room temperature, but you could gently reheat it in the oven or a saucepan.

ALONGSIDE: *Gem lettuce, mint and spring onion* (page 86); *Boulangère potatoes* (page 168); *Cheesy polenta* (page 238); *White beans with fennel seeds, chilli and rocket* (page 274); *Lemon and olive oil fregola* (page 284)

Leeks vinaigrette with crisp-fried leeks

PREPARATION: *on a hob*
TIME NEEDED: *15 to 30 minutes*

I'd forgotten about leeks vinaigrette until I spied it in a friend's fridge. 'We pretty much always have some in there,' they told me, I think partly because it tastes better when left long enough for the ingredients to get to know one another, and they're forward planners. As it happens, leeks vinaigrette suits fridge living because it's an excellent accompaniment to *cold meats* and *terrines*. It's rather good with still-warm *poached fish* and *cooked ham* too.

Two further things to note: use baby or relatively young leeks, since larger, older ones are loose, flop apart and become dull in taste and colour when cooked; and do try the twist of sprinkling shredded fried leeks on top, as they add great crunch and an extra seasoning. You could make them a day in advance and store in an airtight container at room temperature, though they're best fresh and warm from the fryer.

Serves 4–6

8–10 (750g) small, young leeks
2 teaspoons Dijon mustard
2 tablespoons red wine vinegar
1 tablespoon maple syrup
3 tablespoons extra-virgin olive oil
Sunflower or vegetable oil, for shallow frying
Sea salt

Bring a saucepan of salted water to a gentle simmer. Reserve 100g of the leeks for the crisp garnish, then cut the remaining leeks into batons about 6cm in length, discarding any particularly fibrous dark-green ends. Put the leek batons in the pan and cook gently for 6–8 minutes, or until they soften to no more than al dente. Drain and put them in a bowl of iced water or rinse them under running water until cool.

———

Make the dressing by whisking the mustard, vinegar and maple syrup together until they're emulsified. Add the olive oil in two or three splashes, whisking so that the liquids combine. Cut the leek batons in half lengthways and arrange on a plate. Spoon the dressing over and set aside while making the garnish.

———

Slice the remaining leeks widthways very thinly to make a heap of thin circles. If they're muddy, wash and dry them thoroughly. Pour the frying oil into a heavy-bottomed saucepan to a depth of 2–3cm and set over a high heat.

———

Line a bowl or tray with kitchen paper. Test the oil temperature by dropping a couple of leek strands in: if it bubbles, it's ready. Fry the sliced leeks in batches until brown and crisp. Remove with a slotted spoon and transfer them to the kitchen paper. Once all are fried, remove the kitchen paper and sprinkle 2–3 good pinches of salt over the leeks. Mix well, then sprinkle generously over the leeks vinaigrette.

———

ALONGSIDE: *Pink radicchio with pear and almonds* (page 82); *Green tomato, salted celery and chervil salad* (page 100); *New potatoes with pickled samphire and sorrel* (page 174); *Seeded rye and honey soda bread* (page 232); *Herb-loaded lentils* (page 262)

Blue cheese leeks

PREPARATION: *on a hob*
TIME NEEDED: *15 to 30 minutes*

Growing up, one of my favourite Sunday lunch accompaniments was 'leek sauce': leeks softened in butter and combined with a milky white sauce. They were soft and sloppy but so comforting on a wet British weekend, and particularly good with lamb. But it was also quite heavy. I now do something slightly different by adding a few tablespoons of crème fraîche and blue cheese to the pan; it's a much quicker and sharper sauce than a classic bechamel.

This is an excellent side dish for *roast and grilled meats*, *smoked haddock* or *baked mushrooms*. If a cheese sauce doesn't seem right for your meal, but leeks do (alongside most fish, for example), just ignore the blue cheese and crème fraîche – sautéed leeks are an excellent simple side in their own right.

Serves 4–6

1kg leeks, trimmed
40g butter
1 small garlic clove, crushed
75g blue cheese, such as Stilton, Danish Blue or Bleu d'Auvergne
150g crème fraîche
1 heaped teaspoon Dijon mustard
Juice of ¼ lemon
Sea salt and freshly ground black pepper

Cut the leeks on an angle into pieces about 3cm long. Wash them thoroughly to remove any mud or grit. Set a large heavy-bottomed saucepan or frying pan with a lid over a medium heat, add the butter and, once it has mostly melted, the still-wet leeks, along with a pinch of salt. Cook for 2–3 minutes, stirring occasionally.

———

Add the garlic and cook gently for 2 more minutes. Reduce the heat to low and cover the pan. Cook very gently until softened and sweetened for 8–10 minutes, lifting the lid to stir only after 6 minutes, and just a couple of times after that. The leeks are ready when tender and sweet; avoid cooking them for so long they turn to a dull, stringy mush.

———

If not using the crème fraîche and blue cheese, season the leeks with salt, pepper and a squeeze of lemon and serve. Those aiming for something more decadent need simply crumble in the blue cheese, add the crème fraîche and mustard, stir and cook very gently for 1–2 minutes, no more. Season with the lemon juice and a grind or two of black pepper. Taste. The blue cheese will be salty, but add more salt if you think it's required.

———

ALONGSIDE: *French-ish peas* (page 58); *Portobello mushrooms baked with oregano* (page 152); *Maple and pecan roast squash* (page 186); *'Young Turk' celeriac* (page 196); *Carrot-juice carrots* (page 218)

Vermouth-braised red onions

PREPARATION: *in the oven*
TIME NEEDED: *30 minutes to an hour*

Perhaps because we use it as the base for so many of our dishes, we forget that the humble onion can play a more prominent role. I personally love picking at any (and all) of the onions that have been used as a trivet under my roast meats; they're caramelised, tender and juicy. These braised red onions derive from that treat, and they're a natural fit with *any roast meat*, or *offal like flash-fried beef heart or a kidney pie*. *Mushrooms*, too.

In addition to caramelising at the edges and becoming ever sweeter as they soften and collapse in on themselves, they take on the gorgeous vermouth and thyme flavours and become a treat for everyone to enjoy, not just the cook.

Serves 6

6 medium red onions
8–10 sprigs thyme
40g butter, sliced
100ml sweet vermouth
Sea salt

Preheat the oven to 200°C/Fan 180°C/Gas 6. Peel the onions and trim the base of each one just enough so that they will sit flat, but the root will still hold the layers together. With the onions resting upright on a chopping board, cut each one in half from top to bottom, stopping two thirds of the way down. Make two further cuts so that the onion opens up into six even-sized 'petals'.

Sprinkle a little salt over the base of an ovenproof dish that holds the onions snugly in one layer. Sit the onions on top, push a sprig or so of thyme and two slices of butter into each one, and add a few flakes of salt. Pour in the vermouth and bake for 50–60 minutes, basting the onions with the cooking juices every 10–15 minutes. They're done when that liquid has been mostly absorbed and the onions are sweet, soft and just a little charred on top. Serve each one with a spoonful or two of any remaining cooking juices.

ALONGSIDE: *Boulangère potatoes* (page 168); *Colcannon* (page 178); *Honey and Marmite-glazed parsnips* (page 182); *'Young Turk' celeriac* (page 196); *Nutmeg neeps* (page 202)

Anise-braised spring onions

PREPARATION: *in the oven*
TIME NEEDED: *30 minutes to an hour*

For those of us accustomed to finding raw spring onions harsh and astringent in a green salad (and discarding them upon discovery), it might be a surprise to find that these alliums can also make a gentle, soft and warming side. When braised, as in this recipe, their inner cores become tender and sweet and resemble cooked leeks or Spanish *calçots*. *White fish*, *chicken* and *lamb* are particularly big fans.

You'll get the best results from generously bulbed and thick-stemmed onions, especially the purple-tinged ones if you can find them. A mass of thin salad onions is okay too, though. Whichever you use, be sure to spoon the buttery, anise-infused sauce over the top when serving.

Serves 4–6

600g large-bulbed spring onions, preferably a mix of red and white
3 garlic cloves, skin on
1 lemon, zest peeled off in long strips
10 stems tarragon
50g butter, sliced
1 teaspoon fennel seeds
75ml Pernod, or white wine or vermouth
Sea salt

Preheat the oven to 200°C/Fan 180°C/Gas 6. Trim the spring onions to fit the length of a cast-iron skillet or other ovenproof dish, ideally keeping them around 20cm long. Put the onions in the dish, no more than 2 layers deep.

———

Press the garlic cloves with the back of a heavy knife to flatten them just a little. Add these to the cooking dish. Tuck the lemon zest and tarragon in between the onions, reserving the flesh of the lemon for another recipe. Put the butter on and around the onions, scatter the fennel seeds over the top and pour in the Pernod. Top up with enough boiling water so that the liquid reaches halfway up the onions.

———

Take a piece of greaseproof paper or baking parchment that's marginally bigger than the oven dish. Crumple it up, run it under the tap to wet it, then unwrap it and place it over the onions, tucking the edge in like a blanket. Bake undisturbed for 35 minutes, then remove the paper, gently turn the onions and cook for 10–15 minutes more, or until they are completely tender, sweet, succulent and just a little browned. Season with a good pinch or two of salt. Pick out the straggly tarragon sprigs and serve the onions with the braising juices spooned over the top.

———

These are fine kept at a low temperature for 20 minutes, or reheated later on if that suits the timing of your meal better.

———

ALONGSIDE: *Chopped kale with edamame, miso and sweet chilli* (page 26); *Charred Romanesco* (page 46); *Quick romesco* (page 106); *Chorizo roast potatoes* (page 170); *Roast butternut squash purée* (page 188)

Burnt sweet onion petals with cucumber

PREPARATION: *on a hob*
TIME NEEDED: *15 to 30 minutes*

If you see French sweet onions (Roscoffs, ideally) in the shops or online, snap them up. They're naturally sugary and need only a little heat to make them agreeable to eat. That said, here their cut faces are given more than a little, as they're left to blacken fully in a hot pan. During that time, the rest of the onion softens just enough and then, when it is pushed apart, you're left with the prettiest of charred, tender, sweet petals, which cup cooling cubes of cucumber and a nutty, sharp dressing. The whole thing is reminiscent of lip-puckering pomegranate molasses-dressed onions at a Turkish restaurant.

There's a little crunch, making them a joy both texturally and aesthetically, and they're particularly enjoyable with *ox heart*, *faggots*, *calves' liver*, *red meat* and generally anything that's also been charred. Also, what a pleasure it is to leave something to burn, knowing that is the aim from the outset!

I should note that arranging them on a platter as per the picture is pleasing. But it will be quicker to serve the petals from a communal bowl, and let people spoon up the cucumber and dressing themselves.

Serves 4–6

2 tablespoons sunflower or vegetable oil
6 sweet French onions, unpeeled and halved from root to tip
5 tablespoons cold-pressed rapeseed oil
2 tablespoons sherry vinegar
1 teaspoon golden caster sugar
½ cucumber, peeled, seeded and finely diced
Sea salt and freshly ground black pepper

Place a heavy-bottomed frying pan over a high heat and add the sunflower oil. Put the onion halves in the pan cut-side down, pushing them over the oil, and cook for 8–10 minutes, or until thoroughly blackened. Press down on each onion occasionally and don't panic – the idea really is for the cut sides to char. Just make sure your extractor fan is on full blast. Once the onions are well blackened, turn them over to sit on the skin side for 5 minutes, during which time the onions will soften, then remove the pan from the heat.

———

While the onions are charring, make a dressing in a bowl by whisking the rapeseed oil, sherry vinegar, sugar and a good pinch of salt and black pepper until emulsified. Add 1 tablespoon tepid water, whisk again, then stir the diced cucumber through the dressing.

———

When the onions are just cool enough to touch, remove and discard the skins. Separate the petals and serve immediately, spooning the dressing and cucumber into the onion petals.

———

ALONGSIDE: *Purple sprouting broccoli with ricotta and orzo* (page 44); *Aubergine purée* (page 138); *Celeriac baked in a salt and thyme crust* (page 198); *Butter-glazed turnips with horseradish* (page 204); *Carrots with brown butter and hazelnuts* (page 220)

Portobello mushrooms baked with oregano

PREPARATION: *in the oven*
TIME NEEDED: *30 minutes to an hour*

Portobellos have a unique ability (among mushrooms at least) to become more juicy, more meaty and more intense when cooked, making them a stellar side dish for meat-focused meals, particularly *beef steaks* and *veal*; though they sit nicely next to *vegetable stews*, *rice dishes* and *white fish* as well.

You could skip the browning stage if you're pushed for hob space, though you'll need to bake the mushrooms for longer and the end flavour won't be quite as good.

Serves 6

50g butter, sliced
6 large Portobello mushrooms
2 garlic cloves, thinly sliced
4 stems oregano, cut into 2–3 pieces
15g flaked almonds
Sea salt and freshly ground black pepper

Preheat the oven to 160°C/Fan 140°C/Gas 3. Melt half the butter in a large skillet or frying pan over a high heat until foaming and browning. Add the mushrooms, curved-side down, and cook for 2 minutes, until browned. You may need to cook them 2 or 3 at a time and add extra butter if you think it needs it.

———

If your pan is not ovenproof or does not fit the mushrooms in one layer, transfer them to a larger ovenproof dish, ensuring the gills face upwards, then scatter the sliced garlic into the cups. Do the same with the oregano. Season generously with salt and pepper and dot the remaining 25g butter inside the mushrooms.

———

Pour boiling water into the pan or dish to a depth of 1cm. Take a piece of greaseproof paper or baking parchment slightly bigger than the dish, wet it under the cold tap, screw it up then unravel it and place it over the mushrooms, tucking it in at the edge. Bake for 25 minutes, then remove the paper. Sprinkle the mushrooms with the almonds and bake for 10–15 minutes more, or until the almonds are turning golden and the mushrooms are yielding and juicy. Turn the mushrooms over a few times in the cooking liquid and serve, ensuring everyone has a fair share of the garlic, oregano and almond flakes, plus a spoonful or two of that delectable liquor.

———

If required, you could prepare them in advance and keep them warm for 20–30 minutes in a very low oven, or simply reheat with a quick oven blast when needed.

———

ALONGSIDE: *Chard with chilli, shallot and cider vinaigrette* (page 6); *Quick romesco* (page 106); *Butter-glazed turnips with horseradish* (page 204); *Baked Jerusalem artichokes with yoghurt and sunflower seeds* (page 206); *Cheesy polenta* (page 238)

Za'atar mushrooms with curd

PREPARATION: *on a hob*
TIME NEEDED: *less than 15 minutes*

King oyster mushrooms (also known as eryngii or trumpet royale) are all about the thick, meaty stems. Sliced and fried in oil and butter, they turn golden and become crisp but remain soft within. The ricotta and cream is like a homemade curd and its cooling creaminess lifts the earthy mushroom flavour. Both of those elements work really well with a liberal dusting of za'atar, a heady spice mix made from dried wild herbs, sesame and salt, which is becoming ubiquitous for good reason, and is now available in many supermarkets.

If it's the right time of year and you have the cash, try this with fresh ceps. Frankly, good old chestnut mushrooms enjoy being matched with curd and za'atar too. The dish is well suited to *spatchcocked and chargrilled quail or guinea fowl*, *lamb chops*, or as one of those sides from which a *full mezze-style meal* could be assembled, not least the 'Alongside' recipes listed below.

Serves 4–6

500g king oyster mushrooms, ceps or good chestnut mushrooms
4 tablespoons cold-pressed rapeseed oil
50g butter
Juice of ½ lemon
2 tablespoons za'atar
Sea salt and freshly ground black pepper

Curd
160g ricotta
80ml double cream

Mix the ricotta and cream together to make the curd and keep in the fridge until needed.

Wipe the mushrooms with a damp cloth to remove any dirt. If using king oysters or ceps, slice them lengthways into 5mm-thick slices – aim for 4–5 from each mushroom. If using chestnut mushrooms, slice them in half from top to bottom.

Heat the oil in a large heavy-bottomed frying pan that fits all the mushrooms in one layer (or be prepared to cook in batches) over a high heat. Wait 45 seconds for the oil to heat up, then add the mushrooms and cook them for 45 seconds. Turn them over and sprinkle with salt and cook for 30–45 seconds longer, or until they begin to turn opaque; moisture and oil will begin to be released back into the pan and the mushrooms will start frying. Add the butter to the pan and turn the mushrooms once or twice more as they turn golden brown in the frothing butter. When the mushrooms are a good colour and just starting to crisp, turn the heat off, grind over a little black pepper and squeeze the lemon juice over the top.

Spoon the curd onto a serving plate or bowl and liberally sprinkle with half the za'atar. Top with the mushrooms, drizzle with a little more rapeseed oil or any juices left in the pan, then sprinkle with the remaining za'atar.

ALONGSIDE: *Dijon-dressed green beans* (page 64); *Anchovy-dressed chicory* (page 78); *Roast Romano peppers* (page 104); *Burnt sweet onion petals with cucumber* (page 150); *Spinach and preserved lemon freekeh* (page 248)

Fish sauce watermelon salad

PREPARATION: *on the counter*
TIME NEEDED: *less than 15 minutes*

This is one of those occasions when a sweet fruit, more traditionally eaten for breakfast or after a meal, crosses over into the savoury realm. Watermelon does it successfully here because it's fresh and cooling. Therefore, although there's plenty of heat in the dressing, it's the perfect antidote to hot and spicy and/or fatty food, or simply as a mezze-style dish on a sweltering day.

The fish sauce is instrumental in flavouring and binding the salad; don't hold back. The squeeze of *sriracha* (a hot chilli sauce from Thailand) is essential too because it adds an addictively piquant mix of chilli and garlic, putting this squarely in the side-dish (rather than pudding) camp. If you can't find sriracha, double the fresh chilli in the recipe and add half a clove of crushed garlic.

I love this with *pork belly*, *fried chicken* or *pan-fried crisp-skinned salmon fillets*.

Serves 4–6

1kg watermelon, rind removed, cut into 3cm cubes, chilled
300g cucumber, peeled, seeded and cut into 1cm crescents, chilled
3 tablespoons sriracha chilli sauce
6 tablespoons fish sauce
3cm fresh ginger, peeled and finely grated
2 teaspoons palm sugar or golden caster sugar
Juice of 1 lime
1 bird's eye chilli, thinly sliced
Leaves from 10–15 stems mint, rolled and finely shredded
15–20 basil leaves (preferably Thai), torn
A handful of bean shoots (optional)

Ensure the watermelon and cucumber are fridge-cold before preparing the salad. Mix the chilli sauce, fish sauce, ginger, sugar and lime juice in a large bowl. Add the watermelon, cucumber and bird's eye chilli. Toss gently, but thoroughly enough to ensure they are well coated. Let this sit in the fridge for a few minutes.

Add three quarters of the herbs and the bean shoots, if you're using them. Mix and serve immediately, with the remaining herbs scattered over the top.

ALONGSIDE: *Chopped kale with edamame, miso and sweet chilli* (page 26); *Courgettes with soy, sesame, mint and chilli* (page 112); *Gochujang mayo and coconut corn on the cob* (page 126); *Sesame soba noodles* (page 254); *Three pepper rice* (page 294)

Smacked cucumbers

PREPARATION: *on the counter*
TIME NEEDED: *15 to 30 minutes*

Smacked cucumbers are cooling and refreshing; traditionally a Sichuanese appetiser, they are in many ways a palate cleanser as much as they are a side dish. But they work so well alongside *sizzling-hot or spicy meat*, *fish*, *vegetables* and *tofu dishes* – hot and cold foods alike. I'm keen on them whenever I'm serving noodles or plain rice and want something to cut through the meal and provide extra spark. That's quite a regular occurrence for me, so it's fortunate that they're also quick, easy and fun to prepare.

Serves 6

750g cucumbers
1 teaspoon sea salt
2 garlic cloves, crushed
1 tablespoon light soy sauce
1 tablespoon black Chinkiang vinegar
2 teaspoons golden caster sugar
1 tablespoon sesame oil
2 teaspoons white or black sesame seeds

Wash the cucumbers but don't peel them, then place them on a solid board or work top. Use a mallet, rolling pin or cleaver to smack them, so that the centres get squashed and turn a little mushy, and they split in several places lengthways. You can be pretty brutal.

Chop the smacked and split cucumbers into 3–4cm pieces along their length. Put them in a bowl and add the salt. Toss well and chill in the fridge for at least 10 minutes, and up to 1 hour.

Mix the remaining ingredients, except the sesame seeds, together in a bowl. A few minutes before eating, pour the sauce over the cucumbers and the water that has been drawn out by the salt, sprinkle with the sesame seeds and mix well.

ALONGSIDE: *Chinese cabbage with black vinegar* (page 16); *Baby pak choi with sticky garlic and ginger* (page 48); *Asian greens with shrimp paste* (page 50); *Garlic oil pea shoots* (page 56); *Almond and anise rice* (page 298)

Quick cucumber and daikon kimchi

PREPARATION: *on the counter*
TIME NEEDED: *more than an hour*

Traditional Korean kimchi made with cabbage takes a month or two to achieve the requisite levels of sourness and fizz that make it so addictive. But the key flavours of *gochugaru* (Korean red chilli flakes), fish sauce and garlic can be combined with crunchy vegetables like cucumber and daikon to great and almost instant effect. The rice vinegar adds a little of the sourness that classic kimchi brings, and the chilli remains addictively hot in this non-fermented version. I love it as a cooling condiment (in temperature, if not chilli heat) alongside *slow-cooked spiced beef*, *seafood-stuffed omelettes* and, in particular, as part of a mid-week supper of *plain rice, stir-fried vegetables and a fried egg*.

Serves 4–6

1 cucumber, peeled
10–15cm daikon, peeled
½ teaspoon sea salt
2 teaspoons gochugaru red chilli flakes
1 teaspoon golden caster sugar
½ garlic clove, crushed
1 tablespoon fish sauce
1 tablespoon rice vinegar
1 tablespoon sesame oil
2 teaspoons black or white sesame seeds

Cut the cucumber in half lengthways. Use a teaspoon to scoop out the seeds, then place each half flat on its cut side. Cut it into 1cm crescents. Do the same with the daikon (although there are no seeds to scoop out), then put both in a bowl with the salt. Mix them together and very quickly the salt will begin to draw out moisture from them. Leave for 30 minutes, then drain off the liquid.

———

Add the gochugaru, sugar, garlic, fish sauce, rice vinegar and sesame oil. Mix well. Cover and leave for at least another hour, or up to 2 days. Serve fridge-cold with the sesame seeds mixed through at the last minute.

———

ALONGSIDE: *Chinese cabbage with black vinegar* (page 16); *Asian greens with shrimp paste* (page 50); *Courgettes with soy, sesame, mint and chilli* (page 112); *Sesame soba noodles* (page 254); *Black bean, coriander and lime rice* (page 292)

ROOTS, SQUASH & POTATOES

The likes of carrots, parsnips, pumpkins and, of course, potatoes are present at most meals. It's easy to see why. Yes, they're carbs that add bulk and energy, but they also provide a range of flavours, colours and textures that leave our bellies, taste buds and minds sated. The spectrum runs from super-sweet squashes and parsnips at one end, through more neutral potatoes, and eventually to peppery turnips and radishes. There's a huge variety and yet, broadly speaking, roots, squash and tubers (potatoes are technically the latter) can be treated in similar ways: boil, bake, roast, fry, slice, dice, mash and purée. These are adaptable and fairly forgiving ingredients.

Boiling is as good a place to start as any. This is the most efficient way to turn fibrous, often inedible-when-raw ingredients into tender, enjoyable mouthfuls. Boiled roots, squash and tubers can either be left whole, or mashed or puréed, depending on your needs. For each of those treatments, a dressing of butter or extra-virgin olive oil and a heavy hand with salt and pepper are usually necessary. The cooking liquid, or milk or cream, can be useful additions when it comes to mashing and puréeing.

Although they're forgiving, over-boiling roots, squash and tubers is a no-no – they tend to break down into watery mush if you're not careful. The general rule for tough vegetables that grow underground is to start the boiling process in cold water, so as not to overcook the outside before the inside has a chance to tenderise. For the starchiest of these ingredients, potatoes in particular, you need to use as much water as possible, to help disperse the starch. Conversely, it's best to boil carrots and beetroot in just a little water, and for as short a time as possible, to reduce the leaching of colour and flavour into the surrounding waters.

Baking roots, squash and tubers is possibly the simplest way to achieve grand results. The dry heat of an oven thickens and crisps their jackets while turning the insides to a fluffy mass ready to burst out at the slightest prod. Again, butter, oil and plenty of seasoning help when it comes to the eating part, and the flesh of a baked potato or squash is especially good when whipped up into a purée. Sugar-heavy roots and tubers, such as sweet potatoes and beetroot in particular, are more intensely flavoured cooked like this rather than boiled. See the baking recipes on pages 188, 198 and 206.

Baking also encompasses gratinating. Is there anything more comforting and satisfying than thinly sliced roots, squash and tubers, layered in a dish, drowning in stock or cream and left in the oven to soften in the middle and crisp on top? There are suggestions for cooking potato, beetroot, sweet potato and celeriac in this way (see pages 168, 194 and 224) although you could swap in most roots and tubers to the same effect.

Frying, whether shallow or deep, provides crunch and colour, but unless the ingredients are cut very thinly, an initial blanch in water or medium-temperature oil before frying at a higher heat is usually necessary to ensure the insides are soft and the edges crunchy.

Then, of course, there's roasting. Who can honestly say they'd turn down an extra roast potato at the end of a massive Sunday lunch and not feel as though they're missing out? For potatoes, you need to parboil and fluff the edges before roasting, and make sure you use a cooking fat that reaches a high smoke point, such as rapeseed oil, duck fat or beef dripping. Parsnips, squash, sweet potatoes, celeriac and radishes all enjoy a roast too, but do not benefit from being parboiled first. If roasting different roots, squash and tubers together, they need to be cut to different sizes according to their cooking times. It's also crucial that there's plenty of space in your roasting tin, and don't add salt until the latter stages if you want moreish and crisp rather than soggy results. See pages 182, 184 and 216 for ideas.

Some final words on the potato, the so-called world's most important vegetable. The main thing to remember when selecting them is: waxy varietals for salads and bakes; floury ones for roasting, jackets and mashing. Oh, and no one will ever thank you for an undercooked spud. More controversially, if potatoes are your default carb, have a think as to whether another root might take their place. Would your meal actually be better with the colour and sweetness of a beetroot gratin, sautéed celeriac, roast carrots or a squash purée? Honestly, you don't always need potatoes on the side, and I've found that not including them every time means I enjoy them more when I do.

Boulangère potatoes

PREPARATION: *in the oven*
TIME NEEDED: *more than an hour*

Whisper it: I find dauphinoise potatoes too rich, filling and, well, creamy. They take over a plate and almost always leave me excessively full – although I admit this last issue is possibly a problem of personal restraint. I prefer boulangère potatoes, in which the cooking liquid is chicken stock, rather than full milk or cream. You still get that tender, moist cut-through of multiple layers of spud and a crisp browned top; it's just a lighter and more versatile option. *Roast lamb and beef joints* are obvious partners, but also good are *sausages*, *suet puddings*, *stews* and *bakes*.

Use real chicken stock if you have it, although a good-quality powdered bouillon will do; just check it's not too salty before adding your own seasoning. A mandolin will quickly ensure uniform, thin slices of potato and is much quicker than labouring with a knife.

Serves 4–6

600ml chicken stock
1.5kg waxy potatoes, such as Desiree or Vivaldi
1 large onion, thinly sliced
2 garlic cloves, very thinly sliced
Leaves from 10 sprigs thyme
Leaves from 5 sprigs rosemary, finely chopped
100g butter, thinly sliced
Sea salt and freshly ground black pepper

Preheat the oven to 200°C/Fan 180°C/Gas 6. Bring the chicken stock to a gentle simmer in a pan, then turn the heat off. Peel the potatoes and cut them into 2–3mm slices, ideally using a mandolin.

Choose an ovenproof dish around 5–8cm deep that will fit all the sliced potatoes. Layer the slices in it, using the less uniform slices and end pieces first. Once you have completed the first layer, sprinkle over a handful of onion, a few slices of garlic, a good pinch or two of herbs, 3 or 4 slices of butter and season with salt and pepper. Add another layer of potatoes and flavourings and repeat until all of the potatoes have been used. Use up all the herbs before the final layer of potatoes and don't worry too much about presentation until the final layer or two. Pour the warm chicken stock over the potatoes, then dot any remaining butter on top.

Put the dish on a baking tray (in case of overspill), then bake on the top shelf for 1 hour, until the top is crisp and brown and a fork pushes through the other layers with ease. After 15 minutes, press down the top layer with a fish slice or palette knife and repeat every 10 minutes from then on. This will ensure the potatoes are compressed and the top is crisp and a glossy caramel colour, rather than a dry and unappealing shade of brown.

ALONGSIDE: *Cabbage with juniper butter* (page 20); *Braised red cabbage and beetroot* (page 22); *Sprout tops with Jerusalem artichokes and apple* (page 36); *Blue cheese leeks* (page 144); *Vermouth-braised red onions* (page 146); *White wine and dill carrots* (page 222)

Chorizo roast potatoes

PREPARATION: *in the oven*
TIME NEEDED: *more than an hour*

Does the world need another roast potato recipe? Probably not. Although some writers argue over the minutiae, the method is essentially: a floury potato varietal, parboiled and roughed up; into hot fat with a high smoke point; plenty of space in the tin; cook at the top of a hot oven; and don't add salt at the start (which makes for soggy spuds). That said, it seemed remiss to write a book on side dishes without mention of this crowd-pleasing side. So here's a recipe with a twist: the addition of crumbled soft cooking chorizo halfway through. The nuggets of paprika- and chilli-flavoured pork add colour, seasoning, texture and a secondary hit of oil to help the potatoes crisp up. A scattering of fennel seeds adds a further dimension.

They're not for every meal but do make a pretty vigorous change, and work particularly well with *chicken* and *pork*.

Serves 4–6

1kg floury potatoes, ideally Maris Piper
5 tablespoons vegetable oil
200g cooking chorizo
2 teaspoons fennel seeds
A handful of flat-leaf parsley, roughly chopped (optional)
Sea salt

Preheat the oven to 220°C/Fan 200°C/Gas 7. Peel the potatoes and cut them into halves or quarters roughly 4cm long. Put them in a large pan and fill it with cold water. Bring to the boil and simmer for 10–15 minutes, until you can tease a fork fairly easily through the first centimetre or so of potato, but still meet resistance towards the middle. Drain them, allow to cool, then shake them well to rough up the edges.

Pour the oil into a large sturdy roasting tin – plenty of space is essential to ensure crisp potatoes. Put the tray in the oven for 10 minutes to heat up the oil, then carefully add the potatoes to the tray. Turn them over in the hot oil so they are all glossy, then return to the top shelf of the oven and cook for 45 minutes, giving the tray a shake after 20 minutes.

Meanwhile, cut the cooking chorizo in half with a sharp knife. Peel off the casing and discard it. Use your fingers to rip the sausage meat into balls that resemble large nuggets of minced meat. These will release their oil and crisp beautifully around the potatoes.

Remove the potatoes from the oven, add the chorizo bits and fennel seeds and mix and turn the potatoes. Roast for a further 15–20 minutes, when the chorizo will be crunchy but not dry, and the potatoes are crisp and a rusty shade of brown. Remove from the oven and season with salt (bear in mind that the chorizo will have added some salt already). Sprinkle with chopped parsley if it suits the occasion. They'll remain very hot for 5–10 minutes; try to avoid reheating or covering them with foil, or the crunch will disappear.

ALONGSIDE: *Grilled hispi cabbage with anchovy and crème fraîche* (page 10); *Wilted bitter leaves with blue cheese dressing* (page 76); *Gem lettuce, mint and spring onion* (page 86); *Shaved fennel with tarragon* (page 118); *Warm radishes with anise* (page 212)

Hasselback potatoes with bay and caraway

PREPARATION: *on a hob and in the oven*
TIME NEEDED: *more than an hour*

Disappointingly, some so-called hasselback potatoes turn out to be little more than roast new potatoes with a few cuts in them. That won't do at all. The joy of this type of spud, when done properly, is that the waxy potato (medium-sized Charlottes are best) is soft and flavourful inside, having been braised for much of the cooking process, and the ridges and outer skins are crisp, nutty and caramel brown, because once the stock has been soaked up, the potatoes fry in foaming butter. In this recipe, there's also a distant, warming spice from bay leaves and caraway.

Ideally you would cook these in a cast-iron frying pan or baking dish, though a small roasting or enamel tin would be fine as long as it's solid enough to go on the hob and in an oven. It's important that the potatoes fit in one snug layer.

Hasselbacks are a really flexible spud option, suited to subbing in for a roast potato, chip or even mash. That said, if you've, say, a *roast duck* and need something 'special' to match, these should be first choice.

Serves 4

1kg Charlotte potatoes, or another waxy salad potato such as Maris Peer or Ratte
70g butter
5 bay leaves
3 teaspoons caraway seeds
Sea salt

Preheat the oven to 220°C/Fan 200°C/Gas 7. Sit each potato on its flattest side and use a sharp knife to make incisions every 2–3mm along the length, cutting three quarters of the way down.

Set a cast-iron frying pan or heavy-bottomed roasting tin over a medium heat and add the butter. Once it has melted, roll the potatoes in the fat until they're glossy, then carefully turn each one over so the cut side is facing up. You'll probably want to use a fork to avoid burning your fingers. Tear the bay leaves into a few pieces and put them in the gaps between the potatoes. Sprinkle the caraway seeds over the top. Pour in cold water to a depth of 3cm, bring to the boil, then transfer to the top shelf of the oven.

Roast the potatoes for about 1½ hours, basting them with the buttery cooking liquid every 15 minutes or so. They're cooked when there's no liquid left in the pan, the tops are brown and crisp and the inside is soft and tender. Feel free to roll the potatoes around after an hour or so, to ensure all sides turn golden. Season with plenty of salt and serve.

ALONGSIDE: *Creamed chard* (page 8); *Puttanesca runner beans* (page 68); *Quick romesco* (page 106); *Yeasted cauliflower purée* (page 130); *Baby aubergine, oregano and chilli bake* (page 136)

New potatoes with pickled samphire and sorrel

PREPARATION: *on a hob*
TIME NEEDED: *more than an hour*

I love this potato salad with things like *hot-smoked trout*, *whole baked sea bream or bass* and *roast chicken leftovers*. I bet you a tenner it's good with *steak* too. The salty and sharp pickled samphire punctuates the waxy, mellow potatoes, and the extraordinary citrus flavour of sorrel enlivens things further.

Don't be tempted to mix the sorrel leaves with the potatoes before the spuds are cool, or too long before you intend to eat the dish, as they'll dull in both colour and taste. The samphire pickling takes just a few minutes, though you could do this up to two days in advance (and if you do that, this becomes a 15–30 minute side).

Serves 4–6

500–600g new potatoes, such as Jersey Royals or Ratte, halved
100g sorrel
3 tablespoons cold-pressed rapeseed oil
Sea salt and freshly ground black pepper

Pickled samphire
70g samphire
130ml white wine vinegar
40g caster sugar
2 teaspoons yellow mustard seeds

To pickle the samphire, bring a pan of water to the boil and blanch the samphire for 1 minute. Drain and cool under running water or in an ice bath, drain well again, then put the samphire in a jar or container with a lid into which it fits snugly.

Dry the saucepan, then add the vinegar, sugar and mustard seeds. Bring to a gentle simmer over a low-medium heat to dissolve the sugar. Let this cool for 15 minutes, then pour it over the samphire. Cover and leave at room temperature for at least 1 hour before refrigerating until required (and for up to 2 days). When you need it, drain the samphire through a sieve, reserving the pickling liquor and mustard seeds.

To make the potato salad, put the potatoes in a medium-large pan and cover them with 2–3 times their volume of cold water. Add a good pinch of salt, bring to the boil and simmer gently for 15–20 minutes, or until the potatoes are tender all the way through. Drain and rinse under running water until cool.

Put the potatoes in a large bowl and add the pickled samphire, the mustard seeds from the pickling liquor and the sorrel leaves. Make a dressing by combining 2 tablespoons of the pickling liquor with the oil and plenty of black pepper. Pour this over the potatoes and toss. Check for seasoning and add salt if necessary, though remember the samphire provides occasional salty kicks.

ALONGSIDE: *Tomato tonnato* (page 96); *Sherry cherry tomatoes* (page 98); *Roast Romano peppers* (page 104); *Honey, thyme and lime butter corn* (page 124); *Kohlrabi remoulade* (page 208)

New potatoes with seaweed butter

PREPARATION: *on a hob*
TIME NEEDED: *15 to 30 minutes*

Boiled new potatoes, skin on, seasoned simply and slicked with melting butter… it's one of the best sides out there. But you could occasionally embellish things just a little with a handful of seaweed flakes and smoked salt, both of which add amazing depth and umami quality to your spuds. *Shellfish* and *plainly cooked white fish* spring immediately to mind as things that will enjoy a portion of these next to them, though *lamb*, *hogget*, *mutton* and *cooked hams* are fans too.

There's no need to spend time making a flavoured ('compound') butter: scattering dried seaweed onto piping hot potatoes and letting their steam heat, hydrate and generally make everything smell amazing is all that needs to be done. I like a mix of dulse and wakame seaweed flakes, but using just one type also works well. All are available online, and increasingly at the supermarket.

For perfect potatoes, start them in cold water; if you drop potatoes into already boiling water, the outer edges will overcook in the time it takes for the middles to soften. Arguably the most important thing in this instance is to use really miniature potatoes (or to cut the ones you have quite small), so that the seaweed scent and butter have lots of surface area to cling to.

Serves 4–6

800g–1kg baby new potatoes, such as Jersey Royals, Anya or Pink Fir
60–80g unsalted butter, at room temperature
4 tablespoons (6–8g) dried dulse and/or wakame
1 teaspoon smoked salt
Sea salt and freshly ground black pepper

Put the potatoes in a medium-large pan and cover them with 2–3 times their volume of cold water. Add a good pinch of salt, bring to the boil and simmer gently for 15–20 minutes, or until the potatoes are tender all the way through. Drain.

Add the butter, dried seaweed, smoked salt and a few twists of the black-pepper mill to the empty and still-warm pan. Tip the drained potatoes back in, roll them around in the pan and place a lid on for 3 minutes. The seaweed will start to hydrate, expand and smell amazing as the potatoes steam. Stir well so all the potatoes are glossy, replace the lid and leave for 2 minutes more. Finally, transfer to a serving dish, making sure you scrape any melted butter and seaweed flakes over the top.

ALONGSIDE: *Bacon and buttermilk cabbage* (page 18); *Grilled tenderstem broccoli with umami crumbs* (page 40); *Agretti with olive oil* (page 62); *Chicken stock and orange-braised fennel* (page 120); *Seeded rye and honey soda bread* (page 232)

Colcannon

PREPARATION: *on a hob and in the oven*
TIME NEEDED: *more than an hour*

There is some debate as to whether the best mash comes from baked or boiled potatoes. I'm not sure this is a topic to lose sleep or friends over; it's more important to use floury, not waxy potatoes, and show them a bit of love once they're cooked.

For plain, everyday mash, I prefer simply to beat warmed milk and butter into the mashed potatoes until they're smooth and creamy. But the classic Irish dish colcannon goes a little further, with the addition of cooked kale and a secondary puddle of butter. It's proper, winter-cuddle comfort food: you won't need many (or any) other sides alongside. *Stews* and *casseroles*, *sausages*, *haggis*, *faggots* and *smoked haddock* are the kind of things you should think about eating with it. Although I'd be pretty happy with just a *poached egg* or two.

Back to the bake or boil issue: here I suggest baking, in part because you could reload the colcannon back into the potato skins at the end if you fancy. Feel free to just boil the potatoes instead; you'll need fewer potatoes, though – 1kg should do.

Serves 6

1.5kg floury potatoes, such as Maris Piper or Russet
250–300g kale (200g if pre-shredded)
140g butter
200ml milk
Sea salt

Preheat the oven to 220°C/Fan 200°C/Gas 7. Wash and dry the potatoes and put them on a baking tray. Bake for 1–1¼ hours, depending on their size, until soft all the way through.

If using whole kale, rather than a bag of the chopped stuff, tear the leafy bits off the tough central ribs. Discard the ribs, then roughly shred the leaves. Wash and drain them. Melt 20g butter in a large heavy-bottomed pan over a medium-high heat, then add the kale and cook for 4 minutes, until soft, glossy and dark. Remove from the heat and set aside.

When the potatoes are cooked, remove them from the oven and cut them in half with a sharp knife. Leave them to steam for 2 minutes (to mash them immediately would lead to gloop). Heat 100g butter and the milk in a saucepan over a low-medium heat. Scoop the potato flesh out of the skins into a bowl. Mash or rice the potatoes (they shouldn't need much work), then add them to the milk and butter pan and beat with a wooden spoon until smooth and silky. Add a good pinch of salt. Taste and add more salt if you think it needs it, then stir in the cooked kale.

Decant the colcannon into a large warm bowl. Make a depression in the middle with the back of a spoon and add the remaining butter, which will melt into a gloriously decadent pool. Encourage people to dip their spoon into the butter while helping themselves. Alternatively, load the mash back into the potato skins and add a knob of butter on top of each one before serving.

ALONGSIDE: *French-ish peas* (page 58); *Smoky ratatouille* (page 114); *Nutmeg neeps* (page 202); *Carrot-juice carrots* (page 218); *White wine and dill carrots* (page 222)

Anchoïade mashed potatoes

PREPARATION: *on a hob*
TIME NEEDED: *15 to 30 minutes*

The anchovy and crème fraîche paste gives these mashed potatoes a tangy, salty, umami finish, which makes it way more exciting than a stodgy filler. I think things like *roast lamb*, *white fish*, *cooked ham*, *haggis* and, of course, *sausages* work really well with it. Plus I like to partner it with other sides that have a bit of bite: verdant greens, bitter leaves and/or sides with a crunch.

When boiling potatoes for mash, use a large, full saucepan of water, to disperse the starch; use cold water so the potatoes will cook evenly as it heats; choose a floury potato variety; and mash or rice the potatoes thoroughly before using plenty of elbow grease to beat them to a smooth purée. By all means substitute the flesh of baked potatoes if you prefer (see page 178), although you'll need to start with 1.5kg potatoes, as baked potatoes lose moisture and boiled take it on when cooking.

Serves 4–6

50g tinned anchovy fillets in oil, roughly chopped and oil reserved
1 garlic clove
1 tablespoon white wine vinegar
120g crème fraîche
1kg floury potatoes, such as Maris Piper, Russet or Yukon Gold
150ml milk, warmed
Sea salt and freshly ground black pepper

To make the anchoïade, mash the anchovies, garlic and a pinch of salt to a smooth paste in a pestle and mortar. Add the oil from the anchovy tin a drip or two at a time, stirring with the pestle until it emulsifies. Gradually add the vinegar, still stirring, then season with a couple of grinds of black pepper. Scoop the crème fraîche into a bowl and fold the anchovy paste into it. Set aside until needed.

Peel the potatoes and dice them into 5–7cm chunks. Put them in a large pan of salted cold water. Bring to the boil and simmer for 20 minutes, or until you can crush a potato easily with the back of a fork. Drain and leave them to steam for 2 minutes (to mash them immediately would lead to gloop).

Mash or rice the potatoes thoroughly. Mix the warm milk in, one third at a time, using a wooden spoon to beat the potatoes to a smooth purée. Add the anchoïade, a good pinch of salt and plenty of black pepper. Use that wooden spoon and a bit of elbow grease one more time, then serve.

ALONGSIDE: *Deep-fried Brussels sprouts* (page 32); *Grilled tenderstem broccoli with umami crumbs* (page 40); *Agretti with olive oil* (page 62); *Puttanesca runner beans* (page 68); *PX radicchio Treviso* (page 74)

Honey and Marmite-glazed parsnips

PREPARATION: *in the oven*
TIME NEEDED: *30 minutes to an hour*

My dad's not much of a cook. But I have him to thank for honey and Marmite on toast (Homite™), which he passed on as his secret hangover cure. Not only is it extremely effective in that form, but it's actually a surprisingly tasty flavour combination, and the mix of malty yeast extract and sweet honey has huge potential, including as a glaze for roast parsnips. I'm convinced even Marmite haters will enjoy this, especially next to *slow-cooked beef*, *roast pork* or *anything to do with a chicken*.

After trialling numerous methods, I can announce that parsnips are best roasted from fresh, rather than parboiled like potatoes, and that if you want crisp edges, don't add salt before roasting, as that tends to make them soggy. Also, although there are many recipes out there that add maple or honey to parsnips while they're cooking, their edges never seem to be crisp and they often end up burnt and bitter. Accordingly, this Homite™ glaze is applied once they're out of the oven.

A further geeky detail: my preference is to cut parsnips lengthways for roasting into long pieces. This means they provide several different textures: soft, chewy and crisp. If you like things a little more even, ensure your wedges are all broadly the same thickness by cutting the thinner third off at the point the parsnip begins to thicken, and the rest into equal wedges.

Serves 4–6

4 tablespoons vegetable oil
900g parsnips
2 tablespoons Marmite
2 tablespoons runny honey
2 tablespoons cold-pressed rapeseed oil

Preheat the oven to 220°C/Fan 200°C/Gas 7. Pour the vegetable oil into a shallow roasting tin that will fit the parsnips in one layer, and put the tray in the oven for 5 minutes to heat the oil. Peel the parsnips and halve or quarter them lengthways into long wedges from root to tip, depending on how big your parsnips are.

Take the hot tin out of the oven and carefully roll the parsnips in the sizzling fat. Ensure each rests on one of its flat sides, then roast at the top of the oven for 30–40 minutes, turning them after 15 minutes, until soft and golden, with crisp, brown edges.

Meanwhile, mix the Marmite, honey and rapeseed oil together; gently warm the mixture in a small saucepan if it's rather cold and thick. When the parsnips are cooked, spoon the glaze over them, mix well and serve immediately.

ALONGSIDE: *Braised red cabbage and beetroot* (page 22); *Sweet cauliflower greens* (page 38); *Purple sprouting broccoli with tarragon* (page 42); *Hasselback potatoes with bay and caraway* (page 172); *Nutmeg neeps* (page 202)

Rosemary and chilli roast squash

PREPARATION: *in the oven*
TIME NEEDED: *30 minutes to an hour*

Roast squash or pumpkin is one of my favourite side dishes. I like it, in particular, with meat-heavy meals where I might otherwise have used potatoes and carrots (*beef or lamb stews, roast pork or chicken*, for example); it provides both heft and sweetness, and replacing two vegetables with one makes room for a bigger pile of seasonal greens.

But I also like squash in its own right, as something with a bit of texture to be served with creamy sides such as polenta, or beans and their broth. If you can find them, use winter squash like kabocha (delica), acorn or red kuri (onion). They've a particularly deep, nutty flavour, as well as being wonderfully sweet. Of course, the ubiquitous butternut squash is super-enjoyable too.

A final note: although rosemary has a reputation as a hardy herb, if you include it from the beginning of a roasting process, the leaves will burn, dry out and lose much of their flavour. Much better to add it towards the end to get the best from its aromatic oils.

Serves 4–6

1kg winter squash or pumpkin
5 tablespoons cold-pressed rapeseed oil
1 teaspoon chilli flakes
4 garlic cloves, flattened
5 sprigs rosemary
Sea salt

Preheat the oven to 210°C/Fan 190°C/Gas 6½. Wipe the squash or pumpkin with a damp cloth to remove any dirt. Use a large sharp knife to cut it in half from top to bottom. Scoop the seeds out with a spoon, then cut the halves lengthways again into 4cm-wide wedges (leave the skin on). Put the squash pieces in a bowl with the oil, toss them well, then spread them out on a baking tray or roasting tin large enough to hold them in one layer. Sprinkle with chilli flakes, push the garlic underneath the squash, and scrape any oil left in the bowl over the top.

Roast near the top of the oven for 15–20 minutes, then remove and turn the squash pieces, taking care not to leave any caramelised edges in the tray. Bruise the rosemary sprigs with the blunt edge of a heavy knife and place them around the squash. Roast for another 10–15 minutes, or until the squash is tender, sweet and turning golden at the edges. Season with salt and remove the rosemary sprigs before serving.

ALONGSIDE: *Creamed chard* (page 8); *Turnip tops with burnt lemon and olive oil* (page 52); *Cheesy polenta* (page 238); *Borlotti beans and cavolo nero with basil and hazelnut smash* (page 268); *Butter beans with sage* (page 272)

Maple and pecan roast squash

PREPARATION: *in the oven*
TIME NEEDED: *30 minutes to an hour*

Squash, maple and pecan are natural bedfellows, and when roasted together are one of my favourite low-hassle side dishes. You should serve this with *rich, savoury meat dishes*, or things involving a *creamy or cheesy sauce*; if your meal is already a little sweet, or you're contemplating other sweet side dishes, consider the Rosemary and chilli roast squash on page 184 instead.

This is best with winter squash or pumpkin such as kabocha (delica), acorn and red kuri (onion) squash, whose nutty, earthy flavours suit the maple and pecan well. The more ubiquitous butternut verges on being too sweet to be matched with maple (for my palate anyway), but do use it if you can't find the others.

Serves 4–6

1kg winter squash or pumpkin
4 tablespoons cold-pressed rapeseed oil
2 tablespoons maple syrup
Leaves from 10–15 sprigs thyme
25g pecan nuts, lightly crushed
Sea salt

Preheat the oven to 210°C/Fan 190°C/Gas 6½. Wipe the squash or pumpkin with a damp cloth to remove any dirt. Use a large sharp knife to cut it in half and scoop the seeds out with a spoon. Place each one flat-side down and cut it into 6–8 slices around 2–3cm thick (leave the skin on unless it's really too thick).

Put the oil and syrup in a large bowl and mix well. Add the thyme leaves and then the squash wedges. Get your hands in there and ensure each of the wedges is well glossed. You may need to do this in batches. Put the squash in a roasting tin (you need one that's large enough to fit the squash in one layer; otherwise you'll end up with steamed and soft, rather than nicely coloured and crisp-edged, squash). Drizzle with any remaining syrup and oil and roast on the top shelf for 20 minutes. Carefully flip the squash over and sprinkle with the pecan nuts. Roast for 10 minutes more, or until the edges are charring a little and the flesh is soft but not soggy. Season with a generous pinch of salt.

ALONGSIDE: *Cavolo nero with garlic, chilli and orange* (page 24); *Cauliflower cheese* (page 132); *Anise-braised spring onions* (page 148); *Portobello mushrooms baked with oregano* (page 152); *Roman rosemary polenta* (page 240)

Roast butternut squash purée

PREPARATION: *in the oven*
TIME NEEDED: *30 minutes to an hour*

This purée is much more intense than if it were made from boiled squash, and is therefore a vibrant accompaniment rather than a bulky side. I reckon on one, possibly two, heaped tablespoons being enough for each person when served with another side or two and a rich or fatty centrepiece such as *pan-fried scallops*, *duck breast*, *pork belly* or *lamb*, and the recipe quantity reflects this.

The aim is for a smooth purée: thicker, obviously, than soup, but definitely looser and more silky than crushed root vegetables. The weight of squash after it has been roasted will vary depending on a number of factors, so it's hard to give precise instructions for the amount of butter and water you should add (although it'll be roughly one third of the weight of the roast squash). Follow the instructions below, adding a little extra if necessary to reach the desired consistency. If you add too much liquid, just heat it gently in a saucepan until the excess moisture evaporates.

You could cook this at the last minute, but it's quite a good side to make in advance, not least because of the faff of using a food processor or blender. When you need it, simply reheat the purée over a low heat with an additional tablespoon or two of water and another dash of lemon juice at the end.

Serves 4–6

600g butternut squash
2 tablespoons cold-pressed rapeseed oil
20g butter
Juice of ¼ lemon
Sea salt

Preheat the oven to 220°C/Fan 200°C/Gas 7. Peel and deseed the butternut squash, then cut it into rough 3–4cm dice. Spread them out in a roasting tin or baking tray and drizzle the oil over the top. Mix well so that each piece is well coated, then roast on the top shelf for about 35 minutes, or until the flesh is tender, shrunken a little and caramelised at the edges. Turn the pieces over once or twice during cooking.

Remove the squash from the oven and transfer to a blender with the butter and 70ml just-boiled water. It's important that the squash is still warm so that the butter melts into it and blends easily. Pulse and blitz until silky, smooth and light, adding a little more water if necessary. Depending on the power of your blender, you may need to scrape down and cajole the contents occasionally.

Scrape the purée from the blender (every last bit) and season with salt and just a squeeze of lemon. The purée is not supposed to taste citrusy, but try it before and after adding the lemon and you'll notice how it just lifts things a little.

ALONGSIDE: *Bacon and buttermilk cabbage* (page 18); *Purple sprouting broccoli with tarragon* (page 42); *Chicken stock and orange-braised fennel* (page 120); *Celeriac baked in a salt and thyme crust* (page 198)

Scorched sweet potatoes with sobrasada butter

PREPARATION: *in the oven*
TIME NEEDED: *30 minutes to an hour*

There's not much to say about baking a sweet potato, right? Put it in the oven until soft; remove; add butter. Wrong.

Sweet potatoes can and should take a lot of heat. If you happen to have fired up a barbecue, leave sweet potatoes in the embers until they look burnt; the resulting intensely flavoured and near-molten flesh will be a revelation. At other times, the secret is to double cook it. The second time round, blast it for a few minutes at the hottest temperature your oven can go to. You could do the first stage well in advance if other things are going on in the oven; in that case, just add 2–3 more minutes to the blast time.

If you can get hold of sobrasada, the Spanish cured and spiced spreadable sausage (or alternatively, Italian 'nduja), then definitely use it. Cured pork fat improves most things, and a sweet potato is no exception. You can use the same cooking method without the sobrasada: just double the butter and mix 1 teaspoon smoked sweet paprika into it, and add the dried oregano and freshly ground black pepper as per the recipe. It's great with *lamb chops*, pretty much *anything beefy or porky*, and with *crisp, golden-skinned chicken thighs*, too.

Serves 6

3 large sweet potatoes
2 tablespoons sunflower or vegetable oil
30g butter, at room temperature
60g sobrasada or 'nduja
2 teaspoons dried oregano
Sea salt and freshly ground black pepper

Preheat the oven to 230°C/ Fan 210°C/Gas 8. Rub the sweet potatoes with oil and sprinkle with salt. Put them on a baking tray, prick each potato a few times with a fork and bake for about 40 minutes until soft and sunken. Meanwhile, mix the butter and sobrasada together.

Remove the sweet potatoes from the oven and turn it up as high as it will go. Very carefully (because the insides are piping hot), cut the potatoes in half lengthways and place them cut-side up on the baking tray. Distribute the butter and cured sausage mixture evenly over the halves, give each one a couple of grinds of pepper and sprinkle the oregano over the top.

When the oven is up to temperature, bake the potatoes for a further 6–10 minutes, or until the skin dries and hardens and the top is sizzling and starting to crisp.

ALONGSIDE: *Gem lettuce, mint and spring onion* (page 86); *Gochujang mayo and coconut corn on the cob* (page 126); *Kohlrabi remoulade* (page 208); *Baked beans* (page 280); *Mac 'n' cheese* (page 286)

Sweet potato and rosemary hash-rösti

PREPARATION: *in the oven*
TIME NEEDED: *more than an hour*

It's tricky to pan-fry rösti for more than two people at once if you've other things going on in the kitchen, so I prefer this baked method. This probably prevents them from being strictly authentic, hence the hash brown reference in the name.

They're relatively easy to make and quite hands-off once the patties are prepared, but you do need to begin the process well in advance. A little effort and forward planning results in a cracking partner for *gammon and egg*, *breaded fish and chicken*, *lamb chops* and many more. They're more sweet and flavoursome than a basic potato version, and I think particularly good served next to a pile of wholesome greens.

Serves 6

350g sweet potatoes
350g waxy potatoes, such as Desiree
1 white onion, halved and thinly sliced into crescents
Leaves from 3 sprigs rosemary, finely chopped
3 tablespoons plain flour
1 egg, lightly beaten
2 tablespoons light rapeseed or sunflower oil
Sea salt and freshly ground black pepper

Peel both types of potato, then cut into large chunks around the size of a snooker ball. Put them in a medium saucepan, fill it with cold water, bring to the boil and simmer for 8–10 minutes. You should just about be able to push a fork through, but nowhere near mashing territory. Drain, cool to room temperature, then chill in the fridge for at least 2 hours.

———

Put the onion and rosemary in a large bowl. Grate the potatoes on the largest holes of a box grater into the bowl, and add the flour, a generous pinch of salt and a good grind of black pepper. Mix well with a fork, then add the egg and mix again. Divide the mixture into 6 and use your hands to roll the mixture into ball shapes. Gently compress these into patties roughly 4cm thick and chill in the fridge until needed.

———

When ready to cook the hash-rösti, preheat the oven to 200°C/Fan 180°C/Gas 6. Spread the oil over a baking tray that's large enough to fit them all comfortably. Place the patties evenly on the tray and bake on the top shelf for about 40 minutes, carefully turning them over after 20 minutes (you'll need a fish slice or spatula), and once more with 5 minutes to go. They'll be ferociously hot once cooked, and can therefore sit for 5 minutes while you're pulling the rest of your meal together.

———

ALONGSIDE: *Charred fermented cabbage* (page 12); *Cabbage with juniper butter* (page 20); *Kale, Romanesco, Parmesan and pine nut salad* (page 28); *Sweet cauliflower greens* (page 38); *Blue cheese leeks* (page 144)

Sweet potato, celeriac and porcini bake

PREPARATION: *in the oven*
TIME NEEDED: *more than an hour*

This is an incredibly satisfying and comforting dish – the sweetness of the potatoes and celeriac, and the umami of the mushrooms and Parmesan see to that. It's particularly good in tandem with simply cooked seasonal greens, but also with sides where there's a sharpness that cuts through the dreamy slices of roots and their flavourful cooking stock.

Slow-roast lamb, *confit duck legs* or a *sturdy white fish like monkfish or turbot* are very well suited to this bake, which means your oven – and you – will be busy. No problem: it can be assembled in advance of cooking (add an extra 10 minutes, as the stock will be cold) and also reheats pretty well.

Serves 4–6

25g dried porcini mushrooms
600–700g sweet potatoes
600–700g celeriac
70g Parmesan, grated
Leaves from 10 sprigs thyme
2 tablespoons cold-pressed rapeseed oil
Sea salt and freshly ground black pepper

Put the dried mushrooms in a heatproof mug or small bowl and pour 350ml boiling water over them. Cover with clingfilm and leave to rehydrate and steep for 30 minutes, then drain and reserve both the mushrooms and the still-warm soaking liquid. Meanwhile, peel the sweet potatoes and celeriac and cut into 2–3mm thick slices. This is easier and quicker on a mandolin. Preheat the oven to 200°C/Fan 180°C/Gas 6.

———

The plan from here is to make alternating layers of the celeriac and sweet potato in a 1.5-litre ovenproof dish, with the porcini, Parmesan, thyme, salt and pepper as a seasoning. Aim for 3 layers of each root and 2 of porcini. Begin with the smallest, least regular bits of celeriac. Season with salt, pepper, a sprinkle of thyme and Parmesan, then add the sweet potato. Top that with porcini, salt, pepper, thyme and Parmesan, then repeat, making sure you use all the porcini the second time round. Add a third and final layer of celeriac, season, and then a third and final layer of sweet potato (arranging this one neatly, as it's the top). Carefully pour the mushroom-soaking liquid into the dish – it might not seem like much, but celeriac is full of water and there'll be plenty of cooking juices later on.

———

Drizzle the oil over the top and finish with more salt, pepper, the remaining thyme and Parmesan. Bake for about 60 minutes, or until the top is nicely browned and the middle clearly warm, soft and cooked through. Press the top layer down from time to time with a fish slice or spatula – you'll find that the cooking juices will rise and keep the top glistening and in good shape, rather than dry and curled. Allow to rest for 5–10 minutes before serving.

———

ALONGSIDE: *Chard with chilli, shallot and cider vinaigrette* (page 6); *Kale, Romanesco, Parmesan and pine nut salad* (page 28); *Sweet cauliflower greens* (page 38); *Turnip tops with burnt lemon and olive oil* (page 52); *French-ish peas* (page 58)

'Young Turk' celeriac

PREPARATION: *on a hob*
TIME NEEDED: *15 to 30 minutes*

My first experience inside a professional kitchen was at a pop-up restaurant called The Young Turks at the Ten Bells. I lucked out: although only for a few weeks, I was observing and learning from two chefs, James Lowe and Isaac McHale, who within a couple of years had both achieved Michelin stars, and seeing, from the inside, one of the most influential happenings in east London's rapidly evolving food scene.

The menu changed each week, but I remember one regular component that involved diced celeriac, which was left to sweat, steam and eventually brown in a mass of butter. Over that time, the celeriac loses a considerable amount of water and becomes extremely sweet. I can't remember the exact ratios or even what it was served with – probably *pheasant*, *grouse* or *partridge* – but it's an idea I've replicated as a side numerous times since. The game birds just mentioned, plus *offal dishes like braised oxtail, pork faggots or calves' liver and onions*, get on with it famously.

Serves 6

80g butter
1.2kg celeriac, peeled and cut into 1–2cm cubes
Sea salt and freshly ground black pepper

Put the butter in a large heavy-bottomed saucepan (for which you have a lid) over a medium-high heat. Add the celeriac while the butter melts along with ½ teaspoon salt. Stir the celeriac so that each piece is glossed with melted butter, then reduce the heat to low-medium. Cover, leaving the lid slightly ajar, and cook for 15–20 minutes. During this time the celeriac is largely steaming itself as its natural water content boils and evaporates.

Once much of the moisture has gone you'll hear a change in sound as the vegetable starts to fry. At this point (probably around 15 minutes in), remove the lid and cook for about 10 minutes more, stirring only occasionally and allowing the celeriac to colour a little.

Remove from the heat when you have a few brown edges and the celeriac is sweet, but not so soft that it turns to mush. Season with salt and pepper to taste and serve immediately.

ALONGSIDE: *Grilled hispi cabbage with anchovy and crème fraîche* (page 10); *Braised red cabbage and beetroot* (page 22); *Flower sprouts with lemon and anchovy butter* (page 30); *Sweet cauliflower greens* (page 38); *PX radicchio Trevisano* (page 74)

Celeriac baked in a salt and thyme crust

PREPARATION: *in the oven*
TIME NEEDED: *more than an hour*

Here, a little egg white combines with a sprinkling of thyme and a lot of salt to form a dramatic and extremely effective self-seasoning oven. It's an excellent way of cooking and eating the ugly duckling of the vegetable world, and results in a flavoursome, well salted, tender and surprisingly juicy side. It's the perfect accompaniment to *roast game* or *other roast meats*, but is also great with *white fish like hake, cod and sea bass*. Best of all, although dramatic looking, it's neither difficult nor time-consuming to pull off.

The celeriac will stay fairly warm for 30 minutes once out of its casing if you leave it whole and wrap it in foil. To serve, I like to slice the celeriac into steaks, then drizzle them with peppery olive oil to finish.

Serves 6

1 celeriac (800g–1kg)
120g egg white (about 3 large eggs)
500g fine table salt
Leaves from 8–10 sprigs thyme
Extra-virgin olive oil, to serve

Preheat the oven to 200°C/Fan 180°C/Gas 6. Slice off the gnarly, hairy, rooted base of the celeriac, but leave the rest of the skin on. Give it a quick rinse.

———

Put the egg whites in a bowl. Add a pinch of salt and whisk for about 30 seconds – just enough to loosen the protein in the egg whites. Pour in the rest of the salt and whisk it into the egg whites for 30 seconds or so. This will result in a paste that's a little wet, but just holds its shape if you prod it. Stir in the thyme.

———

Put a spatula-worth of salt paste on the base of a baking tray. Spread it out just a little, then put the celeriac on top (flat-side down). Now cover the celeriac with the paste, as if icing a cake. When it's all on and there are no obvious holes, put your celeriac igloo on the bottom shelf of the oven. Check it after 4–5 minutes. If some of the paste is slipping down, remove it from the oven and patch up any holes. The egg white and salt will hold firm from now on. Bake for 90 minutes. The crust will be brown and the celeriac inside will be tender but not yet mushy.

———

Allow the celeriac to rest for 15–20 minutes in its casing, where it will carry on steaming. Once that time is up and the outside is cool enough to handle, cut round the top with a serrated bread or carving knife. Pull the rest of the shell away and carefully remove your prize. Brush any excess salt off the celeriac's skin. Slice it into 3cm-thick steaks, then cut those into smaller portions and drizzle with oil to serve.

———

ALONGSIDE: *Creamed chard* (page 8); *Spring greens in shiitake dashi* (page 14); *Sprout tops with Jerusalem artichokes and apple* (page 36); *Agretti with olive oil* (page 62); *Blue cheese leeks* (page 144)

Wine-poached salsify with gremolata

PREPARATION: *on a hob*
TIME NEEDED: *15 to 30 minutes*

Salsify doesn't look like the most promising of roots. In fact, it resembles kindling for a fire – all dusty, thin, straggly and hairy – rather than something worth cooking and eating. But, peeled and then boiled, sautéed or roasted, salsify adds great flavour and texture to a meal. It's like a cross between mild celeriac and Jerusalem artichoke, with a touch of oyster minerality. I'm thinking *skate* or *ray wing*, *brown butter-doused sole or trout*, or something a bit different to go with *roast chicken or beef*; not least because the gremolata (a dry mix of lemon zest, parsley and garlic) really brings vibrancy and freshness to the party.

Prepare the salsify one at a time, as they discolour very quickly. You won't want too many pieces per person, if in polite company: salsify shares more than just the flavour characteristics of the aforementioned roots.

Serves 4–6

Juice of 1 lemon
650g salsify
45g butter
2 celery sticks, finely diced
250ml dry white wine
300ml vegetable stock (good-quality instant bouillon is fine)
Sea salt and freshly ground black pepper

Gremolata
Leaves from 6 stems flat-leaf parsley
1 small garlic clove, crushed
Finely grated zest of 1 lemon

Fill a large bowl with cold water and add the lemon juice. Peel the first stick of salsify with a vegetable peeler, cut it into 5–6cm batons and drop it immediately into the lemon-water bowl. Repeat with the rest of the salsify.

Make the gremolata by chopping the parsley as finely as you can – almost to dust. Add the garlic and lemon zest, stir well and set aside.

Melt 10g butter in a wide, high-sided frying pan or saucepan over a medium heat. Add the celery and cook for 2–3 minutes, or until softened. Increase the heat, and when the pan is really hot add the wine and reduce it by a third, then add the vegetable stock. Drain the salsify batons and add them to the pan. Bring to a simmer and cook for around 8 minutes, until tender.

When the salsify seems ready, pour out two thirds of the cooking liquid (reserve it to use in a gravy). Add the remaining butter and return the pan to the heat, stirring until the liquids have emulsified and the salsify is glossy. Stir in three quarters of the gremolata and season with a little salt and a good few grinds of the pepper mill. Transfer to a serving dish or individual plates, spooning the juices over the top and sprinkling with the last bits of gremolata.

ALONGSIDE: *Grilled tenderstem broccoli with umami crumbs* (page 40); *Yeasted cauliflower purée* (page 130); *Anchoïade mashed potatoes* (page 180); *Spelt grains with wild mushrooms* (page 256); *Herb-loaded lentils* (page 262)

Nutmeg neeps

PREPARATION: *on a hob*
TIME NEEDED: *15 to 30 minutes*

Not enough people cook mashed swede (aka neeps), which is a shame. Swedes have a unique flavour and, when matched with butter, nutmeg and lots and lots of black pepper, make a cracking partner for numerous meat and veg dishes. *Haggis* is, of course, the obvious thing to eat with neeps. But *sausages with onion gravy*, *lamb stew and dumplings* and even a *smoked haddock gratin* are well suited too.

If you anticipate being particularly busy just before dinner time, you could make this in advance and reheat it in a saucepan with a little water, or bake it in a low oven for 15 minutes with extra butter dotted on top.

Serves 4–6

1.5kg swede, peeled and cut into 3–4cm chunks
100g butter, cubed
¼ nutmeg, freshly grated
Juice of ¼ lemon
Sea salt and freshly ground black pepper

Put the swede in a large pan of cold water with a good pinch of salt. Bring to the boil, then simmer for around 25 minutes, until the orange colour has intensified and a fork can push through the pieces with relative ease. Drain, add the butter, then smash and mash the vegetable with a hand masher. A little texture is good, so don't be too thorough – it's not supposed to be a smooth purée.

Grate in the nutmeg and season liberally with black pepper (at least 20 firm grinds of your pepper mill). Stir, taste, add a little salt if needed and more nutmeg or black pepper if you fancy. Add the lemon juice, which is there to lift the flavour a little, rather than make the neeps taste of lemon.

ALONGSIDE: *Cabbage with juniper butter* (page 20); *Rosemary and chestnut sprouts* (page 34); *Runner beans with bacon and walnuts* (page 66); *Hasselback potatoes with bay and caraway* (page 172); *Colcannon* (page 178); *Carrots with brown butter and hazelnuts* (page 220)

Butter-glazed turnips with horseradish

PREPARATION: *on a hob*
TIME NEEDED: *15 to 30 minutes*

I don't cook turnips very often, and when I do I wonder why that is the case. They have a delicate sweetness when you first bite into them, with just a hint of mustard at the end; a really interesting root to serve at times when carrots or parsnips aren't quite right. The key is to find and use relatively small turnips – never bigger than a tennis ball – as the larger they grow, the more bitter they become.

To my mind, turnips are best boiled or steamed, rather than roasted or braised; in this instance, butter or oil seems better as a garnish, not as a cooking medium. A snowstorm of fresh horseradish enhances the natural spice.

These work best among a group of vegetables rather than as a main carbohydrate, as they can become monotonous. They're also best eaten when still steaming hot, probably next to some *pan-roasted salmon or trout* or a *hefty beef dish*.

Serves 4–6

500g small-medium white turnips
40g butter
20g fresh horseradish
Sea salt and freshly ground black pepper

Peel and cut the turnips into wedges, quarters or sixths, depending on size. (If you find baby turnips, leave them whole and with the skin on.) Put the turnips in a saucepan that comfortably holds them and fill with cold water. Bring to the boil and simmer for 8–10 minutes until a fork can be pushed through with relative ease. Take care not to overcook them, as they'll turn watery and flavourless. Drain and allow to steam dry for a few minutes.

———

Use the now-empty turnip pan to melt the butter over a medium heat. Tip the turnips back into the pan and turn them in the butter so that all sides are well glossed. Heat through for 1–2 minutes. I prefer them to stay pale, rather than catch and brown. Season very generously with black pepper and a pinch or two of salt, then transfer to a serving bowl. Grate a blanket of horseradish over the top and serve immediately.

———

ALONGSIDE: *French-ish peas* (page 58); *Wilted bitter leaves with blue cheese dressing* (page 76); *White wine and dill carrots* (page 222); *Beetroot gratin* (page 224); *Green pearl barley* (page 260)

Baked Jerusalem artichokes with yoghurt and sunflower seeds

PREPARATION: *in the oven*
TIME NEEDED: *15 to 30 minutes*

Jerusalem artichokes can be prepared in numerous ways: sliced thinly and eaten raw, roasted, boiled, steamed, puréed or deep-fried. But I like baking them, skin on, like jacket potatoes. The skins both harden and become a little sticky, while the inner flesh is soft, fluffy and sweet.

Good-quality peppery olive oil and plenty of salt are really important to temper the sweetness of the cooked artichokes, and the sunflower seeds ensure it remains savoury. You don't have to include the yoghurt, but I think its cooling nature and tang really brings everything together. It's cracking alongside *Middle Eastern-spiced lamb shanks*, *bacon chops*, *chargrilled quail*, or *roast peppers and goat's cheese*. Ensure you've another side dish on hand, though – the quantities here provide only 2–3 artichokes per portion, as eating too many of these tubers has an undesirably windy effect.

Serves 4–6

500g Jerusalem artichokes
3–4 tablespoons extra-virgin olive oil
3 heaped tablespoons Greek yoghurt
4–5 chives, finely chopped (optional)
30g sunflower seeds, toasted
Sea salt

Preheat the oven to 200°C/Fan 180°C/Gas 6. Wash and dry the Jerusalem artichokes, then prick each one a few times with a fork. Put them on a baking tray big enough to hold them in one layer. Drizzle with 1 tablespoon oil, then bake for 20–25 minutes, or until their skins are becoming brown and sticky and their middles are soft and bursting from the jackets.

Meanwhile, mix the yoghurt with 1 tablespoon oil and a generous pinch of salt. Spoon this onto a small serving plate or bowl. Once cooked, cut the artichokes in half lengthways and arrange them over the yoghurt. Drizzle with the remaining oil (don't hold back) and add more salt, and perhaps a few chives.

Finally, add the toasted sunflower seeds. Serve immediately. Ensure everyone takes a little yoghurt and plenty of seeds to go with their artichokes.

ALONGSIDE: *Braised red cabbage and beetroot* (page 22); *Kale, Romanesco, Parmesan and pine nut salad* (page 28); *PX radicchio Trevisano* (page 74); *Sherry cherry tomatoes* (page 98); *Portobello mushrooms baked with oregano* (page 152)

Kohlrabi remoulade

PREPARATION: *on the counter*
TIME NEEDED: *less than 15 minutes*

Kohlrabi looks like the green cousin of a turnip or swede. It has a slightly lighter texture than those two roots, though, and is crisp and sweet when sliced thinly and eaten raw. It's great in a mandolin-style salad (see page 134) or, as here, in a version of the classic French celeriac remoulade. I'd have masses of this next to things like *cold ham*, *grilled or smoked mackerel or trout*, or the *leftovers from a Sunday roast*.

Choose a medium-sized dense kohlrabi. Larger ones can be tough and bitter, and others that feel light for their size will be floury and flavourless. You'll know what I mean if you fondle a few.

Serves 4–6

Leaves from a small bunch (25–30g) flat-leaf parsley
350g kohlrabi
2 teaspoons wholegrain mustard
3 tablespoons Greek yoghurt
Sea salt

Chop the parsley very finely until it's nearly like dust. You should have around 2 tablespoons.

Peel the kohlrabi and use a mandolin to cut it into 3mm-thick slices. Stack these slices on top of each other, 5 or 6 at a time, then cut them into matchsticks of the same thickness. (If you have a julienne attachment for your mandolin, just use that.) Add a good pinch of salt to the kohlrabi, along with all the other ingredients. Mix thoroughly. It's best served immediately, although it is fine in the fridge for a few hours.

ALONGSIDE: *Radicchio with a smoky blood orange and maple dressing* (page 80); *Watercress with pickled walnuts* (page 84); *Za'atar mushrooms with curd* (page 154); *Spiced roast carrots* (page 216); *Wheat berries with capers and tomatoes* (page 250)

Quick-pickled daikon

PREPARATION: *on the counter*
TIME NEEDED: *less than 15 minutes*

Daikon – also known as mooli, white turnip or Japanese radish – looks like an oversized anaemic carrot. It's often finely shredded or spiralised and used to garnish a sushi platter, or cooked down and steamed to make a Chinese turnip cake. You could do either of those things, although I like this approach to using daikon: basically just slicing it and seasoning it a little so that it adds a crunchy, cooling and slightly sour bite next to *pan-fried or poached salmon*, or *spicy tofu, squid or pork dishes*.

A nice variation, if it suits your meal, is to add a little grated ginger and a pinch of finely shredded shiso (the unique-tasting Asian herb that looks like a nettle but tastes like sweet perfume).

Serves 4–6

200g daikon
½ teaspoon sea salt
2 tablespoons rice vinegar

Peel and very finely slice the daikon, ideally with a mandolin. Put the slices in a small bowl with the salt, toss and leave to soften for 5 minutes. Add the vinegar, then toss again and leave for a further 10 minutes–1 hour (not too much longer, or the daikon will be past its best).

ALONGSIDE: *Spring greens in shiitake dashi* (page 14); *Asian greens with shrimp paste* (page 50); *Sesame soba noodles* (page 254); *Three pepper rice* (page 294); *Almond and anise rice* (page 298)

Warm radishes with anise

PREPARATION: *on a hob*
TIME NEEDED: *less than 15 minutes*

The fact that you can cook radishes may surprise some, but once warmed briefly, they become juicy and their pepperiness mellows. For the latter reason, it's important to use good-quality French breakfast or heirloom radishes here, otherwise there's not much flavour in the finished dish, though of course the anise from the Pernod and tarragon will be there.

Braised rabbit, *baked white fish* and *blue cheese omelettes* are among my favourite things to eat with this. Oh, and a *roast rib of beef*.

Serves 4–6

300g French breakfast radishes, leaves removed
20g butter
4 tablespoons Pernod
Leaves from 7–8 stems tarragon, roughly chopped
Finely grated zest of ½ orange
Sea salt

First, wash the radishes thoroughly. Cut most of them in half lengthways, leaving only the very small ones whole.

Put the butter in a medium saucepan or frying pan over a medium-high heat. When the butter has melted and is nearly frothing, add the Pernod. Let it reduce for 10–20 seconds, then whisk in 1 tablespoon water. Add the radishes and cook for 3–4 minutes, turning them frequently in the buttery liquid.

Remove from the heat, add the tarragon, stir and immediately transfer to a serving bowl. Season with salt and the orange zest and pour any cooking juices over the top.

ALONGSIDE: *Grilled tenderstem broccoli with umami crumbs* (page 40); *Asparagus with cured egg yolk* (page 60); *Baby aubergine, oregano and chilli bake* (page 136); *Boulangère potatoes* (page 168); *Carrot-juice carrots* (page 218)

Carrot, cumin and nigella seed salad

PREPARATION: *on the counter*
TIME NEEDED: *less than 15 minutes*

This salad is fresh, crisp, full of lively aromatics and yet takes barely 5 minutes to put together. Its cooling nature works well with *hot, oily dishes such as pulled pork or chicken curry*, with *lighter but still warm ones (spiced bream, for example)*, or as part of a *cold buffet* with, say, *a quiche or puff pastry tart*.

The texture is best if you make it using a julienne peeler, a mandolin with a julienne setting or a spiraliser; there's just something about those long, thin strips. But a box grater does a decent job too.

Serves 4–6

600g carrots
2 teaspoons cumin seeds
Leaves from 7 stems coriander
3cm fresh ginger, peeled and finely grated
1 heaped teaspoon nigella seeds
3 tablespoons cold-pressed rapeseed oil
Juice and finely grated zest of ½ lemon
Sea salt

Use a julienne peeler or mandolin attachment to make a mass of carrot strips, or a box grater or spiraliser for a similar effect.

Put the cumin seeds in a heavy-bottomed saucepan or frying pan over a medium heat. Toast lightly for 4–5 minutes until the seeds are fragrant. Remove them before they brown and become bitter, and tip immediately into a pestle and mortar. Add a good pinch of salt and very lightly crush the seeds.

Combine the carrots, coriander leaves, ginger, nigella and cumin seeds, oil and lemon zest and juice in a large bowl, plus a pinch or two of salt. Toss well and let the flavours mingle for at least 5 minutes, or up to 3 hours before serving.

ALONGSIDE: *Gem lettuce, mint and spring onion* (page 86); *Green tomato, salted celery and chervil salad* (page 100); *Roast cauliflower with chickpeas and lemon tahini* (page 128); *Cinnamon, chickpea and apricot couscous* (page 242); *Curry leaf, cashew and coconut rice* (page 290)

Spiced roast carrots

PREPARATION: *in the oven*
TIME NEEDED: *30 minutes to an hour*

These roasted carrots are absolutely knockout. Of course, pretty much any root vegetable is ace when blistered, sweetened and caramelised in a roasting tin. But the addition here of equally sweet roast onions, fresh coriander, sour lemon juice and the spiced salt makes these carrots a little bit special. To be honest, I'd happily have them as a main course with a spoon or two of curd or ricotta. But serve with something else if you must... most dishes involving *chicken*, *beef*, *pork* or *cod* work nicely, whether heavily spiced or plain.

See if you can get your hands on some heirloom carrots for this: those funny but in fact entirely natural purples, yellows and whites. You could use regular orange ones, but the heirloom varieties are both a visual treat and particularly flavourful when roasted. It's still lovely when at room temperature or even fridge cold, so there's no harm in making more than you need.

Serves 6

1.5kg carrots, ideally a mix of heirloom colours
3 red onions
2 teaspoons cumin seeds
1 teaspoon coriander seeds
1 teaspoon fennel seeds
1 teaspoon sea salt
3 tablespoons vegetable oil
2 teaspoons sesame seeds, toasted
Juice of ½ lemon
Leaves from 12–14 stems coriander

Preheat the oven to 220°C/Fan 200°C/Gas 7. Cut the carrots in half lengthways. Put them in a suitably sized baking tray or roasting tin: not so big that there's loads of space between them, nor so tight that they sit on top of each other and steam rather than roast. Peel and quarter the onions and add them to the carrots.

Put the cumin, coriander and fennel seeds and salt in a pestle and mortar and grind well, but not quite to a powder. Sprinkle half the spiced salt over the carrots and onions. Add the oil and then mix well. Roast on the top shelf for 30–40 minutes, shuffling the tray after 20 minutes. They're ready when tender, but also blistered and a little charred or browned at the edges.

Remove the carrots from the oven and sprinkle over the sesame seeds and half the remaining spiced salt. Squeeze the lemon juice over the top, mix well and decant to a serving bowl or platter. Check for seasoning and add more of the spiced salt if you think it needs it. Add the coriander leaves and gently mix the carrots one last time.

ALONGSIDE: *Cavolo nero with garlic, chilli and orange* (page 24); *Kale, Romanesco, Parmesan and pine nut salad* (page 28); *Chorizo roast potatoes* (page 170); *Wheat berries with capers and tomatoes* (page 250); *Jewelled pearl barley* (page 258); *Chickpeas with garlic oil and spinach* (page 266)

Carrot-juice carrots

PREPARATION: *on a hob*
TIME NEEDED: *15 to 30 minutes*

Have you noticed how carrots lose much of their flavour and colour to the water they are boiled in? This aim in this recipe is not just to reduce that loss, but reverse it. Carrots cooked in carrot juice – and not much of it – result in a super-charged side. I also add a little cold butter at the end, which helps provide a silky sheen.

Glazed roast ham, *gammon steaks* or *slow-cooked meats like beef shin, ox or pig cheeks* are especially grateful for these carrots. You could juice your own, but shop-bought cartons are fine, provided they're not from concentrate.

Serves 4–6

600g carrots
200ml carrot juice
2 star anise
20g cold butter, diced
Leaves from 5 or 6 stems flat-leaf parsley or chervil, roughly chopped
Sea salt

Slice the carrots into 2–3 cm-long pieces on an angle. Put them in a medium saucepan and pour the carrot juice in. It won't cover the carrots, which is fine. Add the star anise and a pinch of salt. Bring to the boil and simmer for 12–15 minutes, turning the carrots occasionally so they all spend some time submerged under carrot juice (the rest of them will steam). The carrots are ready when you can push a fork through (though still with a fair bit of resistance).

Remove the star anise and tip some of the liquid out of the pan so there's just 3–4 tablespoons left. Add the butter, return the pan to the heat and stir until the butter melts and the carrots are glossy. Check for seasoning and add salt if required. Throw in the parsley or chervil and mix well. They're best served immediately.

ALONGSIDE: *Braised red cabbage and beetroot* (page 22); *French-ish peas* (page 58); *Chorizo roast potatoes* (page 170); *New potatoes with seaweed butter* (page 176); *Colcannon* (page 178)

Carrots with brown butter and hazelnuts

PREPARATION: *on a hob*
TIME NEEDED: *15 to 30 minutes*

There's absolutely nothing wrong with serving simply boiled or steamed carrots. If you ever fancy taking that staple up a notch or two, though, try this browned butter and hazelnut trick; the nutty aromas of the garnish add so much flavour to a meal.

As with carrots generally, this side is amenable to many foods, though I especially like it with *pork loin or chops, poached chicken, bavette steaks, pan-fried hake, cod or other white fish*.

Serves 4–6

600g carrots (baby carrots are particularly good)
30g hazelnuts, toasted
Leaves from 15 stems flat-leaf parsley
50g butter
Juice of ½ lemon
Sea salt and freshly ground black pepper

Slice the carrots lengthways (or leave them whole if they're small enough). Put them in a saucepan and add cold water to cover by 3–4 cm. Add a couple of pinches of salt, bring to the boil and simmer for 10–15 minutes, or until tender.

Roughly chop the hazelnuts and chop the parsley as finely as you can.

Drain the carrots and return them to the pan or transfer to a serving dish. Melt the butter in a heavy-bottomed frying pan over a medium-high heat until it starts to froth. After a minute or so the butter will be golden and will smell nutty, and a patch in the middle will become calm. When that happens, throw in the crushed hazelnuts, stir them for 10 seconds, then turn off the heat, squeeze in the lemon juice and add the parsley.

Quickly pour the contents of the pan over the carrots. Sprinkle with a generous pinch of salt, toss well so that all the carrots are glossy and the parsley and hazelnuts are evenly distributed. Serve immediately.

ALONGSIDE: *Sweet cauliflower greens* (page 38); *New potatoes with pickled samphire and sorrel* (page 174); *Celeriac baked in a salt and thyme crust* (page 198); *Bread sauce and parsnip crisps* (page 236); *Spelt grains with wild mushrooms* (page 256)

White wine and dill carrots

PREPARATION: *in the oven*
TIME NEEDED: *30 minutes to an hour*

This carrot dish makes a wonderfully sweet, fragrant accompaniment that suits rich comfort dishes like *beef, venison or game suet puddings and pies*, but also more delicate things like *baked trout and salmon*, or any *grilled white fish*. I really like the fact that it's a hands-off carrot dish that's cooked in the oven rather than on a hob. You can pretty much forget about it once in the oven.

The carrots will stay warm under foil for 15 minutes or so, if the other elements of your meal need more time, but wait until you are about to serve before you add the herbs. On which note, if you're not a fan of dill, or it wouldn't work with the rest of your meal, then try parsley, chervil, tarragon or thyme instead. Sprinkle the first three over at the end, as with the dill; the thyme leaves can be cooked with the carrots.

Serves 4–6

600g Chantenay or baby carrots
1 celery stick, very finely diced
30g butter, diced
175ml dry white wine or Noilly Prat vermouth
Fronds from 6 stems dill, roughly chopped
Sea salt

Preheat the oven to 200°C/Fan 180°C/Gas 6. Scrub the carrots well but don't peel them, then place them in a gratin or baking dish into which they fit snugly in one or two layers. Add the celery, dot with the butter, then pour in the wine. Put a tight-fitting lid on the dish or cover with two layers of kitchen foil and bake for 45–50 minutes.

Once the time is up, check that the carrots are tender, then stir well and season with plenty of salt. Just before serving, sprinkle the chopped dill over the top. Mix and serve, ensuring everyone takes a spoonful or two of the cooking liquor along with their carrots.

ALONGSIDE: *Chard with chilli, shallot and cider vinaigrette* (page 6); *Charred fermented cabbage* (page 12); *Deep-fried Brussels sprouts* (page 32); *Chorizo roast potatoes* (page 170); *Anchoïade mashed potatoes* (page 180)

Beetroot gratin

PREPARATION: *in the oven*
TIME NEEDED: *more than an hour*

This is a comforting gratin for the autumn and winter months. *Venison* and *game birds* are suitably seasonal partners for it, but you won't go wrong with *chicken*, *lamb* or *mushroom-heavy dishes*.

I find candy-striped (Chioggia) and golden heirloom beetroot to be sweeter than the earthier red version, and would use them here in preference, given the choice. No one will complain if you have to use the red ones, though.

The sugary nature of the heirloom varieties softens and mellows over the relatively long cooking time, but it remains a pleasingly sweet dish. The startling bright colours also dull as the dish cooks, but as with any gratin, this is ultimately all about the dual joy of a crisp brown baked top and meltingly soft cream-soaked vegetables underneath.

Serves 4–6

1kg heirloom beetroot, equal parts candy-striped and golden
2 garlic cloves, very thinly sliced
20g horseradish, freshly grated
Leaves from 15–20 sprigs thyme
100ml milk
300ml double cream
Cold-pressed rapeseed oil, for drizzling
Sea salt and freshly ground black pepper

Preheat the oven to 200°C/Fan 180°C/Gas 6. Peel the beetroot and cut it into 3–4 mm slices, ideally using a mandolin (or a sharp knife, if you haven't got one). Layer the beetroot in a gratin dish that will hold it in about 5 layers. Use smaller pieces in the bottom of the dish, then sprinkle with salt, a little pepper, a few slices of garlic, a pinch of horseradish and about a fifth of the thyme leaves. Repeat until all the beetroot is used, saving the best, most uniform-sized slices for the top layer or two, and finishing with a final sprinkle of the aromatics.

Pour the milk and cream into a small saucepan and heat until just simmering. Pour this over the beetroot. Drizzle a little oil over the top, ensuring each beetroot slice gets a coating, then set the dish on a small baking tray (in case the cream bubbles over). Bake on the middle shelf for about 1¼ hours, pressing the top layer down with a fish slice or palette knife every 15 minutes or so. The gratin is ready when a fork can be easily pushed through to the base of the dish and the top is golden with the odd crisp edge. Leave to rest for at least 5 minutes before serving – it will be very hot, and that time allows the bubbling cream to settle.

ALONGSIDE: *Anchovy-dressed chicory* (page 78); *New potatoes with seaweed butter* (page 176); *Nutmeg neeps* (page 202); *Carrot-juice carrots* (page 218); *Spelt grains with wild mushrooms* (page 256)

GRAINS, PULSES, PASTA & RICE

It's easy to overlook grains, pulses, pasta and rice – to consider them merely the basic, bland bits that provide bulk, and therefore the last thing you need to pay attention to.

What a shame, though, if the bread is boring, the couscous underwhelming, the rice stodgy, or the pulse pushed aside, because all those things should at the very least be a comforting foil for the other things you're eating. At their best, they can be the most inspirational, moreish and memorable part of a meal. For me, the thought of sage-infused butter beans sitting in a puddle of peppery olive oil or Persian rice with a crust like pork crackling induces hunger as much as any meat, fish or star vegetable.

The recipes in this chapter feature tweaks and twists to take grains, pulses, pasta and rice to the next level, with lots of ideas for adding flavour, aroma and texture. My intention is to provide ideas for enhancing rice, lentils and dried beans; introduce flavourful, wholesome grains and seeds that might be new to you, such as freekeh, spelt and wheat berries; and prompt you to make polenta and soba noodles part of your everyday repertoire.

That said, please also use the recipes as a guide for cooking grains, pulses, pasta and rice simply. For example, if you don't feel the need to embellish rice but do wish to cook it well, turn to any of the examples on pages 288–298 for guidance as to quantity and method. I'm a firm believer in checking the packet instructions and then undercooking by a couple of minutes before leaving whatever is in the pan to steam to perfection.

If the likes of spelt, pearl barley or freekeh intrigue you but also leave you flummoxed, the recipes on pages 242–260 give cooking times, methods and quantities, so you can also use those to cook the grains plainly. The same is true for the pulse recipes (pages 262–280), where you'll find the basics for cooking lentils and beans in their dried form (the whole soaking-and-simmering thing really isn't that much bother).

What's more, pretty much all of the dressings for these dishes can be happily swapped around. The bean, lentil and chickpea flavourings are interchangeable; what works with barley will also be good with spelt, freekeh, buckwheat and wheat berries; and if it's good with couscous, it's probably ace with bulgar wheat and quinoa too.

As a general rule, I don't think pasta works as a side dish. But there are exceptions, not least Mac 'n' cheese (page 286), Chicken stock orzo (page 282) and Lemon and olive oil fregola (page 284). Breads can complete a meal too, whether in place of rice or potatoes or as a double-carb option. But they still need to suit the other components, so do require a little bit of forward planning if their inclusion is going to be worth it. This isn't a baking book, but the Flavoured butter bread and Seeded rye and honey soda bread on pages 234 and 232 are simple and quick, and can be manipulated to complement numerous occasions.

Mix and match the ideas in the recipes that follow, or keep things simple; just don't neglect this vital genre.

Seeded rye and honey soda bread

PREPARATION: *in the oven*
TIME NEEDED: *more than an hour*

My instinct was that there was no need for made-from-scratch bread recipes in this book. If you're inclined to make your own, you've probably got a go-to baking recipe already. Keep using it.

However, I am a strong believer that bread is a legitimate side, whether with a stew or broth, or with salads, tarts and quiches, which is why this recipe – and the flavoured butters on the next page – slipped through the net.

Homemade soda bread is easy, quick, requires no experience or proving, and is quite unlike the soda bread you'd pick up in a shop. This one's sweet, malty flavour pairs superbly with *crunchy pickles*, *oily fish*, *smoked fish* and *earthy broths*. Give it a go.

Serves 6 generously

2 teaspoons each brown linseeds, golden linseeds and poppy seeds
1 tablespoon each sunflower seeds and pumpkin seeds
220g light malt or wholemeal flour, plus extra for dusting
220g light rye flour
1 teaspoon sea salt
1 heaped teaspoon bicarbonate of soda
450ml buttermilk
3 tablespoons runny honey
15g butter, melted

Preheat the oven to 220°C/Fan 200°C/Gas 7. Put a 16–20cm cast-iron casserole dish with its lid in the hot oven to warm up for at least 5 minutes. Mix the seeds together.

Mix the flours, salt, bicarbonate of soda and three quarters of the seeds in a large bowl. Make a well in the middle, pour the buttermilk into the well and add the honey. Stir the liquids into the dry mixture to create a wet dough, then tip it out onto a lightly floured surface. Gently knead the dough a couple of times, before patting it into a round loaf shape. Don't spend too long doing this – the raising agent has already started to work, so you need to get it in the oven quickly.

Remove the hot casserole dish from the oven and take the lid off. Quickly dust the inside with wholemeal flour, then carefully lower in the dough. Sprinkle the remaining seeds over the top, put the lid on and return the casserole dish to the top half of the oven.

Bake for 45 minutes, then lift the lid to check the top is crisp and golden brown (cook for another 5 minutes if not). Remove from the oven and let it sit for 5 minutes, before turning it out onto a wire rack. Brush the top and sides of the loaf with the melted butter, then leave it to cool for at least 30 minutes. Eat it on the same day; briefly return the loaf to the oven if you want to serve it warm.

ALONGSIDE: *Braised red cabbage and beetroot* (page 22); *Dijon-dressed green beans* (page 64); *Watercress with pickled walnuts* (page 84); *Gem lettuce, mint and spring onion* (page 86); *Leeks vinaigrette with crisp-fried leeks* (page 142)

Flavoured butter bread

PREPARATION: *in the oven*
TIME NEEDED: *15 to 30 minutes*

Piping-hot baguettes slathered with garlic butter are a guilty pleasure that I blame on a 1980s upbringing. But there's no denying it's a damn enjoyable one, and a surprisingly good double-carb option alongside pasta or pizza.

We can go beyond garlic butter, though, and beyond baguettes as the platform too: shop-bought or homemade flatbreads also work well, and are worth 'pimping' to accompany meals inspired by the flavours of the Middle East or Indian subcontinent. Below are a few flavour combinations and butter-to-bread ratios to use as a starting point. This is one of those things you should make up as you go, though, depending on the contents of your fridge and store cupboard.

One further note: I don't subscribe to the make-more-than-you-need-and-store-in-the-freezer-never-to-be-used-again school of thought. Nor do I see the point in trying to beat cold butter that I didn't take out of the fridge early enough. Instead, I gently melt the required amount of butter, add the ingredients and either spread that directly onto the bread with a pastry brush, or refrigerate it for 5–10 minutes before spreading with a knife or spoon.

Makes enough for a 600–800g baguette or 3 large, floury, doughy flatbreads

Za'atar butter
100g butter
2 heaped tablespoons za'atar

Sun-dried tomato and paprika butter
80g butter
50g sun-dried tomatoes, finely chopped
1 mild red chilli, seeds removed, finely chopped
1 heaped tablespoon smoked paprika
20g Parmesan, grated

Cheesy garlic butter
80g butter
2 garlic cloves, crushed
20g strong Gruyère or Cheddar, finely grated
Leaves from 6 stems flat-leaf parsley, chopped as finely as dust

Sesame and cumin butter
80g butter
1 teaspoon sesame oil
1 teaspoon cumin seeds, toasted and lightly ground
1 teaspoon sesame seeds

Preheat the oven to 240°C/Fan 220°C/Gas 9. If using a baguette, cut it into 6 equal pieces, then cut each of these into 3–4 slices, not quite cutting through to the base.

Warm the butter very gently in a small heavy-bottomed pan. Before it's fully melted, remove from the heat and leave to cool for 1 minute. Add your chosen flavouring(s) and stir to incorporate fully.

Take a piece of kitchen foil the length of a baking tray and lay it flat on top of the tray. If using flatbreads rather than baguettes, you'll need a large tray and more foil.

Put the bread on top of the foil and use a pastry brush or spoon to spread the butter liberally over all the cut surfaces of the bread and the remainder over the top. Fold the sides of the foil to the middle, clasping it together. Bake for 10–15 minutes, opening the parcel for the last 5 minutes so that the bread takes on a little colour. Serve immediately.

———

ALONGSIDE (DEPENDING ON THE BUTTER FLAVOUR AND CUISINE STYLE): *Wilted spinach with coconut, ginger and pink peppercorns* (page 54); *Quick romesco* (page 106); *Mangal chopped salad* (page 108); *Chickpeas with garlic oil and spinach* (page 266); *Mustard seed, lemon and thyme rice* (page 288)

Bread sauce and parsnip crisps

PREPARATION: *on a hob and in the oven*
TIME NEEDED: *more than an hour*

Bread sauce is, more often than not, served as an accompaniment to the British Christmas roast dinner, but to cook and serve this just once a year would be something of a travesty. It is soothing and savoury and sits very well next to pretty much anything that once had wings. If you ever have a craving for bread sauce, it ought to inspire you to roast or pan-fry a *chicken*, *guinea fowl*, *pheasant*, *grouse*, *duck* or *partridge*. Alongside, or sprinkled over the top, the baked parsnip crisps add sweetness and crunch and complement the smooth sauce and any poultry perfectly.

In my view, unless you're having it as a cheeky snack straight from the fridge, bread sauce is best when freshly made. But you can make it in advance and reheat it later on – you'll just need to add extra milk to loosen the mixture. The parsnip crisps could also be made a few hours in advance.

Serves 4–6

Bread sauce
700ml milk
100g butter
10 cloves
2 bay leaves
1 onion, quartered
8 black peppercorns
1/6 nutmeg, freshly grated
1 sprig rosemary
150g soft white breadcrumbs
100ml double cream
Sea salt

Parsnip crisps
600g parsnips
3 tablespoons sunflower or vegetable oil
Sea salt

Start with the bread sauce. Put the milk, 60g of the butter, the cloves, bay leaves, onion, peppercorns, nutmeg and rosemary in a medium heavy-bottomed saucepan. Bring almost to the boil, then simmer gently for 5–10 minutes. Remove from the heat and leave to infuse for at least 1 hour, then strain into a clean pan and discard the aromatics.

Meanwhile, make the crisps. Peel the parsnips, then use a mandolin to cut paper-thin circles, starting with the tip. If you don't have a mandolin, use a peeler to strip very thin lengths off the parsnips. Place in a large bowl, drizzle with oil and mix well.

Preheat the oven to 200°C/Fan 180°C/Gas 6 and line 2 baking sheets with silicone baking mats or baking parchment. Spread the parsnip slices out over the baking sheets, ensuring they don't clump together (you may need to do this in batches), and bake for 10 minutes. Turn them over and bake for 10 minutes more, or until golden and crisp. Once cooked, line the large bowl with kitchen paper and tip the parsnips in. Let the paper soak up some of the oil and season generously with salt. Set aside to cool.

To finish the bread sauce, bring the infused milk to a gentle simmer. Add the breadcrumbs and stir or whisk until incorporated. Turn the heat right down to the lowest setting and cook for 10–15 minutes until thickened, stirring occasionally to stop it catching. Add a good pinch of salt, the cream and remaining butter and stir until incorporated. It should

be the consistency of a loose porridge – add more milk if you need to. Taste to check the seasoning and add more salt, pepper and/or nutmeg if you wish.

———

Put the parsnip crisps in a communal bowl, sprinkle with more salt if needed and encourage everyone to take a handful alongside their sauce.

———

ALONGSIDE: *Purple sprouting broccoli with tarragon* (page 42); *Watercress with pickled walnuts* (page 84); *Hasselback potatoes with bay and caraway* (page 172); *Maple and pecan roast squash* (page 186); *Spiced roast carrots* (page 216)

Cheesy polenta

PREPARATION: *on a hob*
TIME NEEDED: *15 to 30 minutes*

Some people consider polenta a boring, sloppy and pointless side. My theory is that those people don't put enough butter or cheese in. In fact, when prepared with a little love, it's a glorious accompaniment to *slow-cooked meats and stews*, masses of *garlicky mushrooms* or *fatty cuts of pork*.

The instructions below are for polenta that hasn't been pre-cooked. If you have the instant or quick-cook type, add the same flavourings but follow the cooking instructions on the packet. Personally, I would only serve one other side dish with this, or sometimes none at all where the braised meat, stew or ragu it's to accompany already contains plenty of vegetables.

Serves 4–6

240g polenta
80g butter, cut into small dice
150g strong mature Cheddar, ideally a good-quality Somerset Cheddar, grated
Sea salt and freshly ground black pepper

Put 1.5 litres water and a hefty pinch of salt in a large pan and bring to the boil, then reduce to a simmer.

———

Sprinkle the polenta into the pan in a slow, steady stream, stirring continuously. For a few moments it will seem as though there's far too much water, but after 3–5 minutes the polenta will swell and thicken. Continue to stir – nay, beat – almost without interruption for 10–15 minutes over a very low heat. Once the grains are less visible and the polenta starts to become smooth and slick, reduce the heat to its lowest setting and cook for a further 10 minutes, beating – nay, whipping – every few minutes to prevent sticking and to keep the polenta smooth. Add an extra glass or two of water during cooking to loosen the mixture if necessary.

———

Add the butter, cheese and a twist of pepper and whisk furiously for 60 seconds. Remove from the heat and serve immediately. It should be loose and smooth, although it will quickly firm up as you ladle it onto a dish.

———

ALONGSIDE: *Chard with chilli, shallot and cider vinaigrette* (page 6); *Cavolo nero with garlic, chilli and orange* (page 24); *Purple sprouting broccoli with tarragon* (page 42); *Puttanesca runner beans* (page 68); *Carrots with brown butter and hazelnuts* (page 220)

Roman rosemary polenta

PREPARATION: *on a hob and in the oven*
TIME NEEDED: *more than an hour*

These rosemary-infused squares of set-then-baked polenta are, to me, more satisfying than polenta 'chips', which never live up to their name. I'd serve them with almost *any tomato sauce-based dish*, but also next to *chargrilled lamb chops*, *chicken thighs in a cheesy sauce* or as part of a *meat-free medley*. There's a bit of work involved, but the first two steps can be done in advance of eating. Also: it's worth it.

The instructions below are to suit polenta that hasn't been pre-cooked. If you have the instant or quick-cook type, follow the instructions on the packet, replacing the water with milk, then pick up the method when the cheese and butter are added.

Serves 4–6

800ml milk
3 sprigs rosemary
150g polenta
Light olive oil, for greasing
70g butter, cubed
80g Parmesan, grated
Sea salt

Put the milk and 2 of the rosemary sprigs in a large saucepan, bring to a rapid simmer and cook for 5 minutes. Remove from the heat and leave to infuse for 25 minutes, then discard the rosemary.

———

Sprinkle the polenta into the pan in a slow, steady stream, stirring continuously. At first it will seem as though there's far too much milk, but after 3–5 minutes the polenta will swell and thicken. Continue to stir vigorously, almost without interruption, for 10–15 minutes over a low heat. Once the grains are less visible and the polenta starts to become smooth, reduce the heat to very low and cook for 10 minutes more, beating it frequently. Add some extra water to loosen the mixture if necessary.

———

Meanwhile, line an approximately 20 x 20cm baking tray with baking parchment, and grease the paper with 1 tablespoon oil. When the polenta is cooked, smooth and slick, add 40g of the butter and 60g of the Parmesan and beat well, season with salt, then pour it into the lined tray. Use a palette knife or the back of a spoon to push and smooth the polenta into the corners to an even depth of around 3cm. Leave to cool, then put in the fridge to set for at least 30 minutes or overnight.

———

Once the polenta has cooled and set, turn it out onto a clean work surface and cut into 5cm squares. Place these smooth-side up on a larger lightly oiled baking tray (or two), leaving a little space around them. Preheat the oven to 250°C/Fan 230°C/Gas 10.

———

Strip the leaves from the remaining rosemary and chop them very finely. Melt the remaining butter and pour or brush this over the polenta squares. Sprinkle the rosemary over the top, then finish with the remaining Parmesan. Bake for 15 minutes, or until golden. Allow to cool and firm up for 5 minutes before serving.

———

ALONGSIDE: *Creamed chard* (page 8); *Kale, Romanesco, Parmesan and pine nut salad* (page 28); *Turnip tops with burnt lemon and olive oil* (page 52); *Wilted bitter leaves with blue cheese dressing* (page 76); *Grilled green tomatoes with oregano and chilli* (page 102)

Cinnamon, chickpea and apricot couscous

PREPARATION: *in the oven*
TIME NEEDED: *15 to 30 minutes*

Though I generally prefer bulgar wheat to couscous, there are many occasions when a bowl of fluffed, steaming couscous is comforting and welcome. Obviously, *tagines and stews* bursting with Middle Eastern spices come to mind, but it also pairs well with *roast chicken* and its juices on a balmy summer evening; *spiced salmon or mackerel*; *succulent, flaking white fish*, and much, much more.

Couscous is easy to prepare. But you must season it well to shift it from bland fodder to something really worth eating. I find it demands generosity with salt, pepper, herbs and acidic condiments, and to be studded with interesting textures and bursts of flavour, such as chickpeas, seeds and jammy and warm or dried fruit. Which, by an extraordinary coincidence, just so happen to feature in this recipe.

Serves 4–6

1 large orange
400g tinned chickpeas, drained
1 heaped teaspoon ground cinnamon
1 teaspoon ground ginger
1 tablespoon maple syrup
2 tablespoons cold-pressed rapeseed oil
300g couscous
Juice of 1 lemon
60g dried apricots, diced
Leaves from 8–10 stems coriander, roughly chopped
50g sunflower seeds, toasted

Preheat the oven to 190°C/Fan 170°C/Gas 5. Cut the orange in half. Place the halves cut-side down and slice into 2–3mm thin crescents.

Tip the chickpeas into a small roasting tray. Add the cinnamon, ginger, maple syrup and oil, mix well and lay the orange slices on top. Bake for 20–25 minutes, or until the fruit is jammy and darkening at the edges.

With 10 minutes to go (if you'd like to eat this warm, otherwise timing is not a worry), put the couscous in a large bowl (since there are many ingredients to be added). Pour 450ml boiling water into the bowl, then cover with a clean tea towel, a lid or clingfilm. Leave for 5 minutes to steam and swell. Once that's happened, use a fork to fluff the couscous.

Remove the cooked oranges from the baking tray and set aside. Scrape the chickpeas and all the sticky, spiced oils and juice from the tray into the bowl of couscous. Add the lemon juice, apricots and three quarters of the coriander, sunflower seeds and orange slices. Mix well, and top with the remaining coriander, seeds and oranges.

This is equally good served warm or at room temperature – just make sure you fork the couscous again before serving, particularly if it has been left to sit for a while.

ALONGSIDE: *Charred Romanesco* (page 46); *French-ish peas* (page 58); *Buttermilk, dill and soy-seed wedge salad* (page 88); *Sherry cherry tomatoes* (page 98); *Burnt sweet onion petals with cucumber* (page 150)

Mum's bulgar wheat salad

PREPARATION: *on a hob*
TIME NEEDED: *15 to 30 minutes*

An authentic tabbouleh contains more herbs than bulgar wheat. Mum's tabbouleh was never like that. But I was always – and remain – fond of it, so I'm replicating it here, just tweaking the name a little.

Couscous is often the side people lean towards when looking for a cooling, filling accompaniment for barbecues and cold meat buffets, but I much prefer the nutty chew of bulgar wheat. This sharp salad – flavoured but not dominated by mint, parsley and cucumber – is one of the first things that comes to mind in those circumstances. It's perfect if *chargrilled lamb chops*, a *roast leg of lamb*, *slabs of feta* or *roasted aubergines and peppers* happen to be nearby.

Serves 4–6

200g bulgar wheat
1 large cucumber, peeled and diced
1 spring onion, very thinly sliced
1 small garlic clove, crushed
Leaves from 12 stems mint, shredded
Leaves from 12 stems flat-leaf parsley, roughly chopped
Leaves from 5 stems tarragon or chervil (optional), roughly chopped
2 tablespoons red wine vinegar
1 tablespoon cold-pressed rapeseed oil
Sea salt and freshly ground black pepper

Three-quarters fill a medium saucepan with water. Add a pinch of salt and bring to the boil. Add the bulgar wheat and simmer gently for around 10 minutes, or until the grains have swollen and become fluffy but still retain a pleasing bite. Drain, then rinse under running cold water until cool. Leave to drain fully.

Add the cucumber, spring onion, garlic and herbs to the cooled bulgar wheat, along with the vinegar and oil. Season with plenty of black pepper and a pinch or two of salt. If you have time, leave the bulgar wheat salad to sit for an hour or longer so the flavours can mingle. Serve at room temperature.

ALONGSIDE: *Grilled hispi cabbage with anchovy and crème fraîche* (page 10); *Tomato tonnato* (page 96); *Roast Romano peppers* (page 104); *Mangal chopped salad* (page 108); *Roast cauliflower with chickpeas and lemon tahini* (page 128)

Mixed quinoa with radish and pea shoots

PREPARATION: *on a hob*
TIME NEEDED: *15 to 30 minutes*

Once quinoa moves on from its role as flag-bearer for the superfood movement, we'll be able to recognise it for what it is: a versatile, flavourful, enjoyable ingredient. It's easy and relatively quick to cook, and can be eaten warm or cool.

There are over 100 varieties of quinoa. I have suggested using three of the more common types in this side, largely to provide a little colour; you could use just one variety to similar effect. I've also suggested toasting some quinoa to provide crunch, but this is entirely optional.

The radish, pea shoots, dill and lemon add crunch and multiple fresh flavours. I love this with things like *grilled halloumi*, *feta cheese* and pretty much any *fish*, *chicken* or *rabbit* dish. If it suits, make it in advance and keep in the fridge until required (though it's best served at room temperature).

Serves 4–6

180g white quinoa
75g red quinoa
75g black quinoa
150g radishes, ideally French breakfast, leaves removed
60g pea shoots
Juice of ½ lemon
2 tablespoons cold-pressed rapeseed oil
Fronds from 8 stems dill
1 teaspoon nigella seeds
Sea salt

Put 150g of the white and all of the red and black quinoa in a saucepan and pour on enough cold water to cover by 3–4cm. Bring to the boil, then simmer for 15–20 minutes, until the grains are tender and the little tails have sprung. Drain and rinse under cold running water until cool, then drain well.

To make toasted quinoa, place a small, heavy-bottomed saucepan over a medium-high heat and let it warm up for 2 minutes. Add the remaining white quinoa and cover with a lid. After a minute or so, you'll hear the quinoa popping. Let this continue for another minute, shaking the pan once or twice. Remove from the heat, check the quinoa isn't burning and, assuming not, put the lid back on to let it toast away in the residual heat.

Put the cooked quinoa in a large serving bowl. Slice the radishes thinly and add to the quinoa with the pea shoots, lemon juice, oil, dill and nigella seeds. Taste to check the seasoning and add a pinch or two of salt and more lemon juice if you wish. Stir in three quarters of the toasted quinoa, then sprinkle the rest over the top and serve.

ALONGSIDE: *Grilled green tomatoes with oregano and chilli* (page 102); *Courgette and edamame salad* (page 110); *Mandolin salad* (page 134); *Maple and pecan roast squash* (page 186); *Kohlrabi remoulade* (page 208)

Spinach and preserved lemon freekeh

PREPARATION: *on a hob*
TIME NEEDED: *15 to 30 minutes*

Freekeh is a roasted wheat grain traditionally found in Middle Eastern cuisine, and it's delicious. It can be used in the same way as rice, quinoa, couscous and bulgar wheat, and the nutty, smoky, earthy flavour and wholesome bite make it a superb side with many different dishes.

Here, the freekeh is flavoured with a spinach and preserved lemon purée, which I've become a little addicted to. It seems to suit *salmon fillets*, *shredded roast chicken*, *hot-smoked trout* and *soft-boiled or fried eggs* particularly well. If you'd rather have a plainer version, cook it as per these instructions but dress it with salt, pepper, a good squeeze of lemon and some peppery extra-virgin olive oil.

This reheats easily if you're struggling for hob space, but it will need an extra tablespoon or two of water, and the colour will have dulled. Alternatively, make the purée in advance and cook the freekeh when you need it. If there's leftover purée, store it in an airtight container in the fridge for up to 3 days and use it as a condiment.

Serves 4–6

200g cracked freekeh
40g defrosted frozen peas
50g sunflower oil
50g extra-virgin olive oil
2 tablespoons white wine vinegar
Juice of ¼ lemon
100g baby spinach
1 small-medium bunch (40g) flat-leaf parsley, including stalks, roughly chopped
75g preserved lemons, seeds removed, all flesh and rind roughly chopped
2 mild red chillies, seeds removed, roughly chopped
2 teaspoons Dijon mustard
1 garlic clove, roughly chopped
4g sea salt

Put the freekeh and 600ml cold water in a medium saucepan (1:2 freekeh to water, if you are measuring by volume). Bring to the boil and simmer gently for 20 minutes, or until most of the water has been absorbed and the grains are tender with a pleasing bite. Once cooked, allow it to rest for 2–3 minutes.

Meanwhile, make the spinach purée by putting the peas, both oils, vinegar, lemon juice and half the spinach in a blender or food processor. Pulse, then blitz until smooth, then add the remaining spinach and blitz again until smooth. You might need to prod and cajole the contents of the blender but it should all come together eventually. Once it's reasonably fluid, add the remaining ingredients and blend for a further 60 seconds or so. Taste for seasoning and add a little more salt if you wish. Stir the spinach purée into the cooked freekeh and serve.

ALONGSIDE: *Charred Romanesco* (page 46); *Pink radicchio with pear and almonds* (page 82); *Green tomato, salted celery and chervil salad* (page 100); *Shaved fennel with tarragon* (page 118); *Spiced roast carrots* (page 216)

Wheat berries with capers and tomatoes

PREPARATION: *on a hob*
TIME NEEDED: *30 minutes to an hour*

You can buy packs of unmilled wheat grains (also known as wheat berries) online and, increasingly, in supermarkets too. Which is excellent news, because they're plump, berry-like and pleasingly chewy if simmered for 45 minutes (a little less if you soak them first, though I'm not sure there's much point). There's a wholesome quality to them, and because they carry aromatics well and hold their own against other robust flavours, I think they make an excellent filling side for a multitude of meals, whether that's as part of a *mezze spread* or with *oily fish like salmon and mackerel*, or *meaty stews*.

I first came across wheat berries at a street food stall called Gourmet Goat, which serves the grains with slow-cooked shoulder of kid goat and massive dollops of cooling yoghurt. Capers, tomatoes, fresh herbs and lemon abound – the flavours work so well that, to be honest, this dish simply apes theirs. They'd work nicely with spelt grain and pearl barley, too.

Serves 4–6

300g wheat grains
Leaves from 8 stems flat-leaf parsley
2 tablespoons light olive oil
1 bay leaf
1 garlic clove, crushed
5 tablespoons capers, roughly chopped
Leaves from 6 stems mint, thinly sliced
250g sun-blushed tomatoes, cut in half, oil reserved
Extra-virgin olive oil (optional), for the dressing
Juice and finely grated zest of ½ lemon
Sea salt and freshly ground black pepper

Preheat the oven to 210°C/Fan 190°C/Gas 6½. Spread the wheat grains out over a baking tray and toast for 10 minutes, or until nutty and slightly browned.

Roughly chop the parsley leaves and set them aside. Chop the stems very finely and put them in a saucepan with the light olive oil; cook gently for 3 minutes. Add the toasted wheat grains and bay leaf and cover with water by 3–4cm. Bring to the boil, then reduce to a simmer and cook, covered, for 35–45 minutes, or until plump, tender and berry-like.

Drain the wheat berries, reserving 3–4 tablespoons of the cooking liquid. Remove and discard the bay leaf. Add the garlic, capers, parsley and mint, tomatoes and 5 tablespoons tomato oil (supplementing with olive oil if there's not enough) and loosen the mix with the reserved cooking liquid. Season generously with salt, black pepper and the lemon zest and juice. Serve immediately, although it holds its temperature for 15 minutes or so, and is still very good served cold.

ALONGSIDE: *Steamed marinated fennel* (page 116); *Mandolin salad* (page 134); *Baked Jerusalem artichokes with yoghurt and sunflower seeds* (page 206); *Kohlrabi remoulade* (page 208); *Spiced roast carrots* (page 216)

Buckwheat with celery and walnuts

PREPARATION: *on a hob*
TIME NEEDED: *15 to 30 minutes*

Perhaps confusingly, buckwheat is not related to wheat and its triangular 'groats' are not a grain (they're seeds). But this does mean it's a suitable option for anyone with a gluten allergy or intolerance. More importantly, buckwheat is delicious: it's earthy, savoury and a little bit nutty. If you buy roasted buckwheat (kasha), those flavours are more pronounced, but I find the seeds can become mushy when you cook them, which doesn't suit this dish at all.

I love the different textural roles the plump cooked buckwheat groats, raw celery and walnuts play here; there's a pleasing crunch to each mouthful. At the same time it's a fairly neutral side that will work well with a variety of dishes: *creamy and meaty sauces*, *rich or light meats*, *most fish*, *salty, sharp cheeses* and any number of vegetable options (especially *sweet tomatoes*, *peppers* and *squash*). Use it wherever you might otherwise have served rice, couscous or pearl barley.

If it suits your meal, jazz up the finished dish by studding it with orange segments or a handful of halved grapes; the occasional burst of a sharp, juicy fruit works really well against the other softer, more wholesome flavours.

Serves 4–6

300g buckwheat groats, not roasted
3 celery sticks (approximately 100g), plus a good handful of celery leaves
1 garlic clove, crushed
50g walnut halves, roughly chopped
4 tablespoons extra-virgin olive oil
Juice of 1 lemon
Sea salt and ground white pepper

Combine the buckwheat and 750ml cold water in a saucepan. Set it over a medium heat and bring to a moderate simmer. Turn the heat down and cook gently for 10 minutes, or until the buckwheat groats have plumped up a little and lost any chalky or grainy bite, but before they turn mushy.

Meanwhile, boil a kettle and prepare the remaining ingredients. For the celery, cut each stick in half lengthways, picking and reserving any leafy tops, then slice into 2–3mm pieces.

When the buckwheat is cooked, drain it and rinse with the contents of a just-boiled kettle. Return the buckwheat to the saucepan and add the celery, garlic, walnuts, oil and a good pinch of salt and white pepper. Mix and leave to sit for 3 minutes, letting the residual heat mellow the garlic and soften the celery. Add the lemon juice and celery tops, mix once more, taste to check the seasoning and adjust if necessary. It's best served immediately, but is still good when left to cool to room temperature.

ALONGSIDE: *Roast Romano peppers* (page 104); *Smoky ratatouille* (page 114); *Burnt sweet onion petals with cucumber* (page 150); *Za'atar mushrooms with curd* (page 154); *Roast butternut squash purée* (page 188)

Sesame soba noodles

PREPARATION: *on a hob*
TIME NEEDED: *less than 15 minutes*

This is not really a recipe, more a plea to use buckwheat soba noodles occasionally when cooking an Asian-inspired (particularly Japanese) meal. The nutty and wholesome flavour and firm texture make a change from the ubiquitous egg noodles or plain rice; they're an excellent accompaniment to things like *grilled oily fish*, *unctuous pork belly*, *poached chicken breasts* or *miso-glazed aubergine*.

Even if the dish they're served with is warm, I prefer to rinse soba noodles with cold water and eat them when cool, as they seem to seize up and become claggy if left warm. In the UK, Clearspring, Akagi and Hakubaku are good soba brands to look for.

Serves 4–6

500g good-quality soba noodles (100 per cent buckwheat)
2 tablespoons light soy sauce
2 tablespoons toasted sesame seeds
2 tablespoons sesame oil

Bring a very large pan of water to the boil. If you put the noodles in cold water or a pan with too little water, they are likely to become starchy and sticky. It might even be best to use 2 pans to cook this quantity.

Cook the noodles according to the packet instructions (which are probably to simmer them for 5 minutes), then drain. Rinse in a sieve under running cold water until cool.

Return the noodles to the saucepan or a serving bowl and add the soy sauce, sesame seeds and oil. Mix well and serve.

ALONGSIDE: *Spring greens in shiitake dashi* (page 14); *Chopped kale with edamame, miso and sweet chilli* (page 26); *Baby pak choi with sticky garlic and ginger* (page 48); *Garlic oil pea shoots* (page 56); *Quick-pickled daikon* (page 210); *Warm radishes with anise* (page 212)

Spelt grains with wild mushrooms

PREPARATION: *on a hob*
TIME NEEDED: *more than an hour*

Spelt is an ancient grain that's best known as a flour for use in baking, but the whole grains are excellent for cooking, too, and sit somewhere between barley and brown rice in terms of texture. It has a nutty, earthy flavour when cooked in plain water, but allowing it to bubble away in ever-reducing mushroom stock takes it to another level; you end up with a dark, richly flavoured grain that works brilliantly with many autumn or winter meats and vegetables.

Combinations that make me salivate while writing include: *all game birds*, *venison*, *offal dishes like haggis or calves' liver*, *halibut*, *turbot* and the Spiced roast carrots on page 216, plus a spoonful of labneh or curd.

It could be made in advance and reheated with a few extra spoonfuls of water – just don't add the lemon juice or parsley until the last minute.

Serves 4–6

35–40g dried wild mushrooms
10–15 stems flat-leaf parsley
2 tablespoons light olive oil
1 onion, finely diced
1 garlic clove, crushed
300g spelt grains
Leaves from 15–20 sprigs thyme
70ml white wine or vermouth (optional)
Juice of ½ lemon
Sea salt and freshly ground black pepper

Put the dried mushrooms in a heatproof jug or bowl and pour 1 litre boiling water over the top. Leave to steep for 15 minutes.

Meanwhile, prepare the remaining ingredients. For the parsley, wash and dry it if your bunch is dusty, then finely chop the stems and pick and roughly chop the leaves, keeping the leaves and stalks separate.

Heat the oil in a medium heavy-bottomed saucepan over a medium heat. Add the onion and a pinch of salt. Cook for 3 minutes, until softened and sweetened, then add the garlic and parsley stems. Cook for 1 minute, then add the spelt and thyme. Stir to coat the grains with oil, then increase the heat and pour in the wine, if using. Allow this to reduce by half before adding the rehydrated mushrooms and their soaking liquid.

Bring to the boil, then reduce the heat and simmer gently for 40–45 minutes, or until the spelt grains are tender and the stock has reduced to 4–5 tablespoons. Remove from the heat. Add the lemon juice, a generous grinding of black pepper and the parsley leaves. Stir and serve.

ALONGSIDE: *Cabbage with juniper butter* (page 20); *Braised red cabbage and beetroot* (page 22); *PX radicchio Trevisano* (page 74); *Watercress with pickled walnuts* (page 84); *Wine-poached salsify with gremolata* (page 200)

Jewelled pearl barley

PREPARATION: *on a hob*
TIME NEEDED: *15 to 30 minutes*

Pearl barley is a brilliant option for times when you might have been thinking 'rice again?' or 'hmmm, perhaps couscous?'. It's wholesome and comforting to eat, and possesses, I think, a joyous texture. While it has a pleasing, subtly nutty taste when simply boiled in plain water, it's particularly good in the company of other ingredients, and a flavourful stock or dressing.

Here, simply cooked barley is adorned with a multitude of aromatics, dried fruits, nuts and herbs; it's a riff on Persian jewelled rice, and is good both when served immediately or later at room temperature.

This side is robust enough to accompany really big flavours like *rich, slow-cooked meats and stews* or a bold set of banquet-style dishes, but it would also sit quietly next to *baked white fish* or other similarly delicate foods.

Serves 4–6

300g pearl barley
30g dried sour cherries, roughly chopped
40g sultanas
30g unsalted shelled pistachios, roughly chopped
40g toasted flaked almonds
Leaves from 20–25 stems coriander, roughly chopped
Leaves from 10–15 stems mint, roughly chopped

Orange blossom dressing
10–15 strands saffron
½ garlic clove, crushed
Juice and finely grated zest of 1 orange
Juice of ½ lemon
2 teaspoons orange blossom water
2 tablespoons runny honey
100ml extra-virgin olive oil
Sea salt

Put the pearl barley in a sieve and rinse it under the tap until the water is clear, then transfer to a saucepan and cover with at least 3 times its depth of water. Add a generous pinch of salt, then set it over a high heat, bring to the boil and simmer gently for 25 minutes, or until plump and tender.

Meanwhile, make the dressing. Put the saffron strands and garlic in a small bowl. Add 1 tablespoon boiling water and leave to steep for 10 minutes. Add the orange juice and zest, lemon juice, orange blossom water, honey and a pinch of salt. Stir to combine, then add the oil and whisk until emulsified. It will seem like a lot of liquid, but the barley soaks it up.

Once the pearl barley is cooked, drain well and return it to the saucepan. Add the dressing and two thirds of the dried fruit and nuts. Mix, add the herbs, mix again, then decant to a serving bowl or platter and sprinkle the remaining dried fruit and nuts over the top.

ALONGSIDE: *Radicchio with a smoky blood orange and maple dressing* (page 80); *Grilled green tomatoes with oregano and chilli* (page 102); *Carrot, cumin and nigella seed salad* (page 214); *Spiced roast carrots* (page 216); *Chickpeas with garlic oil and spinach* (page 266)

Green pearl barley

PREPARATION: *on a hob*
TIME NEEDED: *30 minutes to an hour*

In this side, pearl barley grains are coated in a velvety green sauce. It's a wholesome dish that acts as an accompaniment in a similar way to a loose risotto. The herbs, vegetables and Parmesan enhance the savoury and comforting nature of the grains and because it's quite slick, there's no real need for a sauce or gravy. Well, technically no need, but don't let that stop you...

This feels autumnal to me, something to ladle into a bowl to sit underneath *chicken*, *guinea fowl*, *venison*, *pheasant* or perhaps *monkfish*, ideally eaten in the vicinity of a wood-burning stove and a bottle or two of red wine. Up to you whether you serve any other sides alongside; roast or gratinated roots are perfect, or just a handful of peppery or bitter salad leaves.

You could make the green sauce in advance of the barley, adding a few tablespoons of water and reheating it gently in a pan when required. Hold back from adding the lemon zest and juice until just before serving.

Serves 4–6

200g pearl barley
1 sprig rosemary
1 tablespoon light olive oil
50g carrot, finely diced
½ onion, finely diced
150g kale, leaves stripped from the stems
3 tablespoons extra-virgin olive oil
20g butter
20g Parmesan, grated
Juice and finely grated zest of ½ lemon
Sea salt and freshly ground black pepper

Put the pearl barley in a sieve and rinse it under a tap until the water is clear, then transfer to a saucepan and cover with at least 4 times its depth of water. Bash the rosemary with the blunt edge of a large knife and add it to the pan. Bring to the boil and simmer very gently for 25 minutes, or until plump and tender. Remove and discard the rosemary.

———

Meanwhile, make the green sauce. Heat the light olive oil in a large pan or frying pan, add the carrot and onion with a pinch of salt and cook for 5 minutes. Add the kale and cook for a further 4–5 minutes, stirring occasionally and allowing it to wilt, then remove the pan from the heat.

———

Tip the contents of the kale pan into a blender. Take 150ml cooking water from the barley and add to the blender with the extra-virgin olive oil, butter, Parmesan and ½ teaspoon salt. Blitz until silky smooth – leave the motor running for at least 3 minutes. Add the lemon zest and juice and a good grinding of black pepper. Taste and add a little more salt or pepper if needed.

———

Once the barley is cooked, drain and return it to its pan, then pour in the green sauce. Stir to combine and serve immediately.

———

ALONGSIDE: *Rosemary and chilli roast squash* (page 184); *Butter-glazed turnips with horseradish* (page 204); *Carrots with brown butter and hazelnuts* (page 220); *Beetroot gratin* (page 224)

Herb-loaded lentils

PREPARATION: *on a hob*
TIME NEEDED: *30 minutes to an hour*

This is one of those side dishes that becomes the main event without you realising. Sure, it's the obvious partner to *salty or smoky meats like smoked sausages, bacon chops, porchetta* and *confit duck legs*; tender flakes of *white fish* and *goat's cheese* love being eaten with lentils too. But all of those things, amazing as they are, end up playing second fiddle to these heady, vibrant, moreish, herb-loaded lentils – it's the pulse that people come back to for seconds.

It's much better to cook dried lentils from scratch, rather than reach for soggy, mulchy ones in a tin or packet (and ideally use Puy lentils if you can find them). Be sure to add salt only when they are cooked, and be generous with the herbs and capers.

Serves 4–6

1 large bunch (100g) flat-leaf parsley, including the stalks
4 tablespoons extra-virgin olive oil
½ onion, finely diced
1 carrot, finely diced
1 celery stick, finely diced
300g Puy lentils (brown or green lentils are fine too)
Leaves from 10–15 stems tarragon, roughly chopped
Leaves from 6 stems mint, finely chopped
30g capers, roughly chopped
Juice and finely grated zest of 1 lemon
Sea salt

Pick the leaves from the parsley stalks. Reserve half the stalks for another occasion (stock perhaps?), then chop the rest very finely.

In a medium saucepan, heat a little of the oil, add the onion, carrot, celery and chopped parsley stalks and cook for 4–5 minutes, or until softened and sweetened. Rinse the lentils in a sieve, decant to the saucepan and pour in enough cold water to cover by about 3 cm. Bring to the boil, then simmer gently for 20 minutes, or until the lentils are tender. There won't be much water left by the end, which is preferable to having to drain off the flavoursome cooking liquor. Ideally there'll be the equivalent of a mugful, which ensures the lentils are loose rather than stiff. Add a little extra hot water if necessary.

Chop the parsley leaves very finely. It's quite a large amount, but roll the leaves up tightly, then slice and cross-chop them until they are almost like dust.

Once the lentils are cooked, add the parsley, tarragon and mint and the capers, the remaining oil and lemon zest and juice. Stir, taste, season with salt and enjoy.

ALONGSIDE: *Gem lettuce, mint and spring onion* (page 86); *Smoky ratatouille* (page 114); *Leeks vinaigrette with crisp-fried leeks* (page 142); *Anise-braised spring onions* (page 148); *Burnt sweet onion petals with cucumber* (page 150)

Red wine, anise and orange lentils

PREPARATION: *on a hob*
TIME NEEDED: *15 to 30 minutes*

We think of pulses as a humble food typical of 'peasant cooking', yet the taste of well-seasoned lentils is anything but impoverished. The lentils in this recipe, which are cooked with a glass of red wine (for the pot), is a grand demonstration of the potential of this type of side. They're strongly flavoured but versatile, and suit *rich meats like ox cheeks and beef shin* just as well as more delicate things such as *rabbit, hake, cod, turbot* and *vegetables like wild mushrooms and pumpkin.*

Like the Herb-loaded lentils (page 262), these are most satisfying when served loose and silky, so keep a little of the cooking broth and add a liberal glug of olive oil at the end.

Serves 4–6

1 tablespoon light olive oil
1 onion, finely chopped
350g brown, green or Puy lentils
Leaves from 5 sprigs thyme
1 bay leaf
2 star anise
175ml red wine
2 tablespoons red wine vinegar
Finely grated zest of 1 orange
Fronds from 8 stems dill, chopped
3–4 tablespoons extra-virgin olive oil
Sea salt

Heat the light olive oil in a medium saucepan over a gentle heat, add the onion and cook for 3–4 minutes to soften and sweeten.

Rinse the lentils in a sieve, then decant them to the saucepan along with the thyme, bay leaf and star anise. Turn the heat up and cook for 30 seconds, then make a space in the lentils and pour the red wine directly onto the base of the pan, letting it bubble and reduce a little. Pour in enough cold water to cover the lentils by 2–3 cm, then bring to a gentle simmer and cook for 20 minutes, or until the lentils are tender. There won't be much water left by the end, which is preferable to having to drain off the flavoursome cooking liquor. Ideally there'll be 3–4 tablespoons of liquid, which ensures the lentils are loose rather than stiff. Add a little extra water if necessary.

Once the lentils are cooked, add the red wine vinegar, orange zest, dill and a pinch of salt. Try to fish out the bay leaf and star anise (or just task your guests to do it). Taste to check the seasoning and drizzle liberally with the extra-virgin olive oil.

ALONGSIDE: *Kale, Romanesco, Parmesan and pine nut salad* (page 28); *Butter-braised chicory* (page 72); *PX radicchio Trevisano* (page 74); *Steamed marinated fennel* (page 116); *Carrot-juice carrots* (page 218)

Chickpeas with garlic oil and spinach

PREPARATION: *on a hob*
TIME NEEDED: *more than an hour*

This is an easy way to add interest to chickpeas, which have an enjoyable texture but, let's face it, a flavour that fails to excite after the first forkful. Here, a generous quantity of sliced garlic softens in warm, nutty rapeseed oil, infusing a mellow and sweet scent along with the spinach leaves, which wilt a little in the residual heat of the warm chickpeas. It all culminates in a side that suits *spicy stews and tagines*, anything featuring *lamb*, *hogget* or *mutton*, or *crisp-skinned chicken thighs* and *white fish.*

Cooking your own dried chickpeas from scratch is ideal, but garlic oil and spinach can still be added to good effect to 600–650g tinned or bottled chickpeas. For a slight twist, if you're lucky enough to be in the right place at the right time, replace the spinach and garlic with a few handfuls of wild garlic (ramsons).

Serves 6

300g dried chickpeas
100ml cold-pressed rapeseed oil
4 garlic cloves, very thinly sliced
140g baby spinach leaves
Juice and finely grated zest of 1 lemon
Sea salt and freshly ground black pepper

Put the chickpeas in a bowl and cover with 3 times their volume of cold water. Soak for 10–12 hours, then drain and tip them into a medium saucepan. Cover the chickpeas with at least 3 times their volume of fresh cold water. Bring to the boil, then simmer for 1½–2 hours, or until completely tender. Don't add any salt.

Drain the cooked chickpeas well, reserving the cooking liquor (you need 3–4 tablespoons for this recipe; the rest will make a lovely stock).

Put the oil in a small heavy-bottomed saucepan over a medium-low heat. Add the garlic and cook gently for 5 minutes, allowing the garlic to soften and infuse the oil. (This could be done well in advance of draining the chickpeas.)

Return the drained chickpeas to the pan and gently stir in the spinach leaves, allowing them to wilt a little for 1–2 minutes. Add the garlic and oil, the lemon juice, zest and lots of salt and freshly ground black pepper (it needs plenty of seasoning). Stir again, spooning any oil and liquid from the bottom of the pan over the chickpeas as you serve.

ALONGSIDE: *Okra chips with cumin salt* (page 70); *Za'atar mushrooms with curd* (page 154); *Maple and pecan roast squash* (page 186); *Curry leaf, cashew and coconut rice* (page 290); *Crisp-bottomed Persian rice* (page 302)

Borlotti beans and cavolo nero with basil and hazelnut smash

PREPARATION: *on a hob*
TIME NEEDED: *more than an hour*

Given their striking speckled pink appearance when raw, it seems such a shame that fresh borlotti beans turn a dull shade of brown as they cook. But then, on eating, all is forgiven. The king of the legumes? Perhaps.

The cooking method here is fairly classical: boiled with herbs and a little tomato, a touch of vinegar and a great deal of olive oil in the dressing. But this dish then bulks the relatively small quantity of beans (they can be expensive) with dark slithers of cavolo nero, and a powerful basil and hazelnut paste. There's a lot going on, and you'll need only one other side dish to go alongside it. *Slow-cooked lamb shoulder or shank* is the very best thing to eat with borlotti beans, though I wouldn't complain if they were served to me with pretty much *any white fish*, or *chargrilled courgettes and aubergines*.

If you can only get hold of dried borlotti beans, halve the fresh weight of the beans (so 100g), soak overnight, and cook using twice as much water for around 90 minutes. A drained, rinsed 375g tin of cooked beans would suffice.

Serves 4–6

1 tablespoon light olive oil
2 celery sticks, finely diced
½ onion, finely diced
1 garlic clove, crushed
200g podded fresh borlotti beans (400–500g in their pods)
Leaves from 2–3 sprigs rosemary, finely chopped
3 bay or sage leaves
200g tomatoes
250–300g cavolo nero

Basil and hazelnut smash
1 garlic clove
Leaves from 1 small bunch (30g) basil
30g toasted hazelnuts
160ml extra-virgin olive oil
Finely grated zest and juice of ½ lemon
Sea salt and freshly ground black pepper

Heat the light olive oil in a medium saucepan over a medium-low heat, add the celery and onion and cook for 3–4 minutes, or until softened and sweetened. Add the garlic and cook for 1 minute more. Add the beans, rosemary, bay or sage and 600ml cold water. Bring to the boil, then simmer gently for 30 minutes.

Meanwhile, roughly chop the tomatoes into 2–3cm dice and transfer to a bowl, ensuring you scrape in any juice left on the board too. Remove the central ribs of the cavolo nero leaves by cutting them out with a sharp knife. Discard the ribs and cut each leaf in half lengthways if thin; otherwise, cut each leaf into 2–3cm-wide lengths, which will wind around the borlotti. Set aside.

Make the basil smash in a pestle and mortar. Pound the garlic to a paste, using a pinch of salt as an abrasive. Add the basil leaves and pound these into a mush, so that they release all their oils. Add the nuts and crush them

(leaving some chunks for texture), then slowly stir in the extra-virgin olive oil, a tablespoon or so at a time, using the pestle to emulsify the oil and the paste. Add the lemon zest and juice. Mix well and season with salt and pepper. (You could achieve a similar result by blitzing the ingredients in a small blender.)

After 30 minutes of cooking, add the tomato to the beans and cook for another 10–20 minutes, by which time the beans should be tender and smooth (rather than grainy). Stir in the cavolo nero and cook for 6–8 minutes more, until that too is tender.

Drain the beans, reserving the liquid. Stir a quarter of the basil and hazelnut smash into the beans, then serve on a large platter, along with 100–150ml of the cooking liquid. Blob and drizzle the rest of the smash over the top – it's a real burst of flavour that adds zip to the earthiness of the beans and brassica.

ALONGSIDE: *Anchovy-dressed chicory* (page 78); *Grilled green tomatoes with oregano and chilli* (page 102); *Steamed marinated fennel* (page 116); *Aubergine purée* (page 138); *Maple and pecan roast squash* (page 186)

Butter beans with courgettes and tapenade

PREPARATION: *on a hob*
TIME NEEDED: *less than 15 minutes*

Generally, cooking pulses from scratch is best: the result is more flavoursome and has a better texture than what you find in a tin or pouch. I know, though, that quite often this approach seems like a bit of a faff. If convenience is king, look for *gigantes* beans from Greece, or really large Spanish butter beans – the ones in glass jars rather than tins – which are definitely among the top tier of ready-to-eat beans, then stir a quick tapenade and courgette mixture into them.

The pre-cooked beans seem appropriate because this side feels like it should be a hyper-convenient one. The flavours suit light, simple, quick meals involving things like *steamed salmon*, or a little piece of *baked white fish*, perhaps some *prawns*, *oily merguez sausage* or a *lamb chop*, but nothing more complicated or time consuming than that. Of course, if you're happy to soak and cook your own butter beans in advance, go ahead, and see page 272 for instructions.

Serves 4–6

500g cooked gigantes or butter beans
3 small courgettes (around 400g)
75g Kalamata olives (stone in)
1 garlic clove
Leaves from 10–15 sprigs thyme
2–3 tablespoons extra-virgin olive oil
2 teaspoons sherry vinegar
Sea salt and freshly ground black pepper

Warm the beans gently in a saucepan with the liquid from the tin or jar to stop them sticking.

Meanwhile, slice the courgettes into 2–3mm-thick circles, then add them to the beans, stir and simmer very gently for 5–10 minutes.

To make the tapenade, pit the olives by bashing them with the base of a mug or small bowl – a quick tap splits the olive, then you can push the stone out – then chop the flesh roughly. Put the garlic clove in a pestle and mortar with a pinch of salt as an abrasive. Pound it to a paste, then add the olives and thyme. Pound it to a rough paste, stir in the olive oil and then the sherry vinegar.

Drain the beans and courgettes, return them to the saucepan and stir in the tapenade. Serve warm (although it's good at room temperature or cold, too).

ALONGSIDE: *Dijon-dressed green beans* (page 64); *Gem lettuce, mint and spring onion* (page 86); *Shaved fennel with tarragon* (page 118); *Carrot, cumin and nigella seed salad* (page 214); *Flavoured butter bread* (page 234)

Butter beans with sage

PREPARATION: *on a hob*
TIME NEEDED: *more than an hour*

For all the embellishments of the other pulse recipes in this book, it's hard to argue that this relatively simple approach isn't the best of the lot: butter beans gently bubbled until tender; a portion of them mashed and then stirred back through, with sage, garlic and masses of good-quality extra-virgin olive oil. A bed of these beans is a dreamy resting place for any portion of *pork*, *lamb* or *white-fleshed fish* (well, dreamy for the eater).

If soaking beans for 12 hours before cooking them doesn't fit with your schedule, you could make this with pre-cooked butter beans (although it won't be quite as good) – just begin the recipe at the mashing stage. Alternatively, you could make the dish well in advance and reheat it in a saucepan with an extra tablespoon or two of water.

Serves 4–6

400g dried butter beans
2 bay leaves
12 sage leaves
2 tablespoons light olive oil
1 onion, finely diced
3 garlic cloves, thinly sliced
150ml extra-virgin olive oil
Sea salt and freshly ground black pepper

Put the butter beans in a bowl and cover them with 3 times their volume of cold water. Soak for 12 hours, drain, then put them in a large pan with 4 times their volume of fresh cold water. Bring to the boil, add the bay leaves and 2 of the sage leaves and simmer for 1½–2 hours, or until tender. Don't add any salt until they're fully cooked.

———

Drain the cooked beans, reserving 300ml of the cooking liquid (top up with tap water if necessary). Remove the bay and sage leaves. Put a quarter of the beans and 200ml of the cooking liquid in a small food processor or blender and blitz to a thin purée (or use a stick blender submerged in a suitable vessel).

———

Heat the light olive oil in a medium saucepan over a medium-low heat, add the onion and a pinch of salt and soften for 3–4 minutes. Add the remaining sage leaves, cook for 2 minutes, then add the garlic. Soften for 1 minute more, then add the whole and puréed beans to the pan. Cook gently for a further 5–10 minutes to let the aromatics mingle, adding more of the cooking liquid if you think it necessary (this should be served wet and loose, so that the beans spread like an oil slick over your plate). Season generously with salt and pepper, then serve the beans with long pours of extra-virgin olive oil (about 2 tablespoons per person).

———

ALONGSIDE: *Chard with chilli, shallot and cider vinaigrette* (page 6); *Grilled hispi cabbage with anchovy and crème fraîche* (page 10); *Kale, Romanesco, Parmesan and pine nut salad* (page 28); *Turnip tops with burnt lemon and olive oil* (page 52)

White beans with fennel seeds, chilli and rocket

PREPARATION: *on a hob*
TIME NEEDED: *more than an hour*

This is one of my favourite ways to dress and serve white beans. The rocket and extra-virgin olive oil add a grassy, peppery quality, the chilli flakes and fresh chilli bring their own gentle fire, and the fennel seeds contribute a warming note of anise. Any white bean will enjoy these flavours, from the smallest *coco de Paimpol*, through to haricot, cannellini, butter beans and beyond.

They provide a cracking base for things like *slow-braised lamb and beef*, *any chicken or pork dish*, *venison* and *fish* too. Serve the beans with as much of the cooking liquid as suits your meal. I think loosening them with a tablespoon or so per person is usually about right. You could go further and serve them with a broth; just don't serve them dry.

Serves 4–6

300g dried white beans
2 bay leaves
150ml extra-virgin olive oil
2 garlic cloves, thinly sliced
2 teaspoons fennel seeds, lightly crushed
4 anchovies in oil, drained (optional, though preferable)
1 teaspoon dried chilli flakes
1 mild red chilli, finely diced
40g wild rocket
Sea salt

Put the beans in a large bowl and cover them with 3 times their volume of cold water. Soak for 10–12 hours, drain, then put them in a large pan with 4 times their volume of fresh cold water and the bay leaves. Bring to the boil and simmer for 1½–2 hours, or until the beans are tender. Don't add any salt until they're fully cooked. Drain the beans, reserving the cooking liquid.

Put the cooked beans in a medium-large pan with 150ml of the cooking liquid (or more if you'd like a broth – although that will dilute the dressing). Warm over a medium heat for 10 minutes, stirring occasionally.

Heat 6 tablespoons (90ml) olive oil in a heavy-bottomed saucepan or high-sided frying pan over a medium-low heat. Add the garlic, fennel seeds and anchovies (if using) and warm gently for 3–4 minutes. Add the chilli flakes, cook for 1 minute more (taking care not to let the garlic brown), then remove from the heat.

Scrape the garlic, fennel seeds and oil into the beans and stir well, adding 3 or 4 generous pinches of salt and the remaining olive oil for luck. Stir the diced chilli and rocket through the beans, and serve up before the greens wilt beyond recognition.

ALONGSIDE: *Turnip tops with burnt lemon and olive oil* (page 52); *Agretti with olive oil* (page 62); *Steamed marinated fennel* (page 116); *Shaved fennel with tarragon* (page 118); *Caponata* (page 140)

Cannellini beans with sweetcorn and pickled mushrooms

PREPARATION: *on a hob*
TIME NEEDED: *more than an hour*

There's a little bit of forward planning involved in this dish (i.e. pickling mushrooms; soaking and cooking dried beans), but not very much hands-on effort. When it comes to serving up, you only need 5–10 minutes to warm it through, and that's it.

To my mind, it's absolutely worth the admin: the pickled mushrooms and their dressing add a brilliant tang to the dish, cutting through the sweetcorn and plainer beans. Salty meats like *bacon chops* and *gammon* love this kind of thing, as do *brisket*, *white fish*, *scallops* and *prawns*. You'll need just one other side dish (if anything at all).

Serves 4–6

Pickled mushrooms
150–200g girolles or chanterelle mushrooms
75ml rapeseed oil
1 garlic clove, crushed
40ml sherry vinegar
1 teaspoon golden caster sugar
2 sprigs thyme
Sea salt and freshly ground black pepper

Cannellini beans and sweetcorn
250g dried cannellini beans
300g drained tinned or defrosted frozen sweetcorn
8 stems tarragon
Sea salt and freshly ground black pepper

Brush or wipe any mud off the mushrooms. Tear any large ones in half lengthways.

Heat 1 tablespoon of the oil in a pan, add the mushrooms and sauté for 4 minutes, or until they release their juices. Scrape them into a clean glass jar or plastic container.

In a small bowl or jug, mix the garlic, vinegar, sugar and a pinch each of salt and pepper with 1 tablespoon tepid water and the remaining oil, then tip this over the warm mushrooms. Add the thyme sprigs and cover with a lid. Allow to cool, then refrigerate until needed (at least overnight).

Put the beans in a bowl and cover with 3 times their volume of cold water. Soak for 10 hours, drain, then put them in a large pan with 4 times their volume of fresh cold water. Bring to the boil and simmer for 1½–2 hours, or until tender. Don't add any salt until they're fully cooked. Drain, reserving the cooking liquid.

Warm the cooked beans and sweetcorn in a saucepan with 5–6 tablespoons of the reserved cooking liquid and 3 tarragon stems, with the lid on. Stir occasionally, then after 5–10 minutes remove from the heat, take out the tarragon and drain. Add the pickled mushrooms and strip the leaves from the remaining tarragon. Mix these into the beans, season with salt, plenty of black pepper and the mushroom-pickling liquor.

ALONGSIDE: *Bacon and buttermilk cabbage* (page 18); *Cavolo nero with garlic, chilli and orange* (page 24); *Flower sprouts with lemon and anchovy butter* (page 30); *Grilled tenderstem broccoli with umami crumbs* (page 40); *Roast butternut squash purée* (page 188)

Haricot beans with tomato and persillade

PREPARATION: *on a hob*
TIME NEEDED: *more than an hour*

Beans like these should be served in individual bowls, with a ladle or two of stock per person, and topped with something like *confit duck leg*, *unctuous pork belly* or *pan-fried salmon* – you know, things that can be easily pulled apart with a spoon. It's the kind of side I like to gorge on, without bothering to think of additional vegetables to go with it: the bacon, persillade (a dry mixture of finely chopped parsley and garlic) and diced tomatoes really bring the beans to life. That said, the 'alongside' ideas below could be rather good (although the quantity of haricots assumes those sides will be light).

As with all the dried bean recipes, to save time you could soak and cook the beans in advance, or use tinned versions (although these won't be quite as tasty). When you're nearly ready to serve, simply begin the recipe at the point when the bacon is added.

Serves 4–6

350g dried haricot, coco de Paimpol or flageolet beans
10g butter
½ onion, finely diced
4 garlic cloves, 3 peeled and left whole, 1 crushed
2 bay leaves
2 cloves
5 thyme sprigs
100g smoked lardons
Leaves from 15 stems flat-leaf parsley, finely chopped
3 large tomatoes, cut into 1–2cm dice
3 tablespoons extra-virgin olive oil
Sea salt and freshly ground black pepper

Put the dried beans in a bowl and cover them with 3 times their volume of cold water. Soak for 8–10 hours, then drain.

———

Melt the butter in a medium-large pan over a medium heat. Add the onion and cook for 3–4 minutes, until softened and sweetened. Add the whole garlic cloves and cook for 90 seconds more, then tip in the beans, bay, cloves, thyme and 1.4 litres water. Bring to the boil, then reduce the heat and simmer gently for 1½ hours, or until the beans are tender and cooked through but still have a little bite. Now add the lardons, season with salt and simmer gently for 15 minutes longer.

———

Drain the beans, reserving the cooking liquid, then return them to the saucepan. Stir in the crushed garlic, chopped parsley and the tomatoes and season with salt and pepper. Return much of the cooking liquid back to the beans – about 1 ladle per person, plus another couple for the pot – check the seasoning, then divide the beans and broth between individual bowls. Drizzle each portion with olive oil.

———

ALONGSIDE: *Chard with chilli, shallot and cider vinaigrette* (page 6); *Butter-braised chicory* (page 72); *PX radicchio Trevisano* (page 74); *Smoky ratatouille* (page 114); *Warm radishes with anise* (page 212)

Baked beans

PREPARATION: *on a hob and in the oven*
TIME NEEDED: *more than an hour*

Most people will tell you, with sound logic, that there's no point making your own baked beans: Heinz trumps all comers. I have some sympathy with this view. Yet shop-bought baked beans are rammed with sugar and salt, and also don't seem quite right as a side to anything other than a low-effort banger, pie, jacket potato or a full English breakfast. For occasions when you've spent a bit of time cooking *BBQ ribs*, *pulled pork*, *chicken pot pie* or maybe just some *good-quality sausages*, then a smoky home-cooked version does the job very nicely indeed.

You could use pre-cooked cannellini and haricot beans, though they'll break up in the bake somewhat more than is ideal; just multiply the dried bean weight by three and begin at the second step below. The beans can be reheated or cooked in stages to suit your timings.

Serves 4–6

100g dried cannellini beans
150g dried haricot beans
3 rashers smoked streaky bacon, cut into thin strips
4 tablespoons extra-virgin olive oil
1 onion, sliced into thin crescents
1 garlic clove, crushed
400g tinned plum tomatoes
2 bay leaves
Leaves from 3 sprigs rosemary, finely chopped
2 teaspoons smoked paprika
2 teaspoons Marmite
2 teaspoons Worcestershire sauce
1 tablespoon cider vinegar
1 tablespoon light brown sugar
2 tablespoons tomato purée
Sea salt and freshly ground black pepper

Put the dried beans in a bowl, cover them with at least 3 times their volume of cold water and leave to soak for 10 hours.

Drain, then tip them into a large pan and cover with 4 times their volume of cold water. Bring to the boil, then simmer for about 1½–2 hours, until tender.

To make the smoky tomato sauce, put the bacon in a cold saucepan with a dash of oil. Set over a medium heat and cook for 5 minutes, or until crisp and much of its fat has melted. Add the onion and cook for 5 minutes, or until softened and sweetened. Add the garlic and cook gently for 1 minute. Tip in the tin of tomatoes, then fill the empty tin with water and add that too, along with the bay leaves and chopped rosemary. Add the paprika, Marmite, Worcestershire sauce, cider vinegar, sugar and tomato purée. Bring to the boil, then simmer the sauce for 30 minutes to reduce and intensify the flavours.

Preheat the oven to 200°C/Fan 180°C/Gas 6. Remove the bay leaves and transfer the sauce into a blender. Blitz until smooth (or use a stick blender to do the same). Add 1 teaspoon salt and plenty of black pepper. Stir in the remaining oil, then tip in the cooked and drained beans and stir well. It should be quite a loose mixture (think of the shop-bought variety) – add

another cup or two of water if you think it's needed. Ladle the beans and sauce into an ovenproof dish and bake for 30 minutes. Stir after 15 minutes, then leave undisturbed until it has a dark, slick and near-crusted top.

———

ALONGSIDE: *Charred fermented cabbage* (page 12); *Portobello mushrooms baked with oregano* (page 152); *Scorched sweet potatoes with sobrasada butter* (page 190); *Baked Jerusalem artichokes with yoghurt and sunflower seeds* (page 206); *Flavoured butter bread* (page 234)

Chicken stock orzo

PREPARATION: *on a hob*
TIME NEEDED: *less than 15 minutes*

Although orzo is a type of pasta, it looks like grains of rice, which should immediately open your mind to its usefulness as a side dish. I'm not normally a fan of pasta accompaniments, preferring it as the focus of a meal, but orzo, fregola (page 284) and macaroni (page 286) are exceptions to that rule.

There's something particularly enjoyable about the naturally silky nature of cooked orzo. The grains roll loosely over and around the tongue and, lubricated by the stock and oil, make a luscious fork or spoonful alongside things like *roast peppers and feta*, *poached chicken*, *roast lamb*, *salmon* and *smoked trout*.

For the stock, a good-quality bought bouillon powder or liquid is fine, but ideally it will be a derivative of a previous meal; there's a depth of flavour and pleasing viscosity to proper stock from a carcass that the rehydrated versions can't replicate.

Serves 4–6

400g dried orzo
300ml chicken stock
6 tablespoons extra-virgin olive oil
Sea salt

Bring a large pan of salted water to the boil, and in another pan bring the stock to a gentle simmer. Cook the orzo for 2 minutes less than the packet instructions advise. Drain and rinse with boiling water from the kettle.

Return the orzo to the pan and add the chicken stock and 4 tablespoons oil. Taste to check the seasoning and add salt if needed (take care, particularly if you are using bought stock or powder, which can be salty). Serve with a little of the stock and another glug of oil over each portion.

ALONGSIDE: *Chard with chilli, shallot and cider vinaigrette* (page 6); *Flower sprouts with lemon and anchovy butter* (page 30); *Purple sprouting broccoli with tarragon* (page 42); *Asparagus with cured egg yolk* (page 60); *Caponata* (page 140)

Lemon and olive oil fregola

PREPARATION: *on a hob*
TIME NEEDED: *less than 15 minutes*

Fregola is a type of Sardinian pasta made from semolina flour. It's essentially the same product as the giant Middle Eastern couscous called *moghrabieh*, so you can use that in this recipe too. The small balls of pasta are around 2–3mm and work well as a side. You could add a host of different leaves (spinach, chard, wild rocket and so on) to wilt in it just after it's been cooked and drained. But this recipe, like the orzo on page 282, is relatively plain, so that it sits in the background as a quietly confident foil to more showy sides and things like *marinated prawns*, *roast chicken*, pretty much *any fish*, *Mediterranean vegetables*, *labneh* or *soft cheese*. There's just a sprinkle of fresh mint and Parmesan at the end, which adds both freshness and a certain savoury depth without clashing with or overpowering anything that gets served alongside.

Serves 4–6

450g fregola
Juice and finely grated zest of 1 lemon
5–6 tablespoons extra-virgin olive oil
20g Parmesan, finely grated
Leaves from 6 stems mint, finely chopped
Sea salt

Bring a large pan of well-salted water to the boil. Add the fregola and cook for 9–12 minutes, until just al dente.

Drain the fregola, reserving the cooking water, then return the fregola to the saucepan or a serving bowl (if using). Add 2–3 tablespoons of the cooking water, along with the lemon zest, juice, oil, Parmesan, mint and a pinch of salt. If your meal involves plentiful and flavoursome cooking juices you might consider adding these to the fregola in place of the cooking water. Stir well, taste to check the seasoning and serve immediately.

You can leave this to cool to room temperature, but you'll need to stir a little to loosen and de-clump the pasta before everyone tucks in.

ALONGSIDE: *Creamed chard* (page 8); *Grilled hispi cabbage with anchovy and crème fraîche* (page 10); *Purple sprouting broccoli with tarragon* (page 42); *Sherry cherry tomatoes* (page 98); *Maple and pecan roast squash* (page 186)

Mac 'n' cheese

PREPARATION: *on a hob and in the oven*
TIME NEEDED: *30 minutes to an hour*

Mac 'n' cheese is something of a controversial entry in this book. I, and perhaps a few of you too, grew up with macaroni cheese as a meal in itself, not as a side dish. But there are few barbecue, steak and burger restaurants that don't have the US version listed on their menu, and I can see the value of having it in your repertoire for those kinds of eats. I also think it goes particularly well with *cooked ham*, *smoked haddock* and *baked tomatoes*. For me, it should be loose and light, and the sauce doesn't need to be massively cheesy when it's a side, or you'll dominate the other things on your plate. This recipe strikes a good balance on both those fronts.

Note that the portion size here relates to its role as team player, rather than main event. If you want a particularly crunchy topping, add a handful or two of umami crumbs (page 40) before baking, though that's not always needed.

Serves 4–6

250g dried macaroni or elbow macaroni
700ml milk
40g butter
½ large onion, finely diced
1 small garlic clove, crushed
40g plain flour
60g Gruyère, grated
40g mature Cheddar, grated
25g Parmesan, grated
2 teaspoons Dijon mustard
60g umami crumbs (optional; see page 40)
Sea salt and freshly ground black pepper

Put a large pan of well-salted water over a high heat. Once it's at a rolling boil, add the pasta and cook for 2 minutes less than the time stated on the packet. Drain and rinse under cold running water until cooled. Set aside.

Put the milk in a saucepan and heat it gently. Melt the butter in a large pan over a medium heat. Add the onion and a pinch of salt and let this cook and soften for 3 minutes before adding the garlic. Turn the heat down a little and cook for 2 minutes more. Stir the flour into the butter and onions to make a paste (a roux), then cook this for 4–5 minutes over a very low heat, stirring constantly, until it is loose, slick and a pale beige colour. Add a ladle of warm milk and stir until the liquid is incorporated. Then add another, again stirring until fully incorporated. Keep adding and stirring until the milk is fully incorporated. Cook, stirring occasionally to prevent sticking, over a low-medium heat for 8–10 minutes, until the sauce thickens and no longer tastes of raw flour. Add the cheese and mustard and stir until melted into the sauce.

Preheat the oven to 200°C/Fan 180°C/Gas 6. If the saucepan is big enough, tip the cooked and cooled macaroni into the sauce and stir well, then transfer to a large ovenproof dish around 4–6cm deep (alternatively, mix the pasta and sauce directly in the ovenproof dish). Sprinkle the umami crumbs, if using, on top, then bake on the top shelf for 20–30 minutes, or until bubbling and golden.

ALONGSIDE: *French-ish peas* (page 58); *Gem lettuce, mint and spring onion* (page 86); *Sherry cherry tomatoes* (page 98); *Vermouth-braised red onions* (page 146); *Baked beans* (page 280)

Mustard seed, lemon and thyme rice

PREPARATION: *on a hob*
TIME NEEDED: *15 to 30 minutes*

It's good to add a little variety to your rice game. This fragrant basmati and wild rice mixture would suit a multitude of meals, whether *meatballs in a tomato sauce*, a *creamy chicken casserole*, *spiced oxtail stew*, or *plain, steamed white fish*. It straddles a variety of cuisines too, thanks to the widely used aromatics of mustard seed and lemon. If you're thinking of a roasted or fried meat without a sauce, consider serving a saucy – or at least buttery – dish on the side too (see 'Alongside' for suggestions).

My general rule of thumb for basmati and long-grain rice is to undercook the rice by a few minutes, then drain, rinse and let it steam to fluffy perfection while finishing the rest of my meal. It seems a reliable and fairly foolproof method.

Serves 4–6

Juice of 1 and zest of 2 lemons
250g mixed basmati and wild rice
4 tablespoons sunflower or vegetable oil
1 onion, finely diced
1 tablespoon black mustard seeds
1 tablespoon yellow mustard seeds
Leaves from 15 sprigs thyme
Sea salt and freshly ground black pepper

Use a vegetable peeler to remove the zest from each of the lemons (leaving any white pith behind), then slice the strips into fine lengths as thinly as you can. Juice 1 lemon and set to one side.

———

Put the rice in a sieve and rinse until the water runs clear, then tip it into a medium-large pan and fill it three-quarters full with cold water. Bring to the boil, then simmer for 3 minutes less than the packet tells you to. Drain, rinse with boiling water, return to the saucepan, put the lid on and leave it for 5 minutes so the rice steams to perfection in its residual heat.

———

Meanwhile, heat the oil in a saucepan over a medium-high heat. Add the onion and cook for 3–4 minutes, or until lightly browned. Add the mustard seeds and wait for about 2 minutes, or until they start popping. Now add the lemon zest and thyme. Cook for 1 minute more, until the lemon begins to turn translucent and it smells as though its oils have been released.

———

Fluff the cooked rice with a fork, then use a spatula to scrape in the oil and aromatics. Season with salt and plenty of black pepper, add the lemon juice and stir well.

———

ALONGSIDE: *Cabbage with juniper butter* (page 20); *Turnip tops with burnt lemon and olive oil* (page 52); *Baby aubergine, oregano and chilli bake* (page 136); *Blue cheese leeks* (page 144); *White wine and dill carrots* (page 222)

Curry leaf, cashew and coconut rice

PREPARATION: *on a hob*
TIME NEEDED: *15 to 30 minutes*

Curry leaves have a unique aroma that bursts to life when they hit hot fat. Combined with flakes of dried coconut and the milky bite of cashew nuts, these strong, musty and, well, curried leaves add a stellar flavour to basmati or long-grain rice and an extra layer of interest to your meal. The natural fit for such a side is food inspired by the Indian subcontinent, whether that's a *microwave korma from the supermarket*, a more adventurous *homemade fish curry*, *dry-spiced lamb chops* or a *soothing dal*.

Serves 4–6

60g cashew nuts
20g coconut flakes
250g basmati rice
5 tablespoons vegetable oil
1 tablespoon yellow mustard seeds
2 cardamom pods
A small handful of fresh curry leaves
1 onion or 2 banana shallots, halved and thinly sliced
Sea salt

Toast the cashew nuts and coconut flakes separately in a dry, heavy-bottomed saucepan or frying pan over a low heat until light brown and fragrant. Tip into separate bowls and set aside.

Put the rice in a sieve and rinse until the water runs clear, then tip it into a medium-large pan and three-quarters fill it with cold water. Bring to the boil, then simmer the rice for 3 minutes less than the packet tells you to. Drain, rinse with boiling water, return to the saucepan, put the lid on and leave it for 5 minutes so the rice steams to perfection.

Meanwhile, heat the oil in a wide saucepan or frying pan over a medium-high heat. Add the mustard seeds, cardamom and curry leaves and cook for 2–3 minutes, or until the seeds start popping and the curry leaves release their amazing aroma. Add the onion or shallots and cook for 2–3 minutes more, or until lightly browned. Remove from the heat.

Fluff the cooked rice with a fork, then use a spatula to scrape in the oil and aromatics. Add a pinch or two of salt, two thirds of the cashews and coconut and mix well. Transfer to a serving bowl, if using, and sprinkle with the remaining cashews and coconut flakes.

ALONGSIDE: *Charred Romanesco* (page 46); *Wilted spinach with coconut, ginger and pink peppercorns* (page 54); *Okra chips with cumin salt* (page 70); *Flavoured butter bread* (page 234); *Chickpeas with garlic oil and spinach* (page 266)

Black bean, coriander and lime rice

PREPARATION: *on a hob*
TIME NEEDED: *more than an hour*

I love how the sweet-sour zestiness of lime juice perks up a bowl of plain rice. If I'm ever reaching around the kitchen trying to think of a way to make rice more interesting, and there's a lime rolling around, there's a good chance I'll squeeze it in. Similarly, if I have a bunch, I like to throw in a handful of roughly chopped fragrant coriander to lift basmati or long-grain rice.

But this isn't just a convenient receptacle for leftover herbs and citrus. Rather, it's one of my favourite things to have alongside meals that involve a bit of fat and spice. The black beans provide an extra savoury punctuation, and the aforementioned lime and coriander are more than the sum of their parts when used together, but it's still all very simple. This is a side that would work equally well with food that's inspired by the cuisines of Mexico, the Caribbean, the Indian subcontinent, Korea and the United States' Deep South (or a mixture of them all). Think *grilled oily fish*, *curries*, *sticky American BBQ ribs and slow-cooked meats*, *spicy stews* and more.

If soaking and cooking your own black beans doesn't fit with your timetable, you could use pre-cooked ones, or just cook the beans in advance, rinse them under cold water to cool and reserve until needed.

Serves 4–6

70g dried black beans, soaked overnight (or 160g pre-cooked)
200g basmati or long-grain rice
Leaves from 8–10 stems coriander, roughly chopped
Juice and finely grated zest of 1 lime
Sea salt

Drain the soaked black beans and put them in a medium saucepan. Cover them with 3 times their volume of water. Bring to the boil, then reduce the heat and simmer gently for 60–70 minutes, or until the beans are tender but still have a little bite. Top up the water as it evaporates during the cooking process. Drain and pour boiling water over the beans to rinse off any scum and starch.

About 20 minutes before eating, put the rice in a sieve and rinse until the water runs clear, then tip it into a medium-large pan and three-quarters fill it with cold water. Bring to the boil and cook for 3 minutes less than the packet tells you to. Drain, rinse with boiling water and return to the pan. Add the black beans, stir quickly and put a lid on and leave for 5 minutes, so that the rice continues to steam to perfection.

When ready to eat, stir the coriander, lime zest, lime juice and a pinch of salt into the rice and beans. Mix well with a fork and serve.

ALONGSIDE: *Charred fermented cabbage* (page 12); *Okra chips with cumin salt* (page 70); *Honey, thyme and lime butter corn* (page 124); *Quick cucumber and daikon kimchi* (page 160); *Carrot, cumin and nigella seed salad* (page 214)

Three pepper rice

PREPARATION: *on a hob*
TIME NEEDED: *15 to 30 minutes*

This peppery rice is based on the Italian dish *cacio e pepe*, which contains just pasta, pecorino and black pepper, thus celebrating pepper for what it really is: a fragrant spice, rather than a background seasoning. In this instance, though, I suggest going a little further, adding black Sarawak and numbing Sichuan peppercorns, if you can find them, which leave your mouth buzzing and zinging and, somewhat counterintuitively, desperate for more.

The rice is a relatively natural fit with food inspired by Asian flavours: things like *dry-fried pork mince dishes*, *triple-cooked, sweet and unctuous pork belly*, *slowly braised beef*, *vegetable stir-fries drowning in fish sauce* and so on. It works well alongside European dishes too, such as a *creamy wild mushroom ragu* or *goulash*.

Serves 4–6

250g mixed basmati and wild rice
1 heaped teaspoon black peppercorns
1 heaped teaspoon Sarawak peppercorns
1 heaped teaspoon Sichuan peppercorns
Juice of ½ lemon
Sea salt

Put the rice in a sieve and rinse until the water runs clear, then tip it into a medium-large pan and three-quarters fill it with cold water. Bring to the boil, then simmer for 3 minutes less than the packet tells you to. Drain, rinse with boiling water, then return to the pan and put the lid on. Leave for 5 minutes so that the rice steams to perfection.

Grind all the peppercorns to a fine powder and stir well. An electric spice grinder is ideal but not essential. If you use a pestle and mortar, add a pinch of salt for abrasion. A simple pepper grinder is fine too, but you might be in for a mouth-numbing surprise next time you use it.

Fluff the cooked rice with a fork. Add three quarters of the pepper powder, a pinch of salt and the lemon juice. Mix well, taste and add more pepper if you wish.

ALONGSIDE: *Chinese cabbage with black vinegar* (page 16); *Baby pak choi with sticky garlic and ginger* (page 48); *Garlic oil pea shoots* (page 56); *Courgette and edamame salad* (page 110); *Honey, thyme and lime butter corn* (page 124)

Coconut jasmine rice

PREPARATION: *on a hob*
TIME NEEDED: *15 to 30 minutes*

Fragrant jasmine rice is particularly good with southeast Asian cuisine, acting as a calming counterweight to punchy *chilli- and herb-heavy dishes*. But it's also a fine, gently perfumed partner to *plain grilled or baked fish*, *roast vegetables* or *crisp roast pork belly*.

The rice absorbs the liquid that it cooks in, adding flavour and gloss; this recipe includes coconut milk, which I think lends an extra rich, creamy quality, with the kaffir lime leaves providing a curious but very likeable dimension. If you think a slightly plainer jasmine rice would suit your meal, just substitute the coconut milk with the same amount of ordinary water. Keep the kaffir lime leaves, though!

Serves 4

300g jasmine rice
300ml unsweetened coconut milk
4 kaffir lime leaves
Sea salt

Put the rice in a sieve and rinse it until the water runs clear. Stir the coconut milk in the tin so that the solids are well mixed with the liquid.

Put 125ml water, the coconut milk, rice, kaffir lime leaves and a couple of pinches of salt in a medium-large pan (expect the rice to expand to 3–4 times its volume). Place over a high heat and bring to the boil. Reduce the heat to a gentle simmer, then put the lid on and cook for 3 minutes less than the time stated on the packet.

Remove from the hob and leave to stand for 5–6 minutes longer with the lid still on, so that the rice absorbs all the liquid and steams to perfection. Take the lid off and fluff the rice with a fork. Check for seasoning and add more salt if you wish, then serve.

ALONGSIDE: *Cavolo nero with garlic, chilli and orange* (page 24); *Asian greens with shrimp paste* (page 50); *Courgettes with soy, sesame, mint and chilli* (page 112); *Fish sauce watermelon salad* (page 156); *Spiced roast carrots* (page 216)

Almond and anise rice

PREPARATION: *on a hob*
TIME NEEDED: *15 to 30 minutes*

Cooking basmati rice in almond milk results in a subtly nutty, savoury and silky side dish. It's not as rich or filling as you might imagine on reading the words 'almond' and 'milk'; rather, the anise, tarragon and light creaminess make it comforting, interesting and suitable for numerous cuisines.

This is especially good with *chicken dishes*, whether say, a *grilled breast* or a *creamy casserole*, or *white fish like sole, plaice and hake*. You'll need some verdant greens alongside to add freshness and bite.

Serves 4

250g basmati rice
250ml unsweetened almond milk
2 star anise
Leaves from 5 stems tarragon
30g toasted flaked almonds
Sea salt

Put the rice in a sieve and rinse it until the water runs clear. Drain, then put the rice in a saucepan with the almond milk, 50ml water and the star anise. Bring to the boil, then simmer gently for 5 minutes. Turn the heat off, put a lid on and leave it to steam for another 8 minutes.

Meanwhile, roughly chop the tarragon and toasted almonds. When the rice is ready, fluff it with a fork, add a good pinch of salt and stir the herbs and nuts through it.

ALONGSIDE: *Cavolo nero with garlic, chilli and orange* (page 24); *Rosemary and chestnut sprouts* (page 34); *Turnip tops with burnt lemon and olive oil* (page 52); *Runner beans with bacon and walnuts* (page 66); *Carrots with brown butter and hazelnuts* (page 220)

Red rice with beetroot, feta and wild oregano

PREPARATION: *on a hob*
TIME NEEDED: *30 minutes to an hour*

I remember red rice being a thing in the 1990s: the colour intrigued and promised a great deal. But I also remember that, once cooked, red rice was dull in both colour and taste, perhaps a little too wholesome for its own good. This version is different, largely on account of the beetroot, which adds its extraordinary colour and that earthy-yet-sweet quality. The rice absorbs all the liquid it is cooked in, so you don't lose any flavour down the sink, then it is seasoned with salty, sharp feta, and fresh Greek oregano in oil, sometimes called 'zahtar'. If that's not available, sprinkle the finished dish with lemon thyme or a generous pinch of the spice blend za'atar instead.

Grilled mackerel, *lamb chops*, *rib-eye steaks* and *baked mushrooms* are ideal partners to this side; basically, things with big personalities to match the bold colours and flavours in the pot. You'll only need one other thing alongside; I suggest something crisp and fresh.

Serves 4–6

250g Camargue red rice or a mixture of red and wild rice
2 tablespoons sunflower or vegetable oil
1 red onion, finely diced
300g raw beetroot, peeled and diced
100g feta
Juice of ½ lemon
15g fresh oregano in oil, 1 teaspoon za'atar or the leaves from 4–5 sprigs lemon thyme
Sea salt

Put the rice in a sieve and rinse it until the water runs clear. Heat the oil in a large heavy-bottomed saucepan over a medium heat, add the onion and a pinch of salt and cook for 4–5 minutes, or until softened. Add the beetroot and cook for 1–2 minutes, stirring occasionally before adding the rice, coating it in the oil and beetroot juices.

Pour 500ml boiling water over the rice and beetroot, reduce to a gentle simmer and cook with a lid on, slightly ajar, for 40 minutes. Stir once or twice to check the rice isn't catching on the base of the pan. Remove the lid when there are 5–10 minutes to go. The rice is ready when fully tender with just a little nutty (but not chalky) bite. It should still be fairly loose-grained; if you pushed some to one side in the pan, it would fall back rather than sit prudishly. Turn the heat off.

Crumble half the feta into the rice and stir through until it melts. Taste to check the seasoning, adding the lemon juice and salt if necessary. Transfer to a platter or wide serving bowl. Sprinkle the remaining feta over the top, then the oregano (or lemon thyme or za'atar, plus a drizzle of extra-virgin olive oil). It'll stay warm for at least 5–10 minutes, but is best made just before you eat rather than a long time in advance. It's good cold, mind.

ALONGSIDE: *French-ish peas* (page 58); *Dijon-dressed green beans* (page 64); *Pink radicchio with pear and almonds* (page 82); *Gem lettuce, mint and spring onion* (page 86); *Shaved fennel with tarragon* (page 118)

Crisp-bottomed Persian rice

PREPARATION: *on a hob*
TIME NEEDED: *more than an hour*

At the bottom of a Persian rice pot is a golden, buttery disc of crisp rice, the *tahdig*. When the pot is flipped onto a plate, it tops perfectly steamed, still separate grains of rice. It's one heck of a side: the fluffy bits underneath do the hard yards of soaking up juices and filling stomachs, while the tahdig is a popular showpiece to fight over, like pork crackling for non-meat eaters.

For me, the appeal and usefulness of crisp-bottomed rice is endless. Of course it's amazing in the context of Iranian cuisine, but I'd consider it as a side for almost *any tomato-, cream- or coconut-based stew* (I'm thinking *monkfish, squid or hake*), *slow-cooked fatty meats, salmon* and more. The unifying context, really, is that it's a dish for family meals and feasting.

I'm indebted to my friend Shokofeh Hejazi (who, like me, turned from corporate law to food) for teaching me the cooking process that she in turn had been taught by her mother. Intuition is important in this one, but hopefully the guidelines and tricks below will help. This is best served immediately, though if you have a host of dishes to pull together, the rice will stay warm and the crust crisp for 15 minutes or so if decanted but left intact. Don't attempt it without a 20–24cm-diameter, heavy-bottomed non-stick saucepan.

Serves 4–6

500g basmati rice
15–20 strands saffron
4–5 tablespoons grapeseed, groundnut or vegetable oil
6 tablespoons dried dill
Sea salt

Put the rice in a sieve and rinse it until the water runs clear, then put it in a heavy-bottomed non-stick saucepan and fill the pan three-quarters full with cold water. Add 2 or 3 generous pinches of salt (this is the only chance you'll have to season the rice) and leave to soak for 30–60 minutes. Meanwhile, put the saffron strands in a cup or small bowl and add 2 tablespoons boiling water. Leave to infuse.

———

Once the rice soaking time is up, set the pan of rice and water over a medium-high heat and gradually bring to the boil. When the water starts to hint at boiling, reduce the heat immediately and simmer for just 2 minutes. The rice should be almost fully tender, but with just a hint of a nutty, grainy bite. Drain and rinse until the rice is cold.

———

Rinse out the saucepan. Add enough oil to make a layer 3–4 grains of rice deep – about 5 tablespoons. Add the saffron water, stir well, then ladle a third of the rice into the pan. Scatter half the dried dill evenly over the rice (this might seem a bit keen, but the herb will be distributed through the cooking process). Add another third of the rice, sprinkle this with the remaining dill, then top with the rest of the rice.

———

Put the saucepan on a low-medium heat: less than half power. Fold a clean tea towel in half and place this over the saucepan, put the lid on top of that and fold the tea towel back over

the lid. Steam for 20 minutes. At that point, reduce the heat to nearly but not quite its lowest setting and use the thin end of a spoon or fork to make 3–5 holes two-thirds of the pan deep. Pull the rice around a little, taking care not to disturb the bottom third. This helps loosen the grains and ensures that the steam rises through the rice for even cooking. Place the tea towel and lid back on and steam for another 15–20 minutes.

You should notice a distinct change in the sound coming from the pan after 35–40 minutes (total) of cooking. There'll be a gentle sizzle, which indicates that the crust is beginning to form: a good thing. Repeat the moving-the-rice trick at this time, then be brave and keep cooking it for as long as you dare to ensure a good crust. Essentially, that means cooking for as long as you can before the rice in the middle of the pan looks like it's beginning to turn floury, and therefore overcooked. You'll need to make the call, but 60–70 minutes in total is usually about right.

Mix the top two thirds of the rice once more, then put a plate over the saucepan and carefully flip it (like a tarte Tatin) to invert the rice. You should be left with beautifully fluffed rice with a thick, crisp golden crust. High fives all round.

ALONGSIDE: *Sweet cauliflower greens* (page 38); *Wilted spinach with coconut, ginger and pink peppercorns* (page 54); *Okra chips with cumin salt* (page 70); *Jewelled pearl barley* (page 258); *Chickpeas with garlic oil and spinach* (page 266)

RECIPE DIRECTORIES

I like to browse through cookbooks, flicking through the recipe titles and photos for inspiration, perhaps bookmarking some of them to return to on another occasion. Maybe that's how you'll use this book too.

But I also want to offer some alternative ways in, so here are three directories – each organised by a different principle – to help you choose the perfect accompaniment for whatever you're cooking. Use them to refer to when you've already fixed your mind on a particular element, but need some ideas for how to complete the meal. Each directory lists the recipes according to how they relate to three important questions: What's your main dish? Where is the side prepared? How long does it take to make?

What's your main dish?

This directory sets out which of the book's recipes go especially well with particular meats, fish, vegetables and other well-loved dishes (although that's not to say that there won't be others that could work). I hope you'll find something to inspire, whether you're pan-frying a salmon fillet or making a chicken curry.

You could follow the directory to the letter or use it as a general guide as to which flavours go well together. So if you see, say, asparagus with cured egg yolk listed as a dish that goes well with your meal, you could just take that as a hint to serve asparagus simply, and spend more of your time on another side.

Moreover, check the other entries nearby for additional ideas. For example, if you're roasting a pork joint, have a look at the other categories within pork – there may be things I've recommended to go with chops or slow-cooked pork that'll be good with your roast loin, shoulder or belly. And if I've proposed something like caponata as a good match, browse the recipes near it for other dishes involving similar ingredients (such as grilled green tomatoes, roast Romano peppers, ratatouille or chopped mangal salad), as they could be a tasty match too.

You could also use this directory to take your meal in a direction you might not have foreseen. Do you always serve the same plain vegetables with your grilled chicken breast? Well, here I suggest a variety of different cuisines, taking you to Japan with sesame buckwheat soba noodles, to the Middle East with za'atar mushrooms and curd, or to Italy thanks to white beans with fennel, chilli and rocket.

Where is the side dish prepared?

There's no point deciding to make three amazing side dishes if they all need to be cooked in the oven at the same time as your meat, vegetable or fish main dish, and at three different temperatures, or if you end up needing five hob spaces at the same time. It just won't work. Yes, it's a boring logistical matter, but I've done some of the thinking for you.

You'll note that every recipe in this book indicates whether the dish is prepared on the hob, in the oven or just on the counter (if it's served raw). This directory lists the recipes according to where they are prepared, so you can browse for side dishes depending on where you want, or need, to prepare them.

How long does it take to make?

Each recipe page tells you how long the dish takes to prepare in the 'Time Needed' section. However, if you need to find a side quickly that suits the timescale you have, it may be helpful to look here first.

What's your main dish?

Where is the side dish prepared?

On the counter

On a hob

In the oven

On a hob and in the oven

How long does it take to make?

Less than 15 minutes

15 to 30 minutes

30 minutes to an hour

More than an hour

Index

Suppliers

Vegetables

To my mind, every minute and penny spent on seeking out and buying good fruit and vegetables is worth it. Admittedly I'm spoilt, because my local greengrocer is outstanding. Nevertheless, assuming they're in season, all the vegetables and fruits in the book are accessible. If you can't find them at your local grocery, market or farm shop, try these online sources.

- ocado.com delivers produce nationwide from the quality grocers Natoora and Wholegood
- abelandcole.co.uk and riverford.co.uk both provide excellent organic vegetable box services, again with nationwide delivery
- andreasveg.co.uk delivers quality produce London-wide and along the A3 corridor
- farmdrop.com also delivers fruit and vegetables across London, direct from a number of good independent producers and farms

Many of the Asian-style greens used in this book are now readily available at more general greengrocers and at the supermarket too, though you may find that morning glory, pea shoots and pak choi are cheaper at an Asian supermarket.

Spices, grains, pulses and condiments

If any spice, grain, paste or other exotic condiment in this book appears odd or unusual, you'll be able to get it from these brilliant websites.

- souschef.co.uk for all types of condiments, sweet sherries, seaweed, spices, grains, pulses, rice and more
- belazu.com, in particular for olive oil, ancient grains and deli items
- waiyeehong.com for any Asian condiments

I recommend using Halen Môn's smoked water and smoked salt. You can buy direct from their website (halenmon.com), and from Ocado and Amazon.

Cured meats

Buy the best bacon and lardons you can, ideally from a good local butcher. For cured meats, such as 'nduja, sobrasada and cooking chorizo, try these online sources.

- cannonandcannon.com for high-welfare British versions of sobrasada, 'nduja, chorizo and other smoked and air-dried meats
- brindisa.com for the best cooking chorizo (as well as quality vinegars, sherries, oils, anchovies and more)
- thehamandcheeseco.com for supreme 'nduja, lardo, pancetta and other treats

Cookware

It's ideal if the dishes or pans you cook your sides in function perfectly and also look beautiful. If nothing else, it saves on washing up if you can take a dish straight from the oven or hob to the table. If you covet the cookware in this book, it's likely to be from one of the following places.

- cranecookware.com for the most beautiful yet practical matt black cast-iron pans
- netherton-foundry.co.uk for top-quality, British-made cast- and spun-iron frying pans and saucepans
- lecreuset.com for classic French cast-iron casseroles and gratin dishes and ceramic bakeware
- staub-online.com for yet more classic French cast-iron casseroles, cocottes and ceramic bakeware

Acknowledgements

Fist bumps and thank yous to the following:

On my move into food

Miranda Godfrey, my chef-tutor at Westminster Kingsway; Claire Ford and Kate Howell at Borough Market; Sean, Jamie, Woody and the team at Cannon & Cannon; and pretty much every chef, restaurateur, front-of-house, producer, retailer, editor, writer, blogger, photographer, PR and food enthusiast I've had the pleasure of interacting with and being inspired by, whether in real life, or as I scroll down my phone.

Moreover, a huge thanks to Mum and Dad for your support and enthusiasm for all my food endeavours. Cheers, too, to my brothers Adam, Oli and Henry (and Jen, Flora and Sophie) for your encouragement and readiness to lend a hand. Oli, I'd still be a lawyer if you hadn't given up so much of your time to build websites, think creatively, advise, design and direct – really, thank you (this doesn't mean the loan isn't still outstanding).

On the Side

Jon Elek at United Agents for your counsel and for so efficiently making *On the Side* happen.

The editorial team: Natalie Bellos, for immediately 'getting' the concept and facilitating a book to be proud of; Alison Cowan for oiling the wheels and the early tweaks; Laura Gladwin for grammar, typos and sensitively pointing out that what I write in five words could be done in one (how about here?); and Lena Hall, not least for making sense of my tables and lists. Sorry, everyone, about all the cross-referencing and the £*@&i^$ directories – they seemed so straightforward when I pitched them.

Also at Bloomsbury Publishing: Marina Asenjo for having such a fierce eye for a finish; and Ellen Williams and Sarah Williams for so enthusiastically supporting, pushing and promoting.

Pete Dawson and the Grade team. If people judge *On the Side* by the cover and design, I'm fine with that.

Though they might not know it, through the whole recipe creation, testing, writing and photography process I've enjoyed using the produce of: Newington Green Fruit and Veg (you're a dream); Natoora; Belazu; Sous Chef; The Butchery Ltd; Turner & George; and Jonathan Norris Fishmonger (thanks Sam). Quality ingredients from great producers and suppliers are the best way to fire the imagination.

Elayna Rudolphy, you were 'actually' a total star on the photo shoots. I really appreciate all your hard work. And your enjoyment of Tina Turner.

Joe Woodhouse. I'm not sure what the traditional recipe book photographer role is, but I'm certain you went above and beyond. Thanks for the lifts, for letting us mess up your flat and man cave, for the ceramics, cutlery, pipettes and the succulents, for allowing me to move things and tell you how to angle your camera and crop images, and for showing me what swords, pineapples and bike pumps are really for. Shoot days with you and Elayna were a real collaborative effort, and the results complete the book. Ta.

On all of the above and more

Laura. Thank you, among a mass of other things, for tolerating so many sides, for the dish-washing, for (mostly) ignoring the clutter, and for being you. I'm going to tidy up tomorrow. xxcx

Bloomsbury Publishing

An imprint of Bloomsbury Publishing Plc

50 Bedford Square
London
WC1B 3DP
UK

1385 Broadway
New York
NY 10018
USA

www.bloomsbury.com

BLOOMSBURY and the Diana logo are trademarks of Bloomsbury Publishing Plc

First published in Great Britain 2017

British Library Cataloguing-in-Publication Data

A catalogue record for this book is available from the British Library.

Library of Congress Cataloging-in-Publication data has been applied for.

ISBN: HB: 978-1-4088-7315-1

ePub: 978-1-4088-7316-8

2 4 6 8 10 9 7 5 3 1

Project editor: Laura Gladwin
Designer: Peter Dawson, www.gradedesign.com
Photographer: Joe Woodhouse
Food stylist: Ed Smith, assisted by Elayna Rudolphy
Prop stylist: Ed Smith and Joe Woodhouse, assisted by Elayna Rudolphy
Indexer: Vicki Robinson

Printed and bound in China by C&C Offset Printing Co., Ltd

Bloomsbury Publishing Plc makes every effort to ensure that the papers used in the manufacture of our books are natural, recyclable products made from wood grown in well-managed forests. Our manufacturing processes conform to the environmental regulations of the country of origin.

To find out more about our authors and books visit www.bloomsbury.com. Here you will find extracts, author interviews, details of forthcoming events and the option to sign up for our newsletters.